The World of
Thomas Jeremiah

The World of Thomas Jeremiah

Charles Town on the Eve of the American Revolution

WILLIAM R. RYAN

OXFORD
UNIVERSITY PRESS

2010

OXFORD
UNIVERSITY PRESS

Oxford University Press, Inc., publishes works that further
Oxford University's objective of excellence
in research, scholarship, and education.

Oxford New York
Auckland Cape Town Dar es Salaam Hong Kong Karachi
Kuala Lumpur Madrid Melbourne Mexico City Nairobi
New Delhi Shanghai Taipei Toronto

With offices in
Argentina Austria Brazil Chile Czech Republic France Greece
Guatemala Hungary Italy Japan Poland Portugal Singapore
South Korea Switzerland Thailand Turkey Ukraine Vietnam

Published by Oxford University Press, Inc.
198 Madison Avenue, New York, New York 10016

www.oup.com

Oxford is a registered trademark of Oxford University Press.

Library of Congress Cataloging-in-Publication Data

Ryan, William Randolph, 1975–
The world of Thomas Jeremiah : Charles Town on the eve
of the American Revolution / William R. Ryan.
     p.   cm.
Includes bibliographical references and index.
ISBN 978-0-19-538728-5
1. Jeremiah, Thomas, d. 1775.   2. African Americans—South
Carolina—Charleston—Biography.   3. Charleston (S.C.)—History—
Revolution, 1775–1783.   4. Charleston (S.C.)—Race relations.
I. Title.
F279.C49N476 2010
975.7'91502092—dc22   2009027253

9 8 7 6 5 4 3 2 1

Printed in the United States of America
on acid-free paper

Dominus illuminatio mea
Soli Deo Gloria

Preface

This book is about the port of Charles Town, South Carolina, during the two-year period leading up to the Declaration of Independence. Not enough attention has been paid to this Southern metropolis. When the city is discussed in the historiography of the American Revolution, it is usually in the context of the Southern Campaign during the latter part of the war. This book begins in the summer of 1774 in the wake of increased pressure from the Intolerable Acts and ends in the summer of 1776 with the proclamation of the Declaration of Independence in Charles Town.

Not surprisingly, there is a significant racial dimension to the coming of the War for Independence in South Carolina. Nothing illustrates this better than the dramatic hanging and burning of Thomas Jeremiah, a free black harbor pilot and firefighter accused by the patriot party of plotting a slave insurrection during the turbulent spring and summer of 1775. This book examines the world of this wealthy, slaveholding African-American using a wide array of letters, naval records, personal and official correspondence, memoirs, and newspapers. In order to examine the context of Jeremiah's trials and subsequent execution, it has been particularly valuable to generate a chronological narrative for the period of June 1774 to August 1776. As this work illustrates, the enslaved majority of the South Carolina Low Country managed to assist the British in their invasion efforts, despite patriot attempts to frighten Afro-Carolinians into passivity and submission. Although Whigs attempted through brutality and violence to keep their slaves from participating in the conflict, Afro-Carolinians would become actively involved in the struggle between colonists and the Crown as spies, messengers, navigators, and marauders.

It is a well-worn cliché that Charlestonians consider their grand city to be at the center of the known universe. Although the claim is exaggerated, this study shows that an understanding of what was going on in the vital seaport during the mid-1770s does have broader implications for the study of the Atlantic world, African-American history, the history of Revolutionary America, naval history, urban studies, race relations, labor history, and the turbulent politics of America's move toward independence.

Almost immediately after Jeremiah's execution, accounts of the episode started to be spun. Both sides of the American Revolution—patriot and loyalist—regarded the affair as a "disagreeable" subject. For those aligned with the Crown, such as Lord William Campbell (the last royal governor of South Carolina), Alexander Innes (Campbell's private secretary), Dr. George Millegen (chief surgeon to His Majesty's forts in South Carolina), Sir Egerton Leigh (an important customs official), John Montague, fourth Earl of Sandwich (first Lord of the Admiralty, the overseer of the Royal Navy), John Lind (progovernment pamphleteer), James Simpson (attorney general and subsequent head of the Board of Police in South Carolina), and Thomas Knox Gordon (chief justice of South Carolina), the episode displayed a kind of racial tyranny belying American patriotism. For Henry Laurens (a slave trader, merchant planter, and patriot leader), John Laurens (Henry's son and George Washington's aide-de-camp, who later advocated arming slaves), an anonymous gentleman from Charles Town, Peter Timothy (a radical patriot and printer of the *South Carolina Gazette*), and John Drayton (William Henry Drayton's son, who published his father's memoirs related to the American Revolution), the episode showed the depths to which a "wicked" British administration would stoop in order to undermine the social order of a slave society. From reading the few extant primary documents related to the trials and the execution, one gets the impression that contemporaries of Jeremiah familiar with his story sensed the import of the affair and wanted to shape public opinion accordingly.

For historians working on the American Revolution, the case sometimes merits a footnote or several paragraphs. However, a number of authors have described the story in detail or analyzed some aspect of it. Among these are Pauline Maier, Peter H. Wood, David M. Zornow, Robert M. Weir, Sylvia Frey, Philip D. Morgan, Walter Fraser Jr., Walter Edgar, Robert Olwell, Eliga Gould, Peter Linebaugh and Marcus Rediker, Ray Raphael, Simon Schama, Benjamin L. Carp, Gary B. Nash, and Jim Piecuch. All of these authors have drawn upon, and occasionally added to, a slim number of primary sources that shed light on the incident. I have benefited greatly from earlier assessments in developing my own arguments. Although these writers have described various facets of the Thomas Jeremiah incident, this book is the first to fully explicate the context of the trials and their aftermath.

Acknowledgments

There are many people I would like to thank: David A. Weir, Alastair J. Bellany, Cynthia B. Herrup, Elizabeth A. Fenn, Susan E. Thorne, Holly Brewer, Kathleen DuVal, John Thompson, Ron Witt, Jack Cell, the participants of the TEAHS, Michael Ferraro, Revonda Huppert, the Bristol family, Michael O'Connor, Robert Parrish, the Gilrane family, Ian Wise, Greg Cumbee, Dan Bartel, the members of FRPC, Richard Romm, Christopher Graham, Jess Usher, Joseph Moore, Margaret Brill of Perkins Library, and Charles Lesser at the SCDAH. All of you have helped me in diverse and innumerable ways, and I am truly grateful. My life and this book are better for my having known you.

To Peter Wood: You are the best adviser and friend a person could have. Your wisdom is exceeded only by your benevolence and generosity. Thanks for believing in this project and for pushing it in the right directions when necessary. I will never be able to thank you sufficiently. I hope this book will contribute to your wonderful and enduring legacy.

To Robert Calhoon: For reasons that are not entirely clear to me, you have taken this young academic under your wing and have been a great mentor. Thanks so much for being a kind and gentle soul. Your help, especially with respect to chapter 5, has improved the book substantially. You are a great person and an exceptional scholar—thank you for all of your astute advice.

To Nancy Toff: You are a fabulous editor. Thank you for your enthusiasm, hard work, and commitment to this project. Thanks also to Leora Bersohn and Caitlin Craven at Oxford University Press.

Thanks to James Cronan at the National Archives, U.K.; to Sean Flynn; to Andrew Sparling; Aaron Gore; and Joe Mobley. Thanks also to UPF for permission to use excerpts of an essay of mine printed in the 2003 volume *George Washington's South*. Thanks also to Duke University Libraries and UMI Pro-Quest for allowing me to publish a revised version of my dissertation on Thomas Jeremiah accepted December 2006 by the Duke History Department.

To my parents, Bill and Barbara, and my sister, Christine: You are all very dear to me. Thanks for everything. I love you and am so grateful for having each of you in my life.

To my wife, Tara: You mean more to me than you can ever know. I would not have been able to do this without you. Your steadfast love and support have seen me through some tumultuous times. From the bottom of my heart, thank you. Know this: I will always love you.

To my son, Jack: May you never lose your thirst for knowledge. May you always interrogate everything and look to the author of history for all of your answers.

I am especially grateful to an anonymous OUP reviewer who pointed out that "the SC pound was one of the most stable colonial currencies and prior to 1775 generally traded at a ration of 7-1." With that ratio in mind (and with the help of my colleague Andrew Sparling), we deduced that Jeremiah's personal estate (worth approximately £1000 BP in 1775) was essentially the equivalent of $200,000 in today's U.S. dollars. More important, we inferred that Henry Laurens's estimate of the financial damage that blockade of Charles Town Harbor would inflict upon the seaport and its surrounding countryside ("half a million" in 1775 S.C. currency) would roughly equal $15 million in 2009 U.S. dollars. As Holly Brewer put it to me, obviously such conversations are always necessarily approximate and must be taken with a grain of salt because they fail to account for the drastic change in the relative value of certain individual commodities.

Contents

The World of
Thomas Jeremiah

Introduction

A Different Port of Entry

In the 1770s, sailing into Charles Town by way of the Atlantic was menacing proposition. No one knew that better than Henry Laurens. On blustery winter's eve, as he made his way home from Falmouth, the merchant planter nearly perished when a pilot in his employ panicked and dashed their packet boat into the rocks. Stranded for hours at the mouth of Charles Town Harbor, the states-man reportedly resigned himself to a grim death at sea. Much to his surprise, he and his crewmembers narrowly escaped when a favorable tide and a second pilot intervened, bringing their vessel, *Le Despenser* safely to port. Undoubtedly, this near brush with fatality left an indelible imprint on merchant planter's mind as he nestled into his sprawling Ansonborough residence at Rattray Green ready to seize the reigns of a long-standing struggle that was about to cascade into outright war.[1]

As part of Charles Town's Pilotage Commission, the de facto head of South Carolina's patriot movement, like all city residents, understood the strategic importance of the profession and that the port would cease to function without the critical labor of these individuals. There were no exceptions. All oceanic vessels coming into or departing from the Carolina capital required a licensed harbor pilot. There was virtually no other way to negotiate the ever shifting bar-rier of sand and stone treacherously guarding the mouth of the harbor. Pilots stationed off of their base of operations at Sullivan's Island would race toward incoming ships in the hopes of procuring a fee. The first pilot boat to reach the approaching vessel would secure imbursement as well as the opportunity to bring the ship across the bar. Such was the method by which all seafaring craft entered the haven of Charles Town (see map 1).[2]

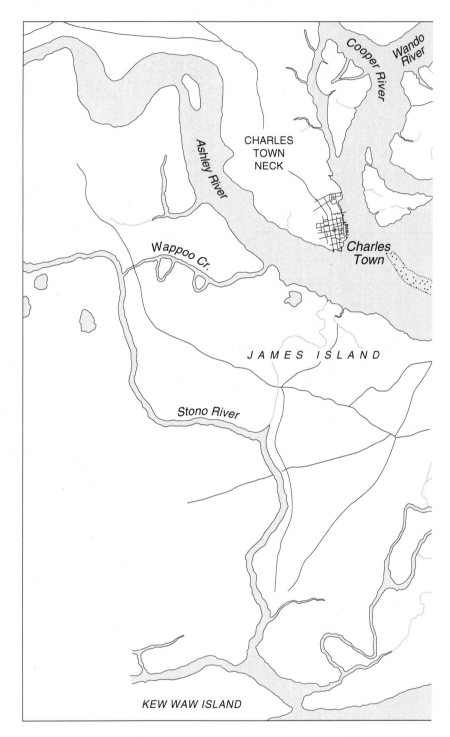

MAP I. "An Accurate Map of North and South Carolina...Printed for Robt. Sayer and J. Bennett...May 30th 1775 (Southern Section) by Thomas Jefferys, 1776." Getting in and out of the port of Charles Town could be incredibly difficult. This inset shows a forty-five-degree line drawn from the top of St. Michael's steeple

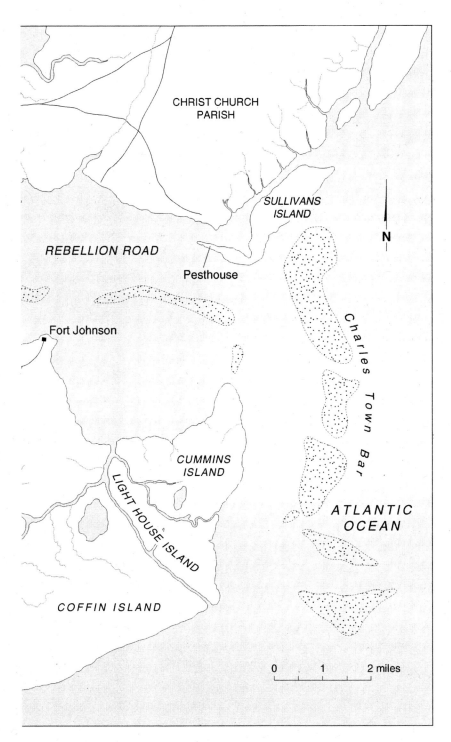

CHRIST CHURCH
PARISH

SULLIVANS
ISLAND

REBELLION ROAD

Pesthouse

C h a r l e s   T o w n   B a r

Fort Johnson

CUMMINS
ISLAND

LIGHT HOUSE ISLAND

ATLANTIC
OCEAN

N

COFFIN ISLAND

0   1   2 miles

down to Lawford Channel. As the tallest building in the skyline, the steeple was used by many boatmen, including Jeremiah, as a way of finding their bearings in the treacherous and tricky waters. *Courtesy of David Rumsey Map Collection*

Piloting in these waters was fraught with great peril. Although one could accumulate wealth rapidly, the undertaking itself was cutthroat and exceedingly dangerous. Besides the strain of competition, day in and day out, pilots were forced to contend with a merciless obstacle capable of bringing down the largest and most seaworthy of vessels. Moreover, depending on the wind and tides, surmounting this obstruction could take days and required an astonishing amount of skill and local knowledge. Given the importance of shipping to the economy of the Low Country, pilots enjoyed a rather privileged position. Simply put, from a strategic standpoint pilots held the keys that unlocked the harbor. Those within the city's confines were painfully aware that if any of the men engaged in this important business should turn and offer their services to an outside enemy, the consequences for Charles Town could be catastrophic. Especially harrowing for white locals was the fact that a number of these boatmen were operating illicitly, of African descent, and had far-reaching ties within the slave community. Adding to the discomfort was gnawing sense that coastal Carolina's black navigators may have been simply better equipped than their white counterparts. Carrying with them seafaring techniques honed on the shores of West Africa, Charles Town's black pilots routinely steered through the channels of the bar with extraordinary aplomb. This was no small feat, considering the harbor's ghastly reputation in eighteenth-century maritime circles.[3] One skilled waterman, who had likely crossed paths with Pilotage Commissioner Laurens, was himself a prominent slave owner with a sizable fortune: a free black by the name of Thomas Jeremiah. Entering the unique world this pilot, fisherman, and firefighter inhabited enables us to better understand why American ultimately broke from Britain.

At some point during the mid-eighteenth century, an Afro-Carolinian named Thomas Jeremiah obtained his freedom and began to distinguish himself as one of the most prominent blacks in the Charles Town community.[4] As he left no diary or papers of his own, little is known about his early life. If not for the controversy surrounding his trials and execution, we would know virtually nothing about the man. Although much about his life remains a mystery, it is patently obvious from the few available records that Jeremiah possessed a number of talents. According to the last royal governor of South Carolina, Lord William Campbell, Jeremiah's "Publick services were universally acknowledged, particularly in cases of fire, where by his skill and intrepidity he had often been remarkably useful."[5] In addition to his duties as a firefighter and protector of property, 'Jerry', as he was often called by contemporaries, made a successful living by transporting soldiers and "piloting in Men-of-War." He was also an accomplished boat maker and the proprietor of a lucrative fishing business. With time, Jeremiah acquired a modicum of fame and a sizeable estate. Eventually, he became a slave owner, employing several men in the city fish market and on the wharfs of the harbor.[6] Fueled by his capacity for self-promotion and an ability to capitalize on his public image, Jeremiah was able to augment his already growing reputation. In 1768, for example, an edition of the South Carolina Gazette contained the following heading: "The Negro Jerry (well known for his extinguishing of fires) has just completed a Well-Boat, in order to supply the inhabitants of [Charles Town] with Live Fish every day."[7] Jeremiah's competence was well known and often talked about in the white community. Campbell observed that he "had by his industry acquired a property upwards of £1000 sterling, was in a very thriving situation, had several slaves of his own, who he employed in fishing, and was one of the best pilots in the harbor."[8] Another contemporary, Royal Surgeon George Milligen, estimated that Jeremiah was worth "six or seven hundred pounds sterling."[9] According to historian Philip D. Morgan, Jeremiah was one of the most affluent blacks in pre-Revolutionary America.[10] Given the extraordinary opulence of the city in which he lived and the value of his personal estate, he may well have been the wealthiest person of color in the entire thirteen colonies.

Regarded as one of the best firefighters in the city and one of the most talented boatmen in the harbor,[11] Jerry's skills earned him the respect of his own community and also gained him a number of prominent white allies.[12] Undoubtedly, the pilot blurred and frequently transcended the boundaries of race that were becoming ever more sharply drawn during the course of his lifetime. Yet the same talents that brought him success and notoriety ultimately made him a target for white suspicion. As a man who had long worked with fire and often "piloted in men-of-war," Jeremiah would come to be viewed by patriots as the most plausible and potentially dangerous link between the Royal Navy and the colony's black majority.[13]

Although he never fit the traditional profile of a radical (according to his loyalist defenders), Jerry was certainly a complex figure. His paradoxical relationship to the white power structure is perhaps best illustrated by an incident that occurred on Wednesday, July 17, 1771. That same year, Jeremiah was convicted (for reasons unknown) of assaulting a white ship captain by the name of Thomas Langen—a bold action for a black man living in the pre-Revolutionary South—and was sentenced to an hour in the pillory and ten lashes with a whip. By dint of his widely acknowledged public deeds, however, Lieutenant Governor William Bull granted him a pardon.[14] Four years later, when open conflict broke out between England and the colonies, such mercies would be harder to come by (figure 3.1).

In spite of the sheer volume of material written on the American Revolution, the story continues to require further explication. Nearly all accounts of the war itself begin in Boston and focus on the northern theater until 1779–80, when the focus of the war finally shifts to the South. One gets the impression from reading most college textbooks and histories of the War for Independence that virtually nothing was going on in the lower South until the British occupied Charles Town and Savannah.[15] However, to truly comprehend the initial years of the war, in all their political, social, and military intricacy, we need to cast our view to the Southeast. Like Mel Gibson's fictional character in the opening scenes of the film *The Patriot*, we need to enter the port city of Charles Town during what are arguably the two most important years in American history, the period between the summer of 1774 and the summer of 1776. And unlike Gibson's reluctant revolutionary, Benjamin Martin, we need to stay there and explore, replacing Hollywood's gauzy fiction with hard-won, and often disconcerting, historical facts.[16] This book, by exploring the world of a hitherto obscure black harbor pilot, will make clear that the coming of the American Revolution had a crucial Southern dimension, and in South Carolina, tension over race and slavery shaped the fight over independence.[17] In recent years, several excellent general studies have attempted to examine the long-neglected racial dynamic of the War for Independence.[18] This monograph attempts to put the topic into sharper focus by bringing to the fore the obscure story of the life and death of Thomas Jeremiah. It places him in the context of his bustling port city and makes clear that his name, like that of Crispus Attucks, Nathan Hale or Molly Pitcher, deserves to be part of the complex iconography of the 1770s.

Those who stood the most to gain from the boatman's execution were those at the helm of South Carolina's nascent patriot movement—dissident statesmen such as Henry Laurens, a confidant of George Washington who would later faithfully serve America as the second president of the Continental Congress.[19] They included men such as Daniel Cannon, a well-to-do planter-artisan, the behind-the-scenes ringleader of the Charles Town Sons of Liberty, who eventually founded the eponymous Cannonsborough in the northwest corner of the city.[20] Naturally, these influential Whigs had a vested interest both in maintaining their own standing at the top the social order and in preserving the prosperity of this incredibly thriving slave port.

While we can never fully know their true motivations, these statesmen must have had a profound sense of impending doom (or that is the impression they frequently gave). Why else would they risk their reputations both at home and in England to ensure that the most successful black man in Charles Town, an individual frequently described as a pillar of the community, would meet with one of the most gruesome fates imaginable?[21] Something was at work here—something manifestly racial in nature—which, despite its elusive character, is critical to our understanding of how the American Revolution unraveled in its Southern theater.

Why is it that South Carolina patriots deliberately ordered the death of this important man at the exact moment the imperial crisis was erupting into outright war? Of what were they so seemingly terrified? And why did they insist, despite the repeated pleadings of Lord William Campbell, the colony's last royal governor (himself a slaveholder), that Thomas Jeremiah needed to be put to death in such a public and brutal fashion?[22] With such overt displays of violence, whom were the patriot leaders trying so hard to intimidate? What were they trying so desperately to preclude? The more I investigated the circumstances surrounding Jeremiah's "trials" and execution, the more it became apparent that the answers had to do with the unique demographic makeup of the province and the fate of Charles Town Harbor.

Few people know that on the eve of the American Revolution, the colony of South Carolina had an enslaved black majority.[23] Fewer still are aware that in 1774, this colony was the richest in all of mainland British North America. The province's capital city, Charles Town (called Charleston after August 13, 1783), was a prized jewel in Britain's imperial Crown and the fourth-largest port in the thirteen colonies.[24] Its wealth was staggering. According to one estimate, the estates of Charles Town merchants were valued at six times that of their Philadelphia contemporaries. Not surprisingly, the affluence of this vibrant Southern port was generated largely by the trade of African slaves and the exportation of its two chief commodities: rice and indigo.[25]

Although technically an entrepôt rather than a full-fledged "commercial center," Charles Town was *the* metropolis of the Southeast. Its reach extended both regionally and to vital ports in the West Indies and along the Atlantic Ocean.[26] Perhaps because the Carolina capital declined so significantly after its "golden age" or because the story of the break from Mother England has been told so frequently from a New England or Virginian backdrop, this city has yet to receive the full scholarly attention it deserves.[27] And yet, by coming at the Revolution through the port city of Charles Town, the story of the War for Independence takes on a different dimension. In other words, a thorough investigation of the Jeremiah affair and its context provides us with a new vantage point from which to view the American Revolution. By looking at this "different port of entry," new questions emerge, new participants come to the forefront of the revolutionary stage, and new problems for the Founding Founders and the British administration are brought to light. Many are aware of the events and key players in Northern port cities. By linking those stories and individuals to the largely unknown world of Charles Town, South Carolina, this book attempts to provide an influx of fresh air.

We must keep in mind, however, that it is absolutely essential when discussing the five most important seaports in colonial America—Charles Town, Newport, Philadelphia, New York, and Boston—to draw down our concept of size. As Nash and Carp have demonstrated, compared with London and the major population centers in Europe, colonial America's cities were in a state of relative infancy. In 1774, the thirteen colonies were predominantly rural. Compared with the metropolises of today, colonial American cities were more like fledgling outposts. On the eve of white independence, Charles Town was barely more than 100 years old and contained only approximately 12,000 souls. For us, it is hard to picture just how intimate these settings were. A quick stroll around Colonial Williamsburg today reminds us, however, that in terms of size and scale, eighteenth-century provincial capitals were a far cry from Gotham. In such environs, face-to-face interactions were indeed common, and many of the residents knew one another well. Given the negligible population of these seaports, this should come as no surprise.[28]

Anyone who has ever stood on the bow of the Staten Island Ferry and taken the twenty-two-minute ride toward lower Manhattan knows how truly breathtaking a harbor in motion can be. And while it was obviously less stunning than the sight of New York Harbor in its current condition, visitors sailing into the port of Charles Town in 1774 would, in many ways, perceive that same sort of kinetic energy. Indeed, like the present-day seaport of New York, the harbor of Charles Town in the mid-1770s teemed with commercial activity, was flanked by neighboring islands, and brimmed with wide assortment of seagoing vessels. Yet unlike Manhattan or the port of Philadelphia—situated on an island and a riverbank, respectively—the city of Charles Town was located at the base of a peninsula in much the same manner as Boston. In contrast to that "city on a hill," the topography of Charles Town was just plain flat. Over time, the phrase "low country" arose to describe the marshy sea-level plain in which the port was nestled.[29]

Twenty-first-century Charlestonians sometimes jest that their beloved city lies "where the Cooper River and the Ashley River come together to form the Atlantic Ocean."[30] And while the harbor has undeniably undergone significant change since the colonial days, the estuarial habitat has long been a world unto itself—a site of incredible biological diversity, where salt and fresh water continually intermingle (although not to the same degree as they once did). This place was and is home to shrimp, oysters, and blue crab. Yet it has also long been a haven for more imposing fauna, including alligators, bull sharks, stingrays, and longnose gar. In the waters surrounding the port, Atlantic manta rays (or devilfish), sometimes spanning twenty-two feet and weighing 2,500 pounds, have been known to breach the surface and leap several feet into the air. The teeming aquatic life of the harbor and it surroundings has made for a centuries-old fishing industry that was first dominated by local Indians and later by imported Africans.[31]

Since the city's shift to its current location in 1680, the space has also swarmed with riverine traffic. In the nineteenth century, the illustrious Charles Dickens, having made the Grand Tour of Europe, likened the Carolina capital to an American Venice—a sparkling city seemingly "growing out of the waves."[32] James Glen, the colony's former governor, once characterized the Cooper River as "a kind of floating market," where "numbers of Canoes, Boats, and Pettygues" plied incessantly. In 1772 and 1773 alone, some sixty-five slaving vessels entered the harbor, their holds crammed with more than 10,000 Africans.[33] At the height of the shipping season that year, Josiah Quincy Jr. spied 350 craft in Charles Town Harbor. The astonished New Englander conceded that the number of ships he had seen in the Carolina capital far surpassed anything he had observed in Boston.[34] In the twelve months leading up to the trade Associations of 1774–75, a total of 507 vessels cleared out in "Charlestown." While generally not buzzing with as much activity during the winter, there were at least 100 vessels at anchor in Rebellion Road at any given time.[35] On a typical day, rice boats, fishing vessels, schooners, and ferries could all be seen cutting through the greenish waters of the estuary.[36]

Activity in the wharf district was often especially frenzied. Strolling down from the top of Bay Street, a hypothetical observer might come upon Christopher Gadsden's Wharf, the largest of its kind in colonial America (map 2). Along the quay, a whole host of warehouses for naval stores, deerskin, cooperage, and cash crops could be seen in full view. There, slave dockworkers could also likely be viewed pulling tierces of rice off boats from inland plantations. Along the waterfront, barrels of prized "Carolina gold" would be watched closely by African bondsmen, who reportedly set fires at night to keep warm. "A practice that exposed the houses near the quays to danger," according to Leila Sellers. Considering how much damage the great fire of 1740 had caused, incinerating 300 homes in just six hours, this behavior was regarded with much suspicion.[37] The newly elected firemaster, Mr. Cannon, may have lain awake at night worrying about the potentiality of a "mishap" on the docks that would set the entire wharf district alight. His anxieties, like those of the white community at large, must have been augmented by fact that gunpowder, a much sought-after explosive (after October 19, 1774), was taken off every incoming ship.[38] Although most of the powder was slated for the magazine at the nearby State House, its proximity to highly flammable pitch, tar, and turpentine made for a potentially

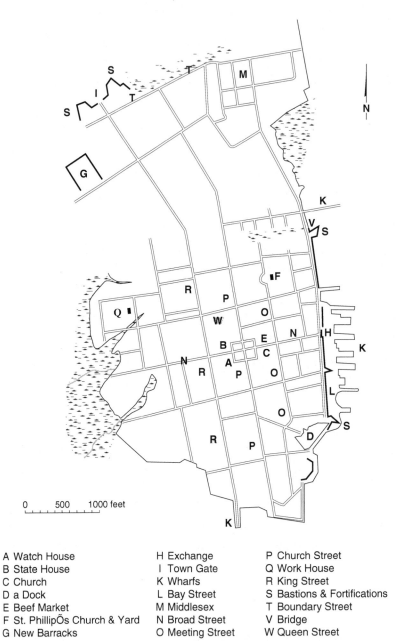

0   500   1000 feet

A Watch House	H Exchange	P Church Street
B State House	I Town Gate	Q Work House
C Church	K Wharfs	R King Street
D a Dock	L Bay Street	S Bastions & Fortifications
E Beef Market	M Middlesex	T Boundary Street
F St. PhillipŌs Church & Yard	N Broad Street	V Bridge
G New Barracks	O Meeting Street	W Queen Street

MAP 2. "A map of the province of South Carolina... by their most obedt. & faithful servt. Jams. Cook. Thos. Bowen, sculpt. 1773." This inset of Charles Town contains one of the best maps of the city from the period. By 1775, Charles Town had expanded beyond its original city walls and was a place where great opulence was juxtaposed with extreme squalor. No other port city in mainland British North America had so much wealth or so many residents ensnared in hereditary bondage. *Courtesy of David Rumsey Map Collection*

volatile concoction.[39] When the black powder was commandeered by patriots in April 1775 in preparation for war, it was at Gadsden's Wharf that the precious article was stored.[40] As we shall see, in the critical two-year period leading up to independence, powder and power became synonymous. In a colony as militarily vulnerable as South Carolina, whoever controlled one controlled the other.

Walking due south along Bay Street, our observer would eventually traverse the curiously named So Be It Lane. [41] Within a few minutes, he or she would eventually see Fitzsimmon's Wharf to the right, a location where our protagonist, Thomas Jeremiah, ostensibly spent much of his time when not at sea, working side-by-side with black fishermen, stevedores, and fellow pilots.[42] Black bondsmen with blue hands could likely be seen there warding off flies attracted by the ghastly aroma of indigo.[43] Slave ships, discharging Gambians fresh from their ten-day quarantine on Sullivan's Island, also likely loosed a fetid stench of blood, vinegar, and urine.[44]

Further afield, "directly opposite to Queen-street," the wafting stink of the city's fish market must have also hit visitors particularly hard. Drawn in by the noisome odor of refuse and rotten fish, turkey vultures circled the skies above.[45] As the foreboding creatures swirled around, they may have spied fishermen converging on the location with their nets, ready to peddle oysters, shrimp, and trout extracted from local waters. As far as whites were concerned, the black boatmen who dominated this marketplace were boisterous and unruly. A statute passed in April 1770 observed that the "business of fishing is principally carried on by negroes, mulattoes and mestizoes, who are apt to be riotous and disorderly." To keep them in line, white justices of the peace erected a pillory on site. The white JPs were also given full "authority to confine all riotous, disorderly or drunken negroes, mulattoes or mustizoes, buying, selling or being in and about the said market, in the stocks…for a space not more than two hours." Repeat offenders were to be "publicly whipped near the said market not exceeding thirty-nine lashes."[46] Incorrigibles were likely sent to the "workhouse" across town for further chastisement.

As one might suspect in a society where melanin determined who constituted a slave, whites were often treated differently under the law. Under the terms of the 1770 statute, whites using "any blasphemous, profane or opprobrious language" or engaging in disorderly behavior in the marketplace were merely fined ten pounds. Those not paying the fine, however, would then be placed in the stocks for a period of up to four hours. The wording of these concerns suggests that the fish market itself may have become a site of interracial commotion. White customers were sometimes irked by black fish vendors unfamiliar with the English language. Of the slave fishermen of Charles Town, the famous botanist Dr. Alexander Garden once groused: "Most or indeed all of them are negroes, whom I find it impossible to make understand me rightly what I want; add to this their gross ignorance and obstinacy to the greatest degree; so that though I have hired several of them, I could not procure anything." Increasingly, white residents such as Garden became agitated by bondsmen and -women haggling with them over the price of seafood and produce. In 1772, an anonymous author, identifying himself as "the Stranger," accused black fishermen of unfairly inflating the price of drumfish by ten times its initial value to the detriment of poor whites.[47] Given the reputation of "fishing negroes" for unruliness, obstinacy, and price fixing, accusing one of plotting an insurrection may have had broad currency with the white populace.

At Prioleau's Wharf, ferries run by black patroons transported passengers across the harbor to the outlying Sea Islands. This, like the contiguous fish market, was an important location, where Jeremiah ostensibly spent much time when not coasting amid the shoals or snuffing out fires.[48] Along the adjacent piers lining the Cooper, crews from Bristol, Liverpool, London, Newport, and Kingston probably fraternized, likely trading tales of their various exploits at sea. Jack Tars, artisans, and shopkeepers may have bewailed the latest injustice at Boston or discussed details of a recent duel. News must have circulated quickly at this site as it poured in from across the ocean, up and down the coast, and around the world. Huguenots, Scots, and Sephardic Jews flooded into the port from the old country. Acadians, later called Cajuns, came down to the metropolis from Nova Scotia.[49] White residents from the backcountry, having traveled two or three weeks down neck to Charles Town, may have resented the perceptible stranglehold of the Low Country grandees on provincial politics. As these upcountry "beggars," as they were sometimes called, rode their wagons along the bay, they must have been struck by the relative opulence, extravagance, and dizziness of their Low Country surroundings.[50]

Across Bay Street, a row of fine houses, alternately built of brick and wood, overlooked the prospect of the commercial district and the waterfront. From the piazzas high above the street, one could reportedly observe the myriad craft in motion and gaze out into "the open sea without the bar." In one of the lavish single houses, a parvenu may have grown cross when his mistress bungled Handel on the harpsichord. Next door, in the drawing room of a Palladian mansion, a company of libertines may have frittered away their fortunes at the gaming table. In a counting house down the street, a merchant planter might have perused folios of *Wells's Register* or the *South Carolina Gazette*, hoping to stay ahead of his competitors. Members of the same set, browsing for the latest finished goods from London, probably had to tread with great alacrity as they passed by raucous taverns overflowing with sailors, slaves, and smoke.[51]

Depending on the time of year, our observer would undoubtedly be taken aback by the city's sultry climate, bloodthirsty mosquitoes, and omnipresent cockroaches scampering along the dusty, sand-covered streets.[52] Scalding heat and various "distempers" were mitigated somewhat by the sight of haunting live oaks draped in gray-green moss, saw palmettos, and the purple hues of flowering wisteria (during the spring).[53] Our onlooker might also be stunned by just how black the city was. Unlike Boston, New York, and Philadelphia, on the eve of the American Revolution, Charles Town had a slight black majority and a quasi-Caribbean feel. Indeed, more than half of the residents in Charles Town were enslaved and African in origin.[54] Given the high number of poor whites and slaves living in the city, interactions among different races and classes were frequent and, in many ways, inevitable.[55] White planters from the "very best" society reportedly held lavish cotillions, where they were said to carouse with slave girls dressed in the latest fineries. Even the speech among Charles Town whites, called "high Gullah" by historian George C. Rogers Jr., may have been tinged by the relative propinquity of imported Africans and creoles.[56]

Surrounding the conurbation itself were outlying parishes established along the same lines as Barbados, from whence many of the original settlers, Africans, and slave codes came. For whites in these Low Country parishes, the demographic circumstances could be downright terrifying.[57] This was especially true for those who had lived through the Stono Rebellion of 1739 and knew full well that servile insurrection was a real possibility. As Peter H. Wood rightly pointed out, unrest in the black community frequently flared up during times of acute strain.[58] In a similar vein to the Irish, who, throughout history, seized on England's difficulties and exploited them as opportunities, the blacks of South Carolina periodically plotted uprisings when whites were distracted or in conflict with one another. Witness the case of Philip John or Jones, a free black or biracial man, who in 1759, at the height of the colony's war with the Cherokee, threatened to "kill all the buckras" or raze all the whites to the ground. The plot was ultimately thwarted and the apparent ringleader killed. But six years later, as the Stamp Act Crisis was raging in Charles Town and blacks were chanting "Liberty!" in the streets, a second alleged conspiracy involving the "troublesome community" was uncovered by colonial leaders. As an added security measure, the Catawba Indians were called down from the backcountry to hunt down runaway blacks who had taken refuge in the nearby swamps.[59]

This tactic of playing Native American tribes and African-American slaves off against one another, first described by William Willis in his pioneering article "Divide and Rule" and later by Gary B. Nash, would, at critical flashpoints, be employed by South Carolina's founders as relations with Britain neared their breaking point. As one white Carolinian described the stratagem earlier in the century, "we make use of a Wile for our pres[en]t. Security to make Indians & Negro's a checque upon each other least[sic] by their Vastly Superior Numbers we should be crushed by one or the other." As unconscionable as it may seem by today's standards, given the demographic makeup of the colony, Whig leaders saw no other way to maintain their hegemony in the face of a potential "British-instigated" race war. To ensure their own survival, it was imperative that blacks and Native Americans residing in and around the colony despised each other and never joined forces against the white revolutionary populace. Acutely aware of their own Achilles heel, South Carolina Whigs were truly concerned that this incredible vulnerability might be exploited at the hands of an external foe.[60]

Perhaps no one articulated this deep-seated fear better than Christopher Gadsden, a leader in and founder of Charles Town's Sons of Liberty organization. In a 1775 letter addressed to fellow radical Samuel Adams, he confided to the Bostonian that South Carolina was "a weak Colony from the Number of Negroes we have amongst us, and therefore exposed to more formid[able] ministerial Tricks."[61] Like Gadsden, the MP for Bewdley, England, William Henry Lyttleton, was intimately familiar with South Carolina's unique (not quite Caribbean) ethnic composition. Previously, he had served as the province's royal governor during the Cherokee War and the John conspiracy and, later, as the governor of Jamaica during the 1765 uprising of Coromantees. He, like other important Britons of his day, including Samuel Johnson (the famed lexicographer and literary figure) and Sir William Draper (who had captured Manila during the Seven Years War), was convinced that if the Americans persisted in rebelling against their king, they could be quickly and unequivocally subdued by turning the South's racial demography against them.[62]

In a speech given before the House of Commons in October 1775, Lyttleton likened the thirteen colonies to a chain. The rings at top of this chain, he argued, representing the Northern colonies, were the strongest on account of the number of white residents. Yet as one moved further down, the former royal governor declared, the chain itself became progressively weaker. The rings at the bottom of the link, representing the Southern colonies, were easily broken as a result of the high proportion of black slaves. By using redcoats and insurgent field hands to vanquish the rebels, Albion might then show mercy to the wayward Americans and thus restore harmony to the empire. Fortunately for the Low Country patriots, this measure was rejected by Lyttleton's fellow MPs. Nevertheless, even before Lyttleton uttered this inflammatory analogy before the Commons, rumors of such a scheme echoed resoundingly in the drawing rooms and dram shops in and around Charles Town.[63]

Indeed, fear of conspiratorial acts by the government of King George III had multiplied in the colonies in the period after 1774. For those living through that time, especially considering the lag in news dissemination, separating fact from fiction must often have been extraordinarily difficult.[64] As the situation grew increasingly grave, there was a kind of "crisis of allegiance"—an intricate web of push-pull interactions in which all of the players on the revolutionary stage were thoroughly enmeshed. Potential alliances, however fragile or born of necessity, weighed heavily on the minds of many. In this local and imperial civil war, enemies of enemies might just be wooed, courted, or turned into strategic collaborators. Would any of the members of South Carolina's black majority align with Britain? Would any of the Cherokee Indians living on the frontier avoid warfare altogether or become British mercenaries? Would any of the Catawba Indians support the Whigs, and if so, could they indeed help frighten the enslaved populace into submission? Would any of the residents in the backcountry stay loyal to the Crown? Or might they aid Charles Town patriots in suppressing alleged attempts by George III's officials to raise an insurrection of the slaves? With conflicting reports, rumors, and tales of ministerial misdeeds circulating, anything was possible, or, at least, so it seemed.

It had only been several years earlier, in June 1772, that the landmark case of *Sommersett v. Stuart* had been decided. Legal academics continue to debate about the exact meaning of the precedent it established. However, for scores of African-American slaves living in the South during the early-to-mid-1770s, the ruling was imbued with real significance.[65] While there were many who opted to stay put, there were numerous others for whom black freedom was often identified more with England and George III than with local masters.[66] Once we come to terms with this fact, the veil obscuring our understanding of the Revolution in the South is suddenly lifted. Let me make it perfectly clear, however, that it is not my desire, or my place, to assert that Britain somehow had a monopoly on benevolence or the moral high ground during this conflict. Nor do I claim that one side's motivations were more humanitarian than the other's, but, rather, I suggest that for all South Carolinians (black, white, Cherokee, Catawba, patriot, and loyalist), actions were often dictated and can best be explained by the contingencies of warfare and Southern demographic conditions. Internal divisions and uncertainty about the best course of action within each of the aforementioned groups made choosing sides a profoundly personal act—one that could have deep and lasting consequences based upon the outcome of the war. Lamentably, for those individuals who were illiterate or lacked access to print, often the only determinant at our disposal is to observe how they voted with their feet.

When on June 15, 1775, George Washington, a former tobacco planter from Virginia, was chosen to lead the Continental Army, the glorious cause was forever intertwined with a seemingly paradoxical position that was, at its heart, proslavery. As hidden as that reality may be today by popular culture, historiography, and tradition, such ironies were not lost on contemporaries. Across the Atlantic, in 1775, the ever caustic Johnson queried, "How is it that we hear the loudest yelps for liberty among the drivers of the Negroes?" The founders, as has been shown by Woody Holton and others, recognized that they had a real conundrum on their hands. Shortly after Lord Dunmore, Virginia's last royal governor, issued America's first partial emancipation proclamation in mid-November 1775, Washington remarked: "If that man is not crushed before spring he will become the most formidable enemy America has; his strength will increase as a snowball by rolling, and faster, if some expedient cannot be hit upon to convince the slaves and servants of the impotency of his designs."[67]

News of Dunmore's proclamation traveled quickly both up and down the slave communication networks of the eastern seaboard. By early December 1775, the situation had become dire, prompting one white Philadelphian to bemoan, "Hell itself could not have vomited anything more black than his design of emancipating our slaves.... The flame runs like wild fire through the slaves." Around the same exact time, a black Philadelphian, elated by such developments, reportedly execrated a white "gentlewoman" walking down the street, telling her she needed to "Stay... 'till Lord Dunmore and his black regiment come, and then we will see who is to take the wall." As patriots rapidly discovered, as the bonds of deference were undermined at the imperial level, those same bonds could just as easily be attenuated among friends, neighbors, and members of the immediate household.[68]

In the days and months leading up to and immediately following Lexington and Concord, South Carolina's slaveholding Whigs had become convinced that their own domestics and neighboring Indian tribes might turn against them if given the chance. As the Crown's Indian agent for the Southern colonies, John Stuart, declared, "nothing can be more alarming to the Carolinians than the idea of an attack by Indians and Negroes."[69] To preclude this nightmarish scenario from taking place, patriot leaders relied on spectacles of violence to try to frighten the black populace into full submission. Often, that meant deliberately fostering antipathy between black and red. In the case of the Sullivan's Island incident in December 1775 and the Tybee Island incident in March 1776, Indians, and/or whites painted and dressed like them, hunted down and reportedly killed an unknown number of blacks who had congregated in and around British warships in the hopes of obtaining their freedom.[70]

With respect to Thomas Jeremiah, it entailed setting a black harbor pilot on fire because he apparently had all of the tools and connections to link a sometimes insurgent slave majority with what was then the most powerful navy in world history. His proven track record as a firefighter and his knowledge of combustibles would also contribute to his eventual demise. Based on his substantial wealth, interracial associations, and access to powder, patriot partisans alleged he intended to ignite a devastating inferno upon the arrival of the British regulars. For white Charlestonians, with memories of the suspicious fire of 1740 fresh in their minds, the threat of black arson was no laughing matter.[71]

The case of Thomas Jeremiah—the protagonist of our story—is incredibly misunderstood. On the rare occasions when the episode is mentioned, the rationale behind this enigmatic boatman's execution is generally limited to his unusually high social status and great "prominence."[72] And while white envy was undeniably a factor in his death, this book makes the argument that his ultimate undoing had less to do with the value of his personal estate and more to do with his strategic occupations. His capacity and rumored willingness to facilitate an impending maritime invasion of Charles Town is what patriots feared (or claimed to fear) more than anything else.

Given the sheer paucity of the source material, we may never be certain of Jeremiah's "guilt" or "innocence." And yet his case and its context are still significant. After the Stamp Act demonstrations of 1765, colonial elites were linked together through far-reaching communiqués. However, in the world of Thomas Jeremiah, patriot leaders were sometimes forced to grapple with issues quite distinct from those of their Northern brethren. For Whigs in Boston, New York, and Philadelphia such as John Adams, Gouverneur Morris, and Benjamin Franklin, respectively, racial demography was never the sticking point that it was for Henry Laurens, Christopher Gadsden, and Arthur Middleton. Recently, one study suggested that in the case of Jeremiah, "crowd action and the criminal justice system worked in tandem, encouraging slaves and free blacks to remain in humble submission...thereby denying them the fruits of Revolutionary political mobilization."[73] And while violence most certainly deterred many from fleeing the Carolina metropolis and its surrounding plantations, there were quite a few black men and women who did defy the odds and participate in conflict as counterrevolutionary spies, messengers, and marauders. Indeed, when the dreaded British invasions finally did come to Charles Town Harbor in June 1776 and again in May 1780, the redcoats depended heavily on the black harbor pilots of the Low Country to surmount the "infernal bar" guarding the port.[74]

In a very real sense, then, what patriots tried to preclude by setting Thomas Jeremiah's body ablaze ultimately came to fruition. That these individuals chose to cast their lot with the side that eventually lost the War for Independence should not vitiate their actions or importance. We can choose to ignore the entire incident as an inconsequential aberration—a bizarre episode better swept under the rug—or we can break it down and dissect it, letting it unfurl carefully and chronologically. Only then will the role of race in South Carolina's War for Independence be more fully understood.

I

White Divisions

June 1774–March 1775

In summer 1774, having learned of the closure of Boston's port by the British, white patriots from across South Carolina made their way into Charles Town. Believing that similar action might be taken against the Southern metropolis, members of the Whig elite called for a "general" meeting of the colony's inhabitants to be held on Monday, July 6.[1] When the appointed day came, 104 gentlemen convened at the foot of the Exchange Building on Broad Street at nine o'clock.[2] Immediately, they settled on resolutions denouncing the recent anti-American legislation.[3] But not long afterward, a rift appeared between the merchants and the artisans. While delegates were being selected to serve at a general congress in Philadelphia, spokesmen for the merchant faction, who opposed the measure to boycott British goods, became embroiled in a debate with Christopher Gadsden, a leading spokesman for the artisan community. After much wrangling, a compromise was reached. Gadsden, Henry Middleton, and Thomas Lynch, along with Edward and John Rutledge, were selected to represent the colony at what would become known as the Continental Congress. Although they had come to an agreement over the issue of representation, spokesmen for the artisans and the merchants remained bitterly divided.[4]

Despite the fissure, the men in attendance took an extraordinary step. Seizing the reins of government from the Crown, the members established a large extralegal body known simply as the General Committee. In keeping with the desire to accommodate the various factions, the patriots in attendance nominated fifteen merchants and fifteen mechanics to represent Charles Town, along with sixty-nine planters to represent the surrounding parts of the province. For the time being, it appeared as though the sharp rivalries among the propertied classes lay dormant.[5]

Around the same time that the General Committee came into being, the issue of nonimportation came to the fore. Captain Richard Maitland had arrived in late June with a cargo of tea in violation of the continental boycott. Maitland was summoned to appear before the committee and was promptly interrogated. When asked why he had imported the tea knowing that "such a conduct was contrary to the sense of this Colony in particular, and of America in general," the captain gave the innocent but dubious response that he did not know the cargo was on his ship until after he had set sail. The members of the committee continued to press him on the issue until Maitland finally agreed that he would not land the tea or tax the citizens of Charles Town for the cargo. Satisfied by his assurances, the General Committee ordered Maitland to set the tea ablaze and pay the duties on the item himself.[6]

The next day, when the captain attempted to reclaim the tea from the Customs House by paying the requisite taxes, the collector refused to relinquish the goods. While the two men were bickering over who should take hold of the tea, the General Committee reconvened. Now, however, a number of merchant members were present who had been absent the day before when Maitland was ordered to destroy the controversial shipment. Feeling that the demand was improper and that the tea should be left untouched, the merchants called for a new vote. After taking a vote, the committeemen decided that the tea should remain in customs. Attempting not to incur the wrath of the lower classes for violating the boycott, the General Committee promptly shifted the blame onto Maitland and publicly denounced him.[7]

That evening, a mob of several hundred Charlestonians stormed onto the wharf where Maitland's *Magna Charta* had come to rest. The makeup of the crowd is hard to determine, but it likely consisted of slaves, sailors, and men from the lowest ranks of society. Maitland had caught wind of the intended assault and, anticipating the arrival of the throng, placed a watch to apprise him of its approach. When the angry multitude reached the end of the quay and was about to stage a raid on the *Magna Charta*, Maitland slipped over the opposite side of his vessel and onto a small boat that he kept ready for the occasion. Under the cover of night, the captain rowed away as the irate horde looked on. After some time, the skipper made his way to a British man-of-war anchored in Rebellion Road.[8] Having reached his destination, Maitland begged the commanding officer for protection. At around two A.M., a pair of armed barges manned by redcoats sailed out to the dock where the *Magna Charta* was still at rest. The British crews proceeded to extricate the vessel from its moorings and tow the ship to a nearby stream out of harm's way.[9]

Shortly after this incident, word reached Charles Town regarding two more "Intolerable Acts" by the British government. The Quartering Act made provincial authorities responsible for accommodating the British army and authorized the army to commandeer vacant buildings or barns in towns that failed to provide adequate housing, and the Quebec Act gave the fledgling province of British Canada control over all of the rich lands west of the Appalachians and north of the Ohio River that had long been coveted by colonial land speculators and frontier settlers. These acts, coupled with the Port Bill, had the effect of alienating colonists up and down the eastern seaboard. They felt that the Quebec Act was particularly egregious in that it limited westward expansion on the part of Americans and allowed the Catholic religion to flourish—something that was anathema to the majority of Protestants in the thirteen colonies. Was George III sanctioning the spread of Roman Catholicism? Were "popery" and French Canadian law about to establish a foothold on the Western frontier? As Drayton noted, such news inflamed the minds of "the people" in Charles Town. Quebec may have seemed a world away, but the act was taken as proof, even in the lower South, that the king was a despot—acting in violation of his coronation oath to protect the Protestant faith. Was this not what the Glorious Revolution had sought to prevent in 1689? Had George III become another James II? Was the Hanover dynasty now repeating the dangerous errors of the House of Stuart?[10]

In addition to fretting about the state of religion, men of all stations in Charles Town's white community speculated increasingly on the state of public affairs. Twenty-one-year-old John Julius Pringle, who would later serve as federal district attorney under Washington and as attorney general of South Carolina, was at that time home for the summer taking a respite from his study of law at the College of Philadelphia. Writing to his classmate William Tilghman, who had remained at the mid-Atlantic port, Pringle noted in late July 1774 that Charlestonians from every rank had begun to weigh in on the larger debate:

> The talk upon the situation of American Affairs and Politics here
> seems to drown all other, no News is sought, and no Conversation so
> much desired as political. The Gentleman & Mechanic, those of high,
> and low life, the learned & illiterate in their several clubs and as they
> casually meet harangue upon the same subjects. The Blessings of
> Liberty—The Miseries of Oppression—the dangerous tendency of
> the measures of Parliament against Boston towards the enthralling of
> America—Rights invaded and grievances to be redress'd are the
> Topics of daily declaration.[11]

The notion of artisans and men from the lower strata of society discussing high politics did not appeal to everyone in Charles Town, as the struggles over patriot leadership during July had made clear. On Sunday, August 14, Reverend John Bullman, assistant minister of St. Michael's Anglican Church, railed from the pulpit against those who had begun to critique the actions of the Crown too vehemently.[12] Taking aim at the "illiterate Clown & low bred Mechanic," the preacher denounced the recent flurry of democratic activity, arguing that Charles Town would return to a state of tranquility only if every man kept "his own rank" and remained firmly within "his own station." Rather than calming his flock with this admonition, the pastor only fueled the controversy for many of the patriot listeners sitting in the pews of St. Michael's. They immediately took offense at this open rebuke, and a ruckus ensued; a cacophony of voices began to drown out the service. As soon as the doors of the church burst open, word spread through the city that Bullman had "inculcated passive obedience" and had "censured popular proceedings."[13]

By Monday morning, the commotion had taken on further momentum. The vestry demanded that the minister produce a written copy of the diatribe for them to examine. Bullman took offense, telling churchwardens that there was nothing derogatory in the text. A heated debate ensued. After exchanging barbs, the irate pastor realized that he was outnumbered by his own vestry and agreed to hand over the sermon. The preacher then stormed out, ranting that no one should be able to dictate the content of his homilies.[14]

Not knowing what steps to take and under pressure from the city's laboring classes, the vestry called for a general meeting of the parishioners the next week. As the mixed crowd of Whig and Tory churchgoers filed into St. Michael's, the vestrymen began to query the congregation about the appropriateness of Bullman's conduct. After considering the matter for some time, there appeared to be universal agreement that the sermon was improper given the turmoil that Charlestonians found themselves in. However, when the minister's character was called into question, most members of the congregation conceded that Bullman was a "moral man" and an "edifying preacher."[15] Suddenly, though, the proceedings took on the flavor of a witch hunt. An altercation ensued, and a number of "mild men" in favor of Bullman walked out in disgust. Some of the more vociferous patriots took over the meeting, intoning, " 'Now we will see, who are the enemies to their country[!]' "[16] In the midst of the hubbub, a tally was taken. Thirty-three members voted in favor of Bullman, and forty-two cast their lots against him. The results, according to Drayton, were met with loud huzzahs and cries of victory. The next day, Bullman was dismissed.[17]

In Charles Town, the dismissal was interpreted as a minor victory for the American cause.[18] Not everyone was pleased, however. A group of wealthy merchants became vexed by the apparent turn of events.[19] How far might this lack of reverence for authority extend exactly? What would happen if men from the middling and lesser sort began to further question their superiors? Even more frightening for the white elite, what if defiant Charles Town slaves began to call openly for their freedom as they had in the wake of the Stamp Act crisis?[20]

If a sense of deference was especially strong among the lower orders in South Carolina, as historians of the period have sometimes asserted, it was by no means universal, and the strains brought on by imperial politics continued to loosen these bonds.[21] Consider, for example, a letter addressed "To the Mechanicks of Charles-Town," which appeared in the *South Carolina Gazette and Country Journal* within twenty-four hours of the Bullman sermon. The document, penned by an anonymous patriot using the evocative shoemaker pseudonym of "Crispin Heeltap," was a scathing indictment of the Anglican minister and the social structure he sought to uphold. The author began his invective by declaring that "a General Contempt of any Order of Men" was a sign of a "bad heart and a weak head." The writer proceeded to attack the preacher with a series of ad hominems. The first of these asserted that Bullman falsely pretended "to be moved by the Holy Ghost" and that he was in fact "instigated by Mammon," having "no other aim than to allay the Insurrection of his own Stomach." Eschewing deference in favor of common sense, Heeltap proclaimed that "a good Cobler is better entitled to Respect than a *bad* Parson." The writer went on to label the reverend "a Monster, composed of both *Bull* and *Man*," and asserted that he abused "those very People who maintain him in all the Conveniences of life, and even furnish him with Rosin for his fiddlestrings." Heeltap concluded that the parson's real crime was introducing "Civil and Ecclesiastical Tyranny, by denying the Priviledge of thinking and acting to the honest and industrious Mechanick."[22]

Several weeks later, another "libelous" piece appeared in the same newspaper. Signed "Philo Clericus," the document was addressed "To the Reverend Mr.*******." Even more vituperative than that penned by Heeltap, the address pulled no punches with respect to Bullman's character. Referring to the parson as "vicious and immoral," the anonymous author alleged that his subject had sought "after debauched Company" and even preferred "the Bottle and Pipe" to his duties as pastor. To make matters worse, Clericus accused Bullman of "hoard[ing] up Riches" at the expense of his congregation. The author even went so far as to claim that the minister openly discriminated against the poor and had refused to perform funeral services for the destitute. "Let them not do as you do," Clericus admonished the preacher, and "refuse to attend some of the Houses of Mourning where poverty dwells, notwithstanding it may be ever so much accompanied with Humility, and every other Virtue."[23]

Clericus, who obviously had personal experience with Bullman, claimed that on one occasion, during a relative's funeral that Bullman presided over, the minister refused to give final prayers at the gravesite because the author's family was slightly late. Clericus advised his fellow worshipers, in dealing with the allegedly inflexible pastor, not to "appoint the Time for a Corps to be brought to the Burying Ground," because if " 'tis not there exactly at the Moment, [Bullman] goes away unconcerned, sauntering about, and [will] leave the Relations waiting perhaps in the hot Sun, or a Shower of Rain, an Hour, or an Hour and a Half," forcing the grieving relatives "to bury the Corps [sic] without a Minister."[24]

Despite these efforts to denigrate the pastor's character, Bullman's wealthy allies continued to lobby for the pastor's reinstatement. The incident became a local cause célèbre and a source of growing friction between Charles Town's patriot and loyalist factions. "The affair grew so serious," John Drayton later recalled, "it was feared blows would ensue."[25] Word of the episode even spread as far as New England. One commentator, writing from Newport, Rhode Island, some of South Carolina's wealthy planters summered, declared:

> A Reverend Divine in Charles-Town, South Carolina, has lately been
> dismissed from his congregation, for his audacity in standing up in
> his pulpit, and impudently saying, that *mechanics* and country *clowns*
> had no right to dispute about politics, or what King, Lords, and
> Commons had done!!!—All such divines should be taught to know,
> that mechanics, and country clowns (infamously so called) are the
> real, and absolute, masters of King, Lords, Commons, and Priests:
> Though (with shame be it spoken) they too often suffer their servants
> to get upon their backs, and ride them most barbarously.[26]

As the quarreling intensified in Charles Town, Lieutenant Governor Bull assented to the demands of the minister's influential friends by appointing a church commission to consider the legality of John Bullman's dismissal.[27]

Meanwhile, as delays of various kinds in the Bullman proceedings kept Charles Town on edge, the First Continental Congress had its initial meeting on Monday, September 5, at Carpenter's Hall in Philadelphia. In one of the opening motions, the members rejected the conservative "Plan of a Proposed Union between Great Britain and the Colonies." The scheme, put forth by Joseph Galloway, was designed to establish an American legislature that would have joint jurisdiction with Whitehall over colonial affairs. A number of resolves and declarations followed, spelling out the rights of the colonists while denouncing the Coercive Acts and the Quebec Act as oppressive and out of step with the British constitution. The most important step to be taken by the Congress was the adoption of the Continental Association, in which Americans pledged to align themselves in a trade embargo against the Mother country. Local committees elected by the people were charged with the task of enforcement up and down the eastern seaboard.[28]

The five delegates from South Carolina—Edward and John Rutledge, Henry Middleton, Thomas Lynch, and Christopher Gadsden—played an important role in the proceedings of the Congress. In terms of personalities, Gadsden and Lynch, probably the two most visible of the contingent, could not have been more diametrically opposed. To the shock of many in Congress, the wealthy radical, Gadsden, proposed a preemptive strike against British troops stationed in Boston. Lynch, on the other end of the spectrum, made three quotidian motions that passed in the affirmative: that Congress meet in Carpenter's Hall, that Peyton Randolph preside, and that Charles Thomson be appointed secretary.[29]

Yet the most remarkable incident that the South Carolina delegates were involved in occurred during efforts to draft the nonexportation provision for the Continental Association. On Thursday, October 20, at a critical juncture when the document was about to be ratified, members of the South Carolina delegation (excluding Gadsden) threatened to leave the proceedings. The representatives told their colleagues that unless their colony was allowed to continue to export rice and indigo, they would drop out. Gadsden was put in an awkward position. His fellow delegates contended that South Carolina would bear a disproportionately heavy burden unless an exemption was granted on the two products. Because rice and indigo were enumerated items, these staples could only be shipped within the confines of the empire. The association therefore threatened to cut off South Carolina rice from its only market besides Portugal. After much discussion, patriot leader John Rutledge and his fellow delegates agreed to a compromise. South Carolina would forgo its right to export indigo in exchange for an exemption on the exportation of rice to Europe. With this exemption included, the delegates from the other colonies, not wanting the fragile alliance among the colonies to fall apart, passed the association in the affirmative. Back in South Carolina, the decision to exempt rice would prove to be controversial.[30]

As the season shifted into autumn and the political winds became more brisk and variable, Charles Town's black community showed telltale signs of unrest.[31] The evidence is scant, but it appears that insurgency among the city's black majority—both enslaved and free—increased as the rift grew wider between opposing parties in the white minority. No sector of the community was less content with the status quo or more attentive to any public stirrings of political unrest from any quarter. Complaints against "Negroes" are numerous in the records of Charles Town's grand jury, and in mid-October 1774, those complaints took on an air of added fear and frustration. In one grievance, anxious jury members lamented that "the negroes in Charles Town are become so obscene in their Language, so irregular and disorderly in their conduct, and so superfluous in their numbers" as to warrant "the immediate attention of the Legislature." How much of this behavior was the result of political unrest is hard to gauge, but enslaved Charlestonians knew better than anyone else that white division could mean black opportunity.[32]

White fears in Charles Town were exacerbated on Monday, October 17, when Captain Richard Grinnell of the slave ship *Maria* arrived from Isles de Los (sometimes called Iles de Los) off the coast of present-day Guinea (near Conakry) with news of a slave insurrection. Grinnell's account was published in the *South Carolina Gazette and Country Journal* just eight days after he unloaded his cargo of thirty-six slaves at Sullivan's Island. He related the story of Captain Daniel Darby and his crew. According to Grinnell, Darby and his men had made several attempts to set sail from the African coastline in their New York brig "but meeting with Misfortunes" were forced to "put back." During the last attempt, Darby got "about Thirty Leagues out at Sea, when his slaves rose, and in the Engagement killed his Chief Mate." As Grinnell related the story, before the crew "could conquer the Slaves, they were obliged to kill a Number of them." Forced to turn around yet again, Darby piloted his vessel back to Isles de Los. Upon his arrival, "his People all left him."[33]

As harrowing as this mutiny might have seemed to white Charlestonians, another captain of a slaving vessel allegedly experienced a far worse fate. Around the same time that the insurrection occurred aboard Darby's vessel, Captain Gideon, commander of a brig from Liverpool, had arrived on the coast of West Africa. According to Grinnell, Gideon then made a voyage "into the River Pungoes [Rio Pongo is an estuary in present-day Boffa, Guinea, north of Iles de Los], in order to Slave off." Having rid the brig of its bondsmen, Gideon had only been in the jungle "but a few Days before he was cut off by the Natives." Perhaps even more disturbing than Gideon's death at the hands of African tribesmen was Grinnell's claim that a "Captain William Boddle, in the Snow Chance, was in the River Pungoes [Rio Pongo]" and ready to set sail for Charles Town with a boatload of restive Guinea slaves.[34]

As the dread of slave insurrection in South Carolina mounted, word spread rapidly of an incident involving a black preacher by the name of David Margate. Sent from England to the Methodist settlement of Bethesda, Georgia, the minister made his way to Charles Town in late 1774, staying at the home of Patrick Hinds, a white bootmaker who had previously been brought before the grand jury for allowing black preachers to deliver subversive doctrines to other blacks.[35] Despite this earlier presentment, Hinds encouraged the preacher to address an audience made up of African-Americans and several whites.

Pandemonium erupted when, apparently to Hinds's surprise, Margate intoned that "God would send Deliverance to the Negroes, from the power of their Masters, as he freed the Children of Israel from Egyptian Bondage." To make matters worse, Margate reportedly dropped "some unguarded expressions" which were construed "as tho' he meant to raise rebellion amongst the negroes."[36] James Habersham, who had been monitoring the preacher's progress from Savannah, suspected that the man was an impostor. The Georgia merchant was convinced that the minister was a slave despite his claim that he was a freeman who had been stolen off the coast of Africa. Although Margate's origins are shrouded in mystery, it is clear that he had certainly spent time in England with Selina Hastings, Countess of Huntingdon. While in Britain, he learned the ins and outs of Methodism and evidently became well acquainted with the landmark decision of *Sommersett v. Stuart*.[37] His familiarity with the case, along with the fact that he could not "bear to think of any of his own colour being slaves" may have prompted him to proclaim, "The Jews of old treated the Gentiles as Dogs & I am informed the people of this Country use those of my Complection as such[.] I dont mean myself Thank God. I am come from a better Country than this, I mean old England but let them remember that the Children of Israel were delivered out of the hands of Pharo [sic] and he and all his host were drowned in the Red Sea and God will deliver his own People from Slavery."[38]

Margate's apparent preference for "old England" may have had a great deal to do with *Sommersett* decision itself. As far as Habersham was concerned, the minister had become "very proud, very superficial, and conceited" as a result of his stay in the Mother country. "I must say it is a pity," the Savannah merchant fulminated, "that any of these People should ever put their feet in England, where they get totally spoiled and ruined, both in Body and Soul, through a mistaken kind of compassion because they are black." Even after the episode, Margate, according to a fellow preacher, persisted in his "shocking delusion" that he was "a second moses…called to deliver his people from slavery."[39] Margate's problem, Habersham believed, was not his faith in British liberty, but the related fact that he preached a "temporal" deliverance and not a "Spiritual" one. After the incident occurred, Habersham reported that the gentlemen of Charles Town "are so possessed with an opinion that his Designs are bad, that they are determined to pursue, and hang him, if they can lay hold of him."[40]

On Tuesday, November 1, 1774, a ship from London, aptly named the *Britannia*, made its way across the Charles Town Bar. Aboard the craft were a number of prominent citizens as well as seven chests of tea. As in the Maitland incident four months earlier, the merchants wanted the tea landed, while the working classes demanded that the cargo be destroyed. The General Committee, sensing unrest from the city's poorer sort who had begun to gather along the wharves yet again, forced the consignees to board the vessel, break open the chests, and dump the contents into the Cooper River. A few days later, several thousand Charlestonians took to the streets, this time burning effigies of Crown officials and denouncing them as "abettors of American taxation."[41]

That week, on November 6, the South Carolina delegation to the Continental Congress returned to Charles Town. Two days later, Lynch, Gadsden, the Rutledge brothers, and Middleton went to the State House to inform members of the General Committee (the same ruling body of Whigs that had convened earlier that summer) about what had transpired at Carpenter's Hall. The next day, an elaborate entertainment was staged in honor of the delegates. Lieutenant Governor William Bull and other royal administrators could merely stand aside and watch as the patriot movement gathered momentum and began to assume control over the colony. On November 9, as the Whigs began to wind down from their celebration, it was decided that 184 representatives from across South Carolina would convene in Charles Town on January 11, 1775. Designed to be even more "representative" than the General Committee of ninety-nine that had first met in the summer of 1774, this new body would be elected by free white males, paying annual taxes of twenty shillings or more. All of the parishes in the colony would be allotted six delegates each except for Charles Town's two parishes—St. Michael's and St. Philip's—which received fifteen apiece.[42]

Six days after these decisions were made, the ship *Fair American*, captained by Joseph Harrington, arrived from Liverpool carrying news that the king had dissolved Parliament on Friday, September 30, and summoned a new Parliament to meet on Tuesday, November 29. More troubling, however, was the information that the king in Council had decided to place a six-month ban on the exportation of arms and ammunition. This important step was interpreted by the colonists as yet another escalation in the Anglo-American crisis. For nearly two months, white patriots braced themselves, observing the winter holidays with more than the usual prayers for peace and waiting intently for January 11 to arrive.[43]

When the appointed day finally came, the delegates packed into the Long Room in Pike's Church Street Tavern. Within the crowd of representatives were thirteen prominent Charles Town artisans, as well as forty members of the gentry who had previously served in the moribund Commons House of Assembly. One of the first things the new body did was to transform itself into the "First Provincial Congress." This new Congress would function as the de facto government of South Carolina, supplanting the de jure Commons House of Assembly and the other remnants of royal authority.[44]

Having stripped the Crown of its official power, the men in the tavern appointed Charles Pinckney to be president and chose the publisher of the *South Carolina Gazette*, Peter Timothy, to be their secretary. In a symbolic gesture, the meeting was moved into the chamber of the defunct Commons House in the west end of the State House.[45] Not long after the delegates had settled into their seats, members of the Whig gathering broached the subject of the Continental Congress. Lynch, Middleton, Gadsden, and the Rutledges were summoned and asked to give account of the proceedings at Philadelphia. Immediately, the members of the provincial body demanded to know why the Continental Congress had only traced the grievances against the Crown back to 1763 and not before. According to Drayton, the South Carolina delegation told its colleagues that the representatives in Philadelphia had wanted to reach farther back, enumerating "the many aggressions which had been committed by Great Britain upon her infant colonies," specifically "the jealousies, monopolies, and prohibitions, with which she was so prodigal towards them." However, they had been overruled by the delegates from Virginia, who wanted to keep the focus on the reign of George III.[46]

This explanation was accepted without controversy. Yet when the subject of the nonexportation agreement cropped up and the conversation turned to the contentious phrase "except rice to Europe," a long and heated debate erupted. Particularly aggrieved by the proviso were the rural and Sea Island representatives, who were appalled by the fact that the interests of the indigo growers had been forfeited in favor of the rice planters. According to Henry Laurens, "Evil Spirits had stirred up the Jealousy of the Indigo Planter who complained that partiality had been Shewn to the Rice Maker." The Whig leader noted that the "Back Woods-Men, unaccustomed to the formalities of parliament," in particular became convinced that the "'Rich Rice-Planter & the Towns-people had Schemed to weary them out in order to thin the House & transact business their own way.'" As John Drayton recalled, the rice "exception had given so general a disgust, that the whole interior of the province, considered their interests as sacrificed to the emolument of the rice planters." The representatives from outside Charles Town demanded that the South Carolina delegation strike the clause from the record upon reconvening at Philadelphia.[47]

Gadsden, not wanting to be the object of derision, attempted to explain himself, telling his fellow patriots that he had nothing to do with the rice exemption. In a lengthy oration, the radical Whig told his colleagues that the exception was not decided on unilaterally and that the phrase itself occasioned much debate among the South Carolina delegates. So controversial was the measure that it had prompted a cessation of business in the Continental

Congress for several days. Gadsden never gave a sufficient explanation for why the interests of the indigo planters were sacrificed, merely telling his compatriots that rice was exempted in a last-ditch attempt to hold the fragile alliance of the colonies together. Backtracking altogether, the Whig leader declared that "for the common good," as well as for the honor of the province, the words "except rice to Europe" should be stricken from the fourth article of the Continental Association.[48]

Upon hearing this, John Rutledge rose to speak in defense of himself and the remaining delegates. The conservative leader argued that South Carolina would bear a disproportionate burden of the nonexportation agreement compared with other colonies. The Northern colonies, Rutledge reasoned, did less business with Britain and therefore had less to lose. To back up his assertions, he claimed that Pennsylvania's port of Philadelphia exported 700,000 pounds sterling worth of goods annually, but only a mere 50,000 pounds of that amount involved trade directly to Britain. Attempting to shift blame away from the delegation and to draw on anti-Northern sentiment, Rutledge declared that on the whole, the nonexportation affair "seemed rather like a commercial scheme, among the flour Colonies, to find a better vent for their flour through the British Channel; by preventing if possible, any rice from being sent to those markets." The adroit lawyer added that he never could consent to South Carolinians becoming "dupes to the people of the north." Conceding that the critical rice exemption was indeed designed to preserve the property of the greater Charles Town elite, Rutledge proposed that the members of the Provincial Congress devise a scheme to compensate the indigo growers.[49]

At this suggestion, according to Henry Laurens, alarm quickly "spread through the Several Classes" to delegates concerned with other sectors of the local economy, such as tobacco planters, lumber cutters, and tar makers. Soon "every Planter & Herdsman considered his Constituent as injured in the Supposed indulgence to Rice." Sensing the discontent, Gadsden, Rawlins Lowndes, and Reverend William Tennant argued that all planters, not just those of indigo, were entitled to some form of compensation. Afraid that economic and regional divisions would irretrievably hamper the proceedings of the Congress, Lowndes, Tennant, and Gadsden pleaded for unity. The statesmen told their bickering colleagues that they should try to set an example by dint of the fact that their Northern counterparts were looking upon wealthy South Carolina "with a jealous eye."[50]

Drayton, the Rutledge brothers, and the Lynches conceded that compensation was indeed practical. They felt that whatever divisions there might be, at the very least, a façade of unity should be presented to the public. In furtherance of this union, members of Congress decided that a committee should be appointed to formulate a plan of redress. At sunset that evening, the ad hoc committee met in the chambers of Congress. As they tried to resolve the indigo problem, it became obvious that there were no easy answers. Instead of coming up with a viable solution to the matter at hand, they got sidetracked and turned their attention to the topic of debt, an equally difficult subject that was equally of special interest to the backcountry delegates. After spending the entire night deciding that provincial committees would have jurisdiction over suits relating to indebtedness, a half-hearted attempt was made to address the issue of compensation for indigo growers.[51]

The next morning at nine o'clock, the Provincial Congress convened in anticipation of the committee's report. For two hours, the congressional representatives waited as the committee members hastily tried to come up with a plan. At eleven o'clock, the committee members filed into the assembly room. After relating their suggestions on debt, which were immediately approved, the men began to deliver their proposals on the matter of indigo. Finding the plans to equalize profits unsatisfactory, the committee's recommendations were rejected outright.[52]

Once again, Congress turned its attention to those controversial four words. The heated and tumultuous debate over the phrase "except rice to Europe" lasted all day. At some point that evening, one of the indigo planters called for a vote on the issue of recompense. Time was running out. In order to see what they were doing, members had to light candles. To expedite the process, representatives decided that the vote should be taken by declaring yeas and nays rather than the usual method of selection. To the horror of the upcountry and Sea Island representatives, there were eighty-seven nays and only seventy-five yeas. At that moment, the interests of all non–rice planters appeared to be in jeopardy.[53]

The next day, however, a concession was made by the Charles Town rice growers. Realizing that they had the upper hand, they agreed to adjust the price of other commodities based on the fluctuation of the cost of rice. Furthermore, the rice planters assented to a new proposal, agreeing that one-third of the rice crop would be exchanged for one-third of the crop of indigo, hemp, flour, corn, lumber, pork, and butter. Under this scenario, rice planters would deliver a third of their crop to a specialized committee. That committee would supply them in return with an equivalent amount of the various South Carolina commodities not exempted by the Continental Association.[54]

In an ironic twist, at the very same moment that the divided Whigs began to contemplate a viable scheme for bringing their crops to market, General Thomas Gage, then governor of Massachusetts, wrote to Indian superintendent John Stuart in Charles Town and issued a distressing warning. Having heard rumors of an extraordinary proposal made in the British House of Commons calling for the general emancipation of American slaves, Gage told Stuart in a private letter that unless South Carolina patriots ceased their revolutionary activities, "it may happen that your Rice and Indigo will be brought to market by negroes instead of white People."[55]

White South Carolinians may have reeled from the debate over nonexportation, but they were nevertheless compliant with the nonimportation article (Article 10) of the Continental Association. As tempting as it may have been to land expensive goods, cargoes in violation of the boycott were promptly turned away. On Monday, February 13, the resolve of Charles Town patriots was initially tried when the snow *Lively*, captained by William Carter, arrived from Tenerife carrying two tons of potatoes. Three days later, the vessel *Charming Sally*, captained by George Fortune, arrived from Bristol carrying 3,844 bushels of salt, 35 caldrons of coal, and 40,500 tiles. On Saturday, February 25, the Charles Town Committee of Observation adopted a strong position, ordering the cargoes to be summarily dumped in Hog Island Creek.[56] Exactly one week later, on Saturday, March 4, the ship *Katherine*, sailed by Captain Fraser, arrived from Angola carrying a human cargo of 300 slaves.[57] Not wanting to violate Article 2 of the nonimportation agreement (which expressly prohibited the importation of slaves), patriot leaders carefully weighed their options and considered their next course of action.[58]

At the same time that provincial authorities were deciding what to do with slaves aboard the *Katherine*, the apparent eagerness of patriots to comply with nonimportation would be put to a further test. On Tuesday, March 14, a snow from London named the *Proteus* made its way into the harbor.[59] Aboard the ship were several thoroughbred horses from England, as well as costly pieces of furniture belonging to the very prominent Charles Town merchant Robert Smythe. A day after the ship first arrived, a thin General Committee of only thirty-three members made an exception to the Continental Association and allowed the goods to come ashore on the grounds that they were for personal use and not intended for sale. Upon hearing this, the city's artisans and laboring classes became enraged and, according to Drayton, "almost generally exclaimed 'The Association was broken!'" Why should one rich man, or anyone for that matter, be permitted to import goods contrary to the nonimportation embargo? The situation quickly worsened. A mob descended on Bay Street, where numerous docks lined the Cooper River. From where they stood, the angry partisans could see the handsome horses, intended for the private satisfaction of the gentry, tethered to the deckrail of the *Proteus*. The crowd, armed and ready for action, vowed to kill the animals if they were allowed to come ashore.[60]

When a second and fuller General Committee meeting was held on Friday, March 17, to reassess the situation, a throng of discontented laborers stormed in and demanded satisfaction. Edward Rutledge tried to dismiss the horde but was shouted down "with a clamour." In the chambers of the assembly room, the situation intensified. Several members of the committee, thinking they had been grossly affronted by the mob, departed from the scene enraged. In a kind of microcosm of what was taking place throughout Charles Town, men of the highest rank clashed vociferously with men from the lowest order. After both sides were finished exchanging rhetorical jabs, a chilling silence filled the room. Eventually, someone worked up the nerve to speak, and the decision was made to postpone the vote until an even fuller meeting of the General Committee could be held.[61]

As the city's inhabitants waited impatiently for the matter to be decided, the town fell into a "universal commotion." Would the mob push Whig leaders into sending Smythe's cargo back to Britain? Or would the elite simply ignore the wishes of "the people" and make an exception to the Association? What role, if any, did poor whites have to play in the realm of high politics? These questions and others likely ran through the minds of Charlestonians as they flooded into the assembly room of the General Committee.[62]

The debates began with a challenge from Christopher Gadsden. The Whig leader, who had his finger on the pulse of popular opinion, argued that the decision to land the horses should be overturned on the grounds "that it would alarm the Northern Colonies" and anger the citizens of Charles Town. According to the radical politician, these reasons, coupled with the fact that there was barely a quorum for the original vote, warranted a reversal. Concurring with Gadsden, Reverend William Tennant and a Mr. Rugely declared that the horses "ought not to be landed."[63]

Their statements were met with harsh opposition by conservatives within the party such as Edward Rutledge, Rawlins Lowndes, Thomas Lynch, and Thomas Bee. The decision should stand, they argued, or the General Committee would lose face and "fall into contempt." The conservatives were of the opinion that temporizing "did not become honest men, and statesmen" and that their fellow members should vote according to their consciences and not according to popular mandate. The wealthy merchants felt that the Association was not meant to be adhered to so strictly. Otherwise, no arms or ammunition could be received from England. In addition, individuals were not meant to be targeted by the Association, and "it never was the idea of Congress to exclude such articles" as personal effects, they declared.[64]

In the most dramatic episode of the debate, William Henry Drayton, the former conservative and Crown supporter, made an about face and, taking the side of the radicals, argued for a reversal. The aristocratic lawyer who had once denounced the lower orders as the *profanus vulgus* now appeared to champion their cause. To the horror of his former colleagues, Drayton cited the precedent of the Roman Senate, "who often yielded to the people" without being brought into contempt. The union of the colonies was the rock "upon which the American political edifice was founded," the Whig leader declared. "Hence, it was evident," according to him, that "landing the horses, hazarded our union: for, the people were in commotion against it. Upon all public and general questions," Drayton concluded, "the people are ever in the right."[65]

After Drayton was finished, John Rutledge took the floor and unsuccessfully attempted to refute his peer's appeal to the people. A vote of the entire General Assembly was taken, and by a narrow margin of thirty-five to thirty-four, the ruling was overturned. Once again, the artisans emerged victorious, and Drayton's shift of position had proved decisive. Eventually, the freight was turned away.[66] Needless to say, the heated debate only seemed to fuel the antagonisms between the classes that had been brimming over since the Bullman incident.[67]

As we can clearly see from the "Smythe Horses Affair," Charles Town merchants were growing impatient with the nonimportation association, though it had only been in effect since Thursday, December 1, 1774. Besides being concerned about the massive loss of profits, patriot elites found themselves at great pains to curtail the spread of liberty or at least to make certain that it stayed within boundaries of their choosing. This sentiment was perhaps best articulated by the young John Laurens. He wrote to his father from London in mid-February:

> Tho' perhaps I may frequently speak treason against my own Party, among other things I must confess it gives me great concern to hear that some of our lowest Mechanics still bear great Part in our Public Transactions. Men who are as contemptible for their Ignorance, as they may be pernicious by their obstinacy, not but that I wish every Citizen to have a Voice, far be it from me when we are struggling against oppression, to wish to make Distinctions unfavorable to Liberty. But when such men as these take the Lead, it argues a Defect on the Part of abler Hands, and brings our Cause into Disgrace...and perhaps it is necessary to tolerate such Presumption in order to preserve Harmony among ourselves. It will be the policy of Wisemen to guide these Upstart Patriots, & let them enjoy the opinion of acting from themselves.[68]

"Guiding" sentient men from the lower classes would prove to be difficult, however. Several days after the Smythe episode, Drayton's uncle William Bull wrote to officials at Whitehall: "The Men of Property begin at length to see that the many headed power of the People, who have hitherto been obediently made use of by their numbers and occasional riots to support the claims set up in America, have discovered their own strength and importance, and are not now so easily governed by their former leaders."[69] John Bullman would have scoffed. But conditions were changing rapidly, and his reinstatement now seemed less likely than ever. On Saturday, March 25, 1775, sensing the shift in the local political winds, he had boarded a vessel bound for England.[70] Less than twenty-four hours earlier, the *Katherine*, with its cargo of 300 Angolans, was sent out of the colony and headed for the West Indies.[71]

2

A Great War Coming

April 1775–June 1775

On Friday, April 14, 1775, word reached Charles Town from England that the British Parliament had declared the colonies to be in rebellion.[1] At the same time, South Carolinians learned that Lord North was dispatching additional troops to America and was taking steps to restrict New England's trade. The news was perceived as a declaration of war.[2] Exactly one week later, with rumors of slave rebellion swirling in the Tidewater, Lord Dunmore of Virginia seized the gunpowder from the colonial powder magazine at Williamsburg.[3] Just hours later, at eleven o'clock at night, two days after the British had opened fire at Lexington and Concord, patriots in Charles Town raided the armory at the State House and the two powder magazines on the outskirts of the city. In a span of less than three hours, all of the functional weapons and military stores in the Carolina capital had been stolen. Eight hundred muskets and 200 cutlasses, along with cartridge boxes, flints, and matches, were reportedly seized. A total of 1,600 pounds of gunpowder was removed from the powder magazines.[4] The next morning, Saturday, April 22, Lieutenant Governor William Bull issued a proclamation denouncing the seizures, offering a reward of 100 pounds sterling for information leading to the incarceration of the offenders.[5]

Most city residents already knew who the conspirators were, however. The lieutenant governor's offer was ignored, largely because the perpetrators consisted of a veritable Who's Who of Charles Town society. Two of Bull's own nephews—William Henry Drayton and William Bull—participated in the raid, along with Arthur Middleton, Henry Laurens, Thomas Lynch, Benjamin Huger, Charles Pinckney, and Charles Cotesworth Pinckney. Although he was not involved in the actual theft, Christopher Gadsden took possession of the purloined gunpowder when it was landed at his wharf on Bay Street.[6] Charles Town's white revolutionaries were now armed but hardly prepared for what was to come next. Just eleven days after Bull issued his proclamation, on Wednesday, May 3, a letter arrived from Arthur Lee, the American correspondent in London, notifying the wealthy merchant-planter Henry Laurens (figure 2.1) of a design by the British administration to foment insurrections among the African slaves of the province.[7] Five days later, the brigantine *Industry*, captained by Edward Allen, arrived in the Carolina port from Salem, Massachusetts, carrying a copy of the *Essex Gazette* with the first published account of Lexington and Concord. On the same day, William Henry Drayton wrote to the General Committee at Philadelphia of the provincial government's intent to levy troops and put itself in a "preparatory posture" against all enemies foreign and domestic. Although such statements did not appear in the formal letter addressed to the Pennsylvania Whigs, Drayton's cancelled paragraph is highly revealing:

> [Lee] speaks of this *black* [emphasis mine] plan before [the British] Administration with great confidence. We have the more readily undertaken this measure of defence[sic], because it will not only awe the particular quarter against which it is immediately provided; but that we hope it will be putting ourselves in a preparatory posture to effect the great affair in hand. A view of such force as an immediate protection, must give confidence to our friends; it must acquire to us those Men who are wavering & damp the Courage of our Enemies.[8]

News of the outbreak of war in Massachusetts and of the British administration's "black plan" threw "the people into a great ferment" and precipitated the opening of the second session of South Carolina's Provincial Congress.[9] Since 1720, the Commons House of Assembly and the various offices of the royal government were the only recognized symbols of authority.[10] But now there were two entities vying for legitimacy and sovereignty over the colony. The problem of allegiance, a contentious issue since the Stamp Act, was now a primary concern.

Driven by fear and a desire for unity, Whig leaders in the General Committee banded together on Thursday, May 11, and drafted an "Association" to bind all white men of property to the patriot cause. Despite their unanimous approval of the document, the authors decided to delay its ratification until the opening session of the Provincial Congress. Even at this early stage, however, it is evident that British-inspired or British-assisted slave revolts were foremost in the minds of the General Committee members, who explicitly referred to "the dread of instigated Insurrections at home" as "causes sufficient to drive an oppressed People [meaning white patriots] to the use of Arms."[11]

FIGURE 2.1. Henry Laurens (1724–1792), by John Singleton Copley, 1782, oil on canvas. Laurens, who had risen rapidly to the pinnacle of South Carolina society as a slave trader and later as a merchant planter, had returned from England in December 1774 to help take charge of the patriot movement in South Carolina. As one of the Commissioners of the Pilotage for Charles Town, he likely knew Thomas Jeremiah well and was convinced that the pilot had masterminded a British-instigated slave insurrection. Laurens would become the president of the Continental Congress in November 1777 and would subsequently be imprisoned for treason in the Tower of London. *National Portrait Gallery, Smithsonian Institution/Art Resource, New York*

In June, as members of the South Carolina Provincial Congress began to consider measures for the defense of the colony, a fissure became apparent in the attitudes of patriot leaders. In a secret communiqué to the Earl of Dartmouth, Alexander Innes, who had arrived in Charles Town on Wednesday, April 19 to make preparations for the arrival of the new royal governor, reported that "the Opulent and Sensible...are opposed by a numerous body of the Low and Ignorant, led by a few desperate Incendiaries, who have nothing to lose, and some hot headed Young Men of fortune whom it will be difficult to restrain."[12] The president of the Provincial Congress, Henry Laurens, described the colonial representatives as follows: "Some are Red-Hot and foolishly talk of arms and there is another extreme who say that implicit Obedience is the Surest Road to redress of Grievances, the great majority of members lie between, and are men of wealth and consideration."[13] Expressing a similar sentiment, Peter Timothy declared, "In regard to War & Peace, I can only tell you that the Plebeians are still for War—but the noblesse [are] perfectly pacific."[14]

When the unanimously approved draft of the Association was brought before the General Assembly, on Saturday, June 3, it immediately sparked controversy.[15] Moderate and more conservative patriots, such as Laurens, called for an ancillary statement of "Duty and Loyalty to the King," while radical incendiaries, such as Reverend William Tennant, wished to hold all non-subscribers "Inimical to the Liberty of the Colonies."[16] Likening the Association to an "Athanasian Test," Laurens argued that the document would "anathematize good men" and turn friends and fellow neighbors into enemies. Despite these objections, however, the next day (George III's birthday), the document was signed by the 170 members in attendance and ordered to be dispersed among the parishes.[17]

On Monday, June 5, the day after Congress formed a committee to investigate slave revolts, the question of naval defense was brought before the General Assembly.[18] Radicals, such as William Henry Drayton, were convinced that the most efficient way to ward off an impending attack by sea would be to sink vessels in the channels of Charles Town Harbor and effectively blockade the entire waterway. The "more opulent" members of the house, those with a stake in shipping and trade, regarded the plan as extremely dangerous and utterly irrational. Although he did not mention it at the time, Laurens feared that the radical proposal to obstruct the harbor would have drastic long-term consequences. The merchant was convinced that the blockade would permanently ruin the harbor and drain the city of nine-tenths of its prosperity. The planter estimated that the measure had the potential to cost the province "half a Million of our Currency"[19] and make the port of Charles Town into "a second Antwerp on the Schelds." Such an action, Laurens predicted, would not only raise the ire of Britain but would make the patriot party an object of derision around the world.[20]

As the debate over the blockade ran its course, a motion was put forth by the radical faction to "immediately purchase & fit out as a Ship of War" the *Maria Wilhelmina* in order to secure the harbor's entrance.[21] According to Leila Sellers, the vessel had a burden of 800 tons and was "the largest ship that had ever entered Charleston harbor." The enormous craft, captained by William Williams, had been tied to one of the wharves since Tuesday, April 4.[22] The radical party wanted to equip the boat with "50 Guns in order to keep out any of His Majesties [*sic*] Ships of War." According to Henry Laurens, there were even "Some whispers" about seizing the *Tamar* (which was also stationed at port) and using it for the same purpose.[23] The latter proposal made by a "violent advocate" reportedly touched off a "confused clamour & dialogue" in the house, which compelled Laurens to intervene. According to the patriot leader, "the Question was put & passed in the Negative by so great a Majority as all the difference between 11 Yeas & about 180. Nays—in consequence of that disappointment a long train of Armed Schooners, Fortifications, & the intended Blockade of the Channels into this Harbour, all the effects of Fear, & Zeal in a delirium was postpond [*sic*] and laid aside."[24]

Of the closed congressional session, Alexander Innes would later write: "After settling the Association it was proposed to purchase, and arm a large ship that lies in the Harbour for the purpose of defending the Bar at the entrance of this Port against His Majesty's Ships but after a whole day's debate this measure was rejected by a great Majority. Had it been adopted no Act of the famous Knight of La Mancha would have been equal to it."[25]

That day, a motion was put forth to oppose the landing of Lord William Campbell, the newly appointed royal governor (figure 2.2). The highest-ranked Crown official in South Carolina during the turbulent summer of 1775, Campbell had served as a Member of British Parliament and was the son of the late John Campbell, fourth Duke of Argyll (who had been one of George III's Privy Counsellors until his death in 1770). Previously, he had been a post captain in the Royal Navy as well as the governor of Nova Scotia. Lord William was well known among members of South Carolina's high society. In the early 1760s, he had been the commander of HMS *Nightingale* in Charles Town Harbor and had married Sarah Izard, who came from one of the province's most illustrious families. Despite the infamous reputation he would later garner for collaborating with Low Country blacks, he was the proud owner of Inverary Plantation on the Savannah, which held nearly ninety people in bondage. That Campbell was linked to the rice belt through both marriage and property ties demonstrates either the incredible degree of fear that had gripped the colony by this point or the extent to which Carolina Whigs were using his arrival as a pretext for military preparedness.[26]

FIGURE 2.2. Lord William Campbell (1731–1778) before 1776, by Nathaniel Hone. This lavish portrait of Lord William Campbell, the last royal governor of South Carolina and scion of one of Scotland's most powerful clans, hung alongside a portrait of Lady William Campbell in the couple's Charles Town library. Despite his many attempts to rein in the government and pardon Thomas Jeremiah, by the time he had arrived in mid-June 1775, his office had been effectively stripped of most of its power. Lord Campbell would be fatally wounded trying to retake the colony in the Battle of Fort Moultrie on June 28, 1776. *The Campbell-Johnston Family, care of Historical Portraits Limited, London*

Vehemently opposed to blocking Governor Campbell's entrance into Charles Town, the ever cautious Laurens queried, "what is to become of Lord W C. & his Suite?" The merchant reportedly argued that such "conduct would be ungrateful, inhumane, & answer no other end but that of Shewing our ill temper." As a concession to firebrands like Drayton, the city's harbor pilots were ordered by Congress not "to board or bring in any Man of War or Transport Ship." Despite the numerous objections of more conservative committee members, the order was eventually confirmed. Embarrassed by the designs of the more ardent patriots, Laurens consoled himself by asserting, "His Lordship will certainly find a Way into the Harbour without the aid of our Pilots." In addition to the restrictions on licensed maritime pilots, several members within the General Assembly wanted to intimidate the new governor by greeting him with a display of force.[27]

One of the assemblymen raised a question over whether or not the Governor would "have the Honour of Seeing our Traind[sic] Bands as a first object." According to Laurens, "much altercation ensued without conclusion on the point."[28] Although we can only speculate, the heated debates that transpired during the first week of the Provincial Congress may have prompted "conservatives" within the patriot party to search for a scapegoat—one whose punishment would simultaneously deter an increasingly insurgent black majority, discourage harbor pilots from collaborating with the British navy, and pacify a growing number of radicals intent on "destroying" the lucrative waterway of Charles Town Harbor.[29]

When news began to circulate that Campbell was on his way to Charles Town, neither whites nor blacks had any idea of what to expect.[30] As the frenzied second session of Congress was still under way, Captain Innes wrote: "The Governor is expected every hour, and although he can do very little, yet I hope his presence with the King's ship under his Command may afford some countenance to the King's friend's, and will I know embarrass the other party, who have at present a clear field."[31] The king's superintendent of Indian Affairs for the Southern District, John Stuart, reported that "Massacres and Instigated Insurrections, were Words in the mouth of every Child."[32] The local merchant and patriot Josiah Smith observed that the entire colony was "in a Ticklish situation" on account of "numerous Domesticks" who had been "deluded by some villainous Persons into the notion of being all set free" upon the arrival of the new governor.[33] This sentiment was reportedly shared by a group of Charles Town slaves, who, according to Drayton, were said to have "entertained ideas that the present contest [with Britain] was for obliging" their masters "to give them liberty."[34] Shortly before the governor reached Charles Town Harbor aboard the sloop of war *Scorpion*, Smith observed that Campbell's arrival was a frequent topic of discussion among the slaves of the province. The merchant was intensely distressed, claiming that such "common talk" among slaves made them act with impertinence. Smith took comfort, however, in the fact that the Provincial Congress was also issuing certificates in the amount of one million pounds, to raise a force of "Two thousand Men Horse and food," for the purposes of keeping those "mistaken creatures in awe" and warding off "coercive" British troops.[35]

Around the same time, the *South Carolina Gazette and Country Journal* made an optimistic report that companies of militia were patrolling regularly, "the salutary Consequences of which are every Day more apparent; The nightly meetings and Riots of the Negroes are entirely suppressed."[36] According to Laurens, Charles Town was filled with "the daily & nightly sound of Drums and Fifes." These harrowing sounds, Laurens told his son, awakened "a Spirit in the People" and resolved them "to do all in their power to resist the force & stratagems of the British Ministry."[37] An anonymous Charlestonian writing to a "gentleman in Philadelphia" noted that the city had taken on "the appearance of a garrison town [rather] than a mart for trade." "In our situation," the author asserted, "we cannot be too watchful, and we may require much strength, for our negroes have all high notions of their liberty."[38]

When Governor Campbell finally arrived on the evening of Saturday, June 17, it did not take him long to realize that his presence was unwelcome.[39] Not only was the sloop he arrived on—the HMS *Scorpion*—"detained off the Bar until the loss of one tide," but the vessel was also expressly prohibited from entering the harbor until the next day, when the patriot-imposed "restraint upon Pilots was taken off." The next afternoon, Campbell was received on the steps of the Exchange Building with minimal fanfare and feigned enthusiasm.[40] Normally, the arrival of such a prominent public official would occasion large crowds and elaborate ceremony. Yet on this day, as John Drayton recalled, "the citizens for the most part preserved a sullen silence":

> They made no *feu de joie*, as had ever been usual in such a case;
> neither was there the loud and hearty acclamation of citizens, when
> his commission as Governor was publicly read before him, from the
> portico of the Exchange. Whatever acclamation was made, was
> trivial.... No gentlemen as was customary, awaited his Excellency's
> landing; or attended his parade, along the streets—save only, three
> Placemen Councilors including the Chief Justice, Gordon and
> Assistant Judge Gregory; three other Assistant Judges, Savage,
> Fewtrell and Coslett; the Colonel of the Militia—the Collector, Robert
> Dalway Haliday—the Clerks of the Council, James Simpson, and
> Common Pleas, James Trail; and some officers of the *Scorpion*: the
> whole of which escort did not exceed fifteen persons.[41]

The gentlemen of Charles Town were not the only ones to slight the newly appointed the Royal Governor. Lieutenant Governor William Bull, the acting royal overseer of the colony for years, adamantly refused to see Campbell and conveniently neglected to attend his reception.[42] Yet the most unexpected affront to His Lordship was probably that which came from patriot foot soldiers on June 18.

That evening, "Just about dusk," Campbell and his personal secretary, Captain Alexander Innes, proceeded on foot through the city. As they turned down Meeting Street and approached the State House, the pair came upon a large company of artillery—the same group of militia raised by the Provincial Congress to suppress instigated slave insurrections. Although most of Meeting Street was barricaded, the governor found a narrow opening and proposed to go between the guns and the wall. But "in commencing this passage," as Drayton recalled, Campbell was hailed by the sentinel on duty, Thomas Harvey, who would not let him pass. Innes immediately rebuked the young officer, informing him that he was in the presence of the royal governor. Reportedly, the sentinel replied, "I am not to know the Governor," and refused to let Campbell and his secretary through. "His Excellency then found himself obliged, to quit the pavement" and in doing so asked the sentinel's name. Without hesitation, the soldier replied, "*Harvey at your service.*"[43] Campbell may have thought of himself as "the Representative of Majesty" in the "unhappy province" of South Carolina, but at that moment, he must have realized once and for all that his authority as governor was stillborn.[44]

Lord Campbell's harsh reception was likely tied to an incident involving John Stuart. A letter from Stuart to his deputy, Alexander Cameron, had been intercepted by Georgia patriots earlier in the year. Reportedly, the letter described a correspondence between Stuart and General Gage over the possibilities of forming a Native American alliance.[45] Shortly before Campbell arrived, the Provincial Congress in Charles Town received word from Georgia of the alleged correspondence, and local patriots became convinced that the wrath of the Six Nations would be used by British forces to crush the "cause of liberty" in South Carolina once and for all.[46] Fearing for his life, Stuart fled his Tradd Street mansion in late May for Savannah. When it was no longer safe for him in the Georgia capital, the British official subsequently made his way to St. Augustine.[47]

In a letter to Secretary of State William Legge, second Earl of Dartmouth, Campbell attributed his chilly reception to the intelligence sent by the patriot correspondent Arthur Lee. According to Campbell, Lee was responsible for circulating rumors that "the Ministry had in agitation not only to bring down the Indians on the Inhabitants of this Province, but also to instigate and encourage an insurrection among the slaves." The royal governor was astonished to find that it was reported and "universally believed, that to effect this plan 14,000 Stand of Arms were actually on board the *Scorpion*, the Sloop of

War" he had arrived in. According to the governor, "the cruelty and savage barbarity of this scheme were the conversation of all Companies." Campbell could scarcely believe "the flame" engendered by this rumor among "all ranks and degrees," lamenting that "no one dared venture to contradict the intelligence conveyed from such respectable authority."[48] The governor's trusted friend the Chief Justice of South Carolina, Thomas Knox Gordon, from Ireland, was convinced that Whigs propagated reports of black insurrection to justify the augmentation of military resistance.[49] George Milligen, Campbell's physician and fellow loyalist, was convinced that the origin of these pervasive rumors could be traced back to the Association and its explicit reference to "instigated insurrections."[50]

According to Milligen, "the people" had been made "to believe that His Majesty's ministers and other servants instigated their slaves to rebel against their masters and to cut their throats."[51] Like Campbell, Milligen was astonished that no one questioned the veracity of these reports, which he claimed were taken as "strong as proofs of Scripture writ," especially by "the ignorant and unwary." As far as the surgeon was concerned, the mob's "fears" and weak "distractions of mind" made it particularly vulnerable to the recent efflorescence of patriot propaganda.[52] Especially seductive, Milligen argued, were the widely circulated tales of plantation slaves who "had refused to work" and of domestics who had "gone and murdered their masters and families." The doctor was convinced that the Whigs had manufactured accounts of blacks obtaining arms and hiding in "the woods" in order to turn the white populace toward the revolutionary cause.[53] Such accounts were bolstered by correspondences such as the one that appeared on Monday, May 29, in the *South Carolina Gazette*, reporting that "there is gone down to Sheerness, seventy-eight thousand guns and bayonets, to be sent to America, to put into the hands of N*****s [Negroes], the Roman Catholics, the Indians and Canadians; and all the ... means on earth used to subdue the colonies."[54]

During the same week, patriot Michael Hubart testified to the Committee of Safety against Catholic loyalists James Dealy and Laughlin Martin. According to Hubart's testimony, on Friday, June 2, Dealy entered the house of Thomas Nicoll in King Street and proclaimed that "good news [had] come to town." When asked what the "good news" was, Dealy replied that "a number of arms" were "sent over to be distributed amongst the Negroes, Roman Catholics, and Indians." Hubart reportedly told Dealy that he thought it was "very bad news, that Roman Catholics and Savages should be permitted to join and massacre Christians." At that instant, Dealy allegedly struck his breast and swore "'he was a Roman Catholic, and that he had arms, and would get arms and would use them as he pleased.'"[55]

Hubart returned to his home. After some time, Dealy appeared at Hubart's door with Martin and one A. Reed. After sitting down and engaging in small talk, Martin reportedly arose and asked, "'So, Mr. Hubart, you'll not allow Roman Catholics to carry guns.[?]'"[56] Hubart informed Martin that his circumstances were too meager to "forbid any party or sect to carry arms." Martin proceeded to damn Hubart for a "false faced villain" and ordered Dealy to drag him out of his house and tear him to pieces in the street. Allegedly, Dealy held Hubart by the throat while Martin brandished a blade. Hubart dropped to his knees and pleaded for his life. Martin vowed to God that he would cut off Hubart's head if he did not beg for Dealy's pardon. Hubart apologized, and Martin exclaimed that "he was a Roman Catholic and vowed to God, that he would cut off the head of any person, who said he should not carry arms." Afterward, Hubart claimed that he saw Martin drinking with Dealy and Reed and reportedly overheard them toasting to *the Damnation of the Committee, and their proceedings.*"[57]

On the morning of Wednesday, June 7, Charles Town residents awoke to the "repeated alarms of the popular Bell." Henry Laurens wrote to his son John that as no man was allowed to ignore the summons, he reluctantly made his way to the State House. When Laurens arrived, he found that "the Call was to collect a proper Court for trying, condemning & executing a Sentence on, two impudent fellows who had not only refused to Subscribe to the Association but threatend [sic] vengeance against the whole Country by exciting an Insurrection." While most of the members of the Congress, including Laurens, "preserved their dignity" by ignoring the matter and went about their usual business, "some of the lower people [prompted by William Henry Drayton] Set up a Judge & called Witnesses." Within less than an hour—on the basis of Hubart's testimony—the Secret Committee of the Council of Safety ordered that Dealy and Martin be tarred and feathered.[58]

The next day, Laurens reported that he witnessed from his "Windows the Shocking Spectacles put into a Cart and driven up & down the Broad Street." The patriot leader expressed his disapproval of the scene and told his son that "I need not describe to you my feelings to you on this occasion."[59] According to another eyewitness, Captain Innes, "this very *well-timed* piece of Justice was attended with the happiest effects, no one since daring even to think of refusing to swallow anything that may be offered."[60] In his study of the Charles Town artisans, historian Richard Walsh would write that "for the first time, the people saw the mob at its worst."[61] Having thoroughly shamed "the shocking spectacles," the Secret Committee ordered that the men be put onboard the vessel *Liberty* and banished indefinitely. Martin was reprieved at the last moment, however, by the intercession of his friends and was allowed to remain in Charles Town pending a public apology. Dealy would not be as fortunate. And on the day that Martin's plea appeared in the *South Carolina Gazette and Country Journal*, the loyalist was whisked away to England just as David Margate had been only a month and five days earlier.[62]

While Charles Town's patriot authorities were in the midst of deliberating over the Dealy and Martin incident, news appeared that a band of several blacks had looted "a schooner loaded with goods," taking "nothing else but [gun] Powder."[63] Was this the precious supply of powder that Whig leaders had themselves confiscated on Friday, April 21? Had Charles Town slaves seized the explosive article that was sitting on Gadsden's Wharf in an effort to start a revolution of their own? Knowing full well that the Council of Safety was going to interrogate and arrest a number of blacks in connection with the incident, Henry Laurens called a meeting of his brother's slaves and "admonished them to behave with great circumspection in this dangerous times [sic], [and] set before them the great risque of exposing themselves to the treachery of pretended freinds [sic] & false witnesses if they associated with any Negroes out[side] of your family or mine."[64]

That same week, a dispatch from New Bern, North Carolina, appeared in the *South Carolina Gazette and Country Journal*, relating Royal Governor of Virginia Lord Dunmore's seizure of gunpowder at Williamsburg earlier in the spring. According to the report, "The monstrous absurdity that the Governor can deprive the people of the necessary means of defense at a time when the colony is actually threatened with an insurrection of their slaves [by claiming the powder to be under the king's jurisdiction] has worked the passions of the people there almost to a frenzy."[65]

As patriot investigations were underway "a Negro fellow of the Angola country" named Jemmy was "taken up" fifty-two miles outside Charles Town when he could not remember his master's name. The runaway was described as "five feet six inches high," having "country marks on both his sides" and a symbol branded on his chest. He was brought back to the city wearing a "white Negro cloth jacket and breeches" and placed in a workhouse for blacks under the supervision of warden Michael Kalteisen.[66]

Loyalists were convinced that the incarceration of blacks by the Council of Safety in mid-June was a deliberate ploy on the part of patriots to substantiate the mob's fears of instigated insurrection. According to Campbell, because the widely reported threats of Indian incursions never materialized, patriots needed "to have recourse to the instigated insurrection amongst their slaves, effectually to gain the point proposed, and they could not be long at loss for pretexts to establish this."[67] George Milligen argued that the white populace became increasingly skeptical about the constant "reports of country insurrections among the Negroes," and many were beginning to doubt "the truth of instiga-tions being used." In order to "carry on the tragedy, several Negroes were taken up on suspicion and were committed to the prison where there is a workhouse for them."[68]

On Friday, June 16, 1775, "a Negro Man Slave" named Jemmy, "the Property of Mr. Peter Croft," testified before the patriot Council of Safety at Charles Town that several weeks earlier at Prioleau's Wharf, a "free Negro" by the name of Thomas Jeremiah, had pulled him aside and asked if he would be willing to smuggle guns to a runaway named Dewar. According to the witness, these guns were to be distributed by the runaway and "placed in Negroes hands to fight against the [white] inhabitants of the province." To make matters worse, the prime suspect had allegedly boasted about having a large stockpile of gun-powder and had proclaimed himself "the Chief Command[er] of the Negroes."[69]

These accusations were corroborated by a second slave witness named Sambo, who reported that "two or three months earlier" (just before news had reached Charles Town of Lexington and Concord), while working on Fitzsimmon's Wharf, the suspect had approached him and asked if he had heard "anything of the war" that was "coming." When the witness declared that he had not yet heard the news, the suspect assured him that "a great war" would most certainly be "coming soon." When the dockworker asked, "what shall we poor Negroes do?" the suspect reportedly advised him to set a "schoo-ner on fire, jump on shore and join the [British] soldiers" and added that "the war was com[ing] to help the poor Negroes."[70]

In a letter written on Sunday, June 18, patriot leader Henry Laurens men-tioned the slave depositions to his son: "Trials of Several Negroes Suspected & charged of plotting an Insurrection have been conducted this Week I mean the past Week." Laurens wrote that "Jerry the pilot is among the most Criminal" and that "two or three White people" were "committed to prison on Strong Negro Evidence." According to the merchant-planter, just as the committee was about to adjourn, Council of Safety members received a letter from Baptist minister Oliver Hart declaring that one of his female slaves and another belonging to Joshua Ward "could make very ample discoveries." Laurens noted that both women were immediately ordered into custody to be examined the next day.[71] Of the slave wit-nesses, loyalist George Milligen would later write: "I am well informed that the witnesses against him declared him innocent, that the evidence they had given against him was not true and given only to save themselves from a whipping, the only punishment they were told would be inflicted on Jerry."[72]

The validity of such scant testimony given by prisoners facing harsh pun-ishments must have been hard to assess, but it did not prevent the Council of

Safety from taking swift action. Within days, Thomas Jeremiah was arrested, brought to the workhouse, and put into solitary confinement.[73] On Thursday, June 22, the committee appointed by the Provincial Congress to investigate reports of black insurrection was ordered to summon freeholders to try Jeremiah under the draconian Negro Act of 1740.[74] The next day, Laurens reported to his son that "one or two Negroes are to be Severely flogged & banished." Laurens noted that "The White Men Suspected will be Set at large, nothing is brought in Evidence against them, yet tis Said that the populace are determined to drive them out of the Country."[75] The fate of the unidentified white suspects was corroborated by Lord Campbell, who later wrote:

> Happy it was for the friends of government in this country that the
> wretched creatures doomed to death could not be prevailed upon to
> accuse any white person though [they were] repeatedly told it was the
> only chance for life and often desired not to be afraid to mention
> names, let their rank or station be what it would. Though this
> evidence could not have been legally used against a white person,
> I am convinced that if any had been accused they must have fallen a
> sacrifice to the fury of the mob.[76]

Relieved that the white suspects were exonerated but puzzled by the Committee's apparent leniency toward the black suspects, Laurens claimed that "if they deserve any punishment, nothing less than Death should be the sentence, & at this critical time no pardon or mitigation should be granted." Laurens was vexed by the reluctance of freeholders to resort to enforcement of the Negro Act which would necessarily entail the sentence of execution. The planter was confident, however, that the committee would eventually find individuals willing to enforce the harsh set of statutes. He told his son there was "no Sign of danger in this, in a Town where the Inhabitants are as suddenly blown up by apprehensions as Gun powder is by Fire."[77]

Laurens's observations were prescient. Within a few days, all obstacles were resolved, and Jeremiah was brought before two justices and five freeholders under the Negro Act. Campbell claimed that "after sitting a week, and taking uncommon pains to get evidence, no proof could be produced to convict him, or [to] give sufficient grounds to believe any attempt of the kind they pretended to fear was ever intended." The matter was put on hold, but as the governor observed, "Jerry was order'd to be remanded to prison and his tryal resumed two months afterwards, by which time they hoped to procure more evidence."[78] According to Milligen, "About the end of June," the black suspects were "dismissed excepting two," who were "remanded to the workhouse till further proof could be got against" them.[79]

3

Under the Color of Law

July 1775–August 1775

The primary sources illuminating Thomas Jeremiah's ordeal reveal little about the two months he spent in the Charles Town workhouse. However, it seems that the incarceration of a black suspect had the effect of temporarily ameliorating white anxieties. At the end of June, Laurens wrote to his son in England, "Jerry is Still to take his trial but he is not in close confinement—this was relaxed as the people's fears abated."[1] In July, the wealthy plantation owner Gabriel Manigault, also writing to kin in England, observed, "We have been alarmed by idle reports that the Negroes intended to rise, which on examination proved to be of less consequence than expected, however a Strick[t] watch has been kept for fear of the worst."[2] His grandson would later write back to Charles Town, "I am very glad to find by Grandpa's Letter, that there was not so much reason to be afraid of the Negroes, as was first suspected."[3]

On Wednesday, July 5, however, the Council of Safety received a letter from Cheraw plantation owner Thomas Hutchinson of St. Bartholomew parish, relating "that Several of the Slaves in the neighborhood, were exciting & endeavoring to bring ab[ou]t a General Insurrection." Just as in Charles Town the month before, the principal leaders of the "Infernal designs" were apprehended and brought before a court of justices and freeholders in accordance with the Negro Act. In similar circumstances to those of Patrick Hinds, John Burnet, a white unorthodox preacher from Scotland, was accused of organizing "Nocturnal Meetings of the Slaves under the Sanction of Religion" and inculcating blacks with subversive doctrines. According to Hutchinson's report, Burnet had been told on more than one occasion that "his conduct was extremely Obnoxious to the People," and there were many within the parish who, being fed up with his mischievous designs, wished that the preacher "had remained in Scotland where he was born."[4]

The letter contained a transcript of the evidence brought against the "Incorrigible" Scotsman, including the testimony of a slave belonging to John Wells, coincidentally named Jemmy. According to the transcript, Burnet oversaw the training of fourteen slave preachers and encouraged them to address "Great crouds of Negroes in the Neighborhood of Chysaw [sic], very frequently." According to Jemmy's testimony, John Burnet's gatherings of African believers had taken place at the plantation of a Mr. Austin and at various locations deep in the woods. At one of these assemblies, Burnet reportedly overheard several slaves discussing plans for "an Insurrection intended & to take the country by Killing Whites" but did nothing because, "as their Preacher," he was to be spared.[5]

The principal witness, Jemmy, related an incident strikingly similar to David Margate's controversial "sermon" of Exodus. The slave witness testified that one of Burnet's disciples—a preacher named George, the property of Francis Smith—told him that God had consigned the old king (George II) to the depths of hell for refusing to abolish slavery, but that the current king (George III) was on the verge of emancipating "the Negroes": "the old King had rece[ive]d a Book from our Lord by which he was to Alter the World (meaning to set the Negroes free) but for his not doing so, was now gone to Hell, & in Punishm[en]t—That the Young King, meaning our Present One, came up with the Book, & was about to alter the World, & set the Negroes Free."[6]

Refusing to believe that blacks could have formulated such revolutionary ideas on their own, the Cheraw authorities alleged that Burnet was responsible for disseminating notions of emancipation among his followers. To compound matters, the preacher was said to be guilty of telling blacks that "they were equally intitled to the Good things of this Life in common with the Whites." In light of these allegations, the committee at St. Bartholomew decreed that the Scotsman be cast out of their parish and sent to Charles Town under the charge of Sir Thomas Deale. The "Prisoner" George and the other black preachers were treated more harshly. George was brought before the gallows and summarily executed, while the others received "exemplary punishments." Upon his arrival in the colonial capital, Burnet was taken into custody by "the Centinel upon duty," so that "other matters" (such as the Jeremiah case) could be better decided for the good of the province by the patriot Council of Safety.[7]

For the first two weeks of July, while Jeremiah was still in the workhouse, Burnet was "put under a guard and confined at the Barracks until he was brought before the Council." According to a letter from Henry Laurens to the

Bartholomew Committee, the only grounds on which the council could judge were the preacher's own narrative and confession. "It appeared," Laurens wrote, "that his Guilt consisted in a strong Tincture of Enthusiasm." It was this enthusiasm that led him "many months ago to read and pray to Negroes in the woods and in private places without the Knowledge or Permission of their Masters." Burnet denied saying anything about George III's alleged intent to emancipate African-American slaves. He claimed he knew nothing "of the pretended book" but acknowledged that he acted "contrary to the Law of the Land and to Policy in calling Negroes to private Meetings." Burnet narrowly escaped execution by claiming to be a proponent of the racial status quo and asserting that his attempts to organize such illegal assemblies had ceased since his first presentiment in August 1773. According to the Council of Safety's report, the preacher asserted that "he had never anything more in View than the Salvation of those poor ignorant Creatures, that he never had a thought of exciting them to Insurrection, on the Contrary that he had endeavored to reconcile them to their Lot in Life in which God had placed them, and to impress upon their Minds; the Duty of Obedience to their Masters."[8]

By dint of his repentance, Burnet was mildly rebuked. For "the evil Tendency" of his former conduct, the Scotsman was forced to make "solemn Promise" that he would behave with more circumspection in the future and never return to the "Neighborhood where his Practices had given Offence[sic], and rendered him obnoxious." According to Laurens, Burnet was then promptly dismissed and "immediately obtained an Offer of Employment in Georgia."[9]

Around the same time that Burnet quietly left the colony, patriot fears came to fruition when British naval forces enlisted the help of a black pilot to cross the Charles Town Bar. According to Henry Laurens, "one of their [meaning the people's] Negro Pilots" was "illegally carried away by the Commander of one of His Majesty's Sloops of War."[10] On July 14, Laurens wrote to his son:

> Captain Talmach [Tollemache] of the Scorpion Sloop carried off a black pilot by way of Reprisal & for worse purposes perhaps—for our refusing to return Some of his Seamen who had enlisted in the Regiments of Foot—I was Singular in my opposition to that impolitic measure & expressly foretold the consequence—but I added, that If I was Captain of the Man of War I would carry off the president of the Council of Safety.[11]

Although Laurens was probably unaware of the fact, Campbell may have been involved in the incident. The governor continued to keep in contact with Tollemache long after their voyage to Charles Town and would elicit the services of black harbor pilots in the fall after absconding to the HMS *Tamar*.[12] On Wednesday, July 19, Campbell wrote to Lord Dartmouth:

> I have just received an anonymous letter assuring me they have determined to destroy the lighthouse and cut down the landmark trees that direct the pilots passing the bar of this [Charles Town] harbour, but that will answer little end in preventing men-of-war as they can sound and lay buoys along the channel, and besides Mr. Tollemache carried off in the *Scorpion* to Boston a black fellow who is by far the best pilot in this harbour and has marks of his own by which he will carry in any vessel in safety despite of what they [patriots] can do.[13]

The controversy engendered by the Tollmache incident illustrates the degree to which both Whigs and Tories regarded the acquisition of a black pilot as tactical advantage.[14]

By mid-August, the tensions among African-Americans, patriots, and loyalists were once again out in the open. On Friday, August 11, Thomas Jeremiah was tried for the second and final time. During the course of this second trial under the same court, Jeremiah allegedly committed perjury. According to Laurens, when first confronted with accusations by a runaway slave named Jemmy, Jeremiah "positively [*sic*] denied that he knew his person," although upon further inquiry, it was revealed that the man was in fact his brother-in-law. It was on this ground that Jeremiah was finally found guilty. For his suspected treason, he was sentenced to be hanged and publicly burned on the next Friday, August 18.[15]

At two o'clock in the afternoon, on Saturday, August 12, the day after the sentence of Jeremiah was handed down, British soldier George Walker was seized by a mob for making an "insolent speech" against the patriot cause.[16] For five hours, the soldier was tarred, feathered, and carted through the city streets just as Dealy and Martin had been in early June. The next day, radical Council of Safety member Arthur Middleton reported, "A Mr. Walker Gunner of Fort Johnson had a new suit of Cloathes yesterday without the assistance of a single Taylor (tarred & featherd) his crime nothing less than damning us all—during his circumcartation, he was stopped at the doors of the principal non-associaters and was made to drink damnation to them, also not excepting our friend Sr. Wm.[Wragg] on the Bay."[17]

According to secretary of the Council of Safety and publisher of the *South Carolina Gazette* Peter Timothy, "there is hardly a street through which he was not paraded, nor a Tory House, where they did not halt, particularly Innes's, Simpson's, Wragg's, Milligan's, Irving's, &c., &c., &c." When the mob came upon the home of royal officer Fenwicke Bull, they allegedly "stopt, called for a Grog; had it; made Walker drink D*******n [Damnation] to Bull—threw a bag of feathers into his Balcony, & desired he would take care of it till his turn came; & that he would charge the Grog to the Acct. of Ld. North."[18] Timothy claimed that the people "were in such a humour" that "there was scarce a non-subscriber who did not tremble." Tory printer and bookseller Robert Wells was reportedly so frightened by the torrent that he temporarily closed his place of business and departed for London.[19]

At six o'clock in the evening on August 12, the mob came upon the residence of the Milligen family. Dr. Milligen, who may have taken care of Walker at some point, recalled that he was sitting outside, attempting to get some respite from the heat, when he noticed a motley crew fast approaching. Being that he "expected no insult," the surgeon remained in his seat. But soon, "from hundreds of mouths" came the incantation: "Here is the scoundrel Milligen, Put him in the cart with the other, He is the greatest villain of the two!" The doctor recalled that he was immediately surrounded by a vast crowd of "three or four hundred snakes" who began "hissing, threatening, and abusing" him. For ten minutes, he was restrained in his seat and unable to resist. By his own account, Milligen finally worked up the courage to stand up and fend off his assailants. As he made his escape, a dozen men advanced toward him. The physician put his hand to a small sword at his side, and the men began to back away. His wife, distressed at the scene, ran up to him and fainted in his arms. As the surgeon recalled, numbers then poured into his residence and began to harass his eighty-year-old mother-in-law. Resolved to take back his own house, the doctor carried his wife through the mob and "with some difficulty" managed to close the door. Gathered outside, the mob rushed the surrounding gate. According to Milligen, one of his black servants, "a faithful creature, opposed them" and was knocked down several times. The doctor stormed out of his house, forcing the attackers off his property and locking the gate as the procession went on its way. As for Walker, the soldier was taken prisoner and would eventually seek refuge on the *Tamar*. Milligen, confronted several days later by patriot authorities for his refusal to subscribe to their Association, promptly left the colony for England aboard the *Eagle* packet.[20]

Campbell, hearing of the grim sentence and knowing the frailness of the evidence, waited "two or three days" to receive a petition in favor of a pardon for Thomas Jeremiah. But when none appeared, he requested a meeting with Justice of the Peace John Coram for the morning of Wednesday, August 16, in order to discuss "the proceedings against this poor man, and the whole of the evidence." Before the meeting commenced, Coram gave Campbell a copy of the slave depositions and the "whole of the evidence" against Jeremiah.

Reportedly, Campbell's blood ran "cold" when he read the grounds on which "they had doomed a fellow creature to death." Realizing that without a petition from one of the patriot judges, he would not be able to save the prisoner, Campbell expressed to Coram "in the strongest terms" his sense of "the weakness of the evidence." The governor entreated Coram that "for his own sake" and that of his fellow judges, he get a petition signed by them. In addition to this request, Campbell ordered Coram to meet with the royal judges and the attorney general and "lay the affair before them" so that they could evaluate the legality of the patriot decision and report back to the governor the next evening.[21]

While it is impossible to know what transpired during this encounter, at twelve o'clock, Coram was dismissed. According to Henry Laurens, the justice "voluntarily acquainted the people that his Lordship had recommended to him to procure or promote a petition in behalf of the Criminal, and that in speaking of the Evidence that had been given against him his Excellency had said, 'the People should consider the Consequence of executing him upon such Evidence in case the times should alter.' "[22]

Word spread rapidly of a bitter confrontation between Coram and the royal governor, and it was soon leaked that Campbell was trying to stay Jeremiah's execution. Laurens claimed that the alleged remark made by the governor "greatly affected the minds of those to whom it was repeated," because it played on patriot apprehensions and made them acutely aware of the dangers inherent in such an openly rebellious stance against "the Representative of Majesty."[23]

"Whilst this was transacting," Campbell would later recall, "my attempting to interfere in the matter raised such a Clamour amongst the People, as is incredible, and they openly declared that if I granted the man a pardon they would hang him at my door." As rumors continued to spread and recriminations continued to fester, Campbell received a letter from "a man of the first Property in the Province, who had always express'd great friendship."[24] According to Campbell, the letter represented in "the strongest terms, the dreadful consequences that would attend my pardoning him, concluding with this remarkable expression, that it would raise a flame all the water in Cooper River would not extinguish."[25]

The next day, Thursday, August 17, Coram openly confronted Governor Campbell over the perceived threat. According to Laurens, "The Justice persisted in the declaration to Lord William's Face, His Lordship said he had mistaken him some how or other—but Mr. Coram is clear & positive & was very prudently cautious."[26]

At noon, Campbell met with Robert Smith, the Anglican rector of St. Phillip's parish. Born in Norfolk, England, and educated at Gonville and Caius

College, Cambridge, Smith was instrumental in the founding of the College of Charleston, serving as the institution's first president. In 1795, the priest would be consecrated as the first American bishop of the diocese of South Carolina. Although he was a devoted patriot, he, like Campbell, had become intrigued by Jeremiah's story over the course of the past few months.[27] At several points between the end of June and the middle of August, the minister had conferred with Jeremiah and his brother-in-law, Jemmy, and spoke to them at great length about their involvement in the alleged "crime." Robert Cooper, the loyalist rector of St. Michael's, who (as we shall see) would speak out against the Whig cause in June 1776, likely also tried to intervene on Jeremiah's behalf. According to Henry Laurens, both clergymen visited the pilot frequently and "became Solicitous for him." Laurens, a staunch Anglican and a vestryman in Smith's church, was apparently irked by the fact that two priests from his own denomination deigned to provide a black man with counsel and assistance. He wrote to his son John that "that Sort of Duty had been generally left to the Dissenting Ministers when White Men were under Sentence of Death."[28]

On the afternoon of the 17th, Robert Smith met with Lord William and reportedly told him that "he attended the Black [meaning Jeremiah] as much from a desire to ascertain the reality of an instigated insurrection as from the motives of humanity." According to the governor, Smith "used every argument every art to draw him to confession, endeavouring to make him contradict himself in the many conversations he had with him but in vain." The Reverend Mr. Smith also informed Campbell that Jeremiah's behavior "was modest, [and] his conversation sensible to a degree that astonished him." When asked about the impending execution, Jeremiah reportedly told the rector that "he was perfectly resigned to his unhappy, undeserved fate." Moreover, "He declared he wished not for life, he was in a happy frame of mind and prepared for death." According to Campbell, "Mr. Smith concluded this afflicting story with acquainting me, that the wretch [who was] one of the evidences against Jerry, and condemn'd with him [Jemmy], retracted what he had said against him, and voluntarily declared his perfect innocence." Based on their conversation, that afternoon, Smith applied to the governor for Jemmy's pardon, and Campbell decided to redouble his efforts to save the accused.[29]

Meanwhile, John Coram and freeholder Daniel Cannon, the driving force behind the Sons of Liberty, laid the affair before the royal judges and the attorney general as Campbell had requested.[30] Chief Justice Thomas Knox Gordon and Attorney General James Simpson conferred with Justices Edward Savage, William Gregory, John Fewtrell, and Charles Matthew Coslett and proceeded to examine the verdict made by the Whig Committee. Given the impending sentence of death looming over Jeremiah's head, the royal officials knew that they had to report back to the governor as quickly as possible.[31]

Yet it appears that they had difficulty reaching a decision, and in fact, the governor found himself receiving not one report but three. The first, drawn up on the evening of the 17th by Gordon, Savage, Simpson, and Gregory, argued in favor of Jeremiah's acquittal. It claimed that the Negro Act of 1740 was "an Act of a very penal nature," which required "a strict and literal construction." The judges opined that the *only* part of the Negro Act that made the crime of attempting to raise an insurrection a capital offense was Section 17. In that section, the judges demonstrated, "The Words are 'And every Slave who shall raise or attempt to raise an Insurrection in this Province, shall upon conviction suffer Death.'" Because Jeremiah was "a *free Negro* and not a slave," they argued, the critical section did not and could not apply. The judges claimed that the "makers of the Law, cou'd never have had it in contemplation to include Free Negroes in the said recited words of the 17th section, because in many parts of the Act there is a plain and palpable distinction made between *Slaves* and *Free Negroes*." They contended that in the "very preceding sixteenth section" free blacks were mentioned, and were "subjected to the [same] pains of death" as slaves. "Had it been the intention of the Legislature" to have included free blacks in the all-important "subsequent section, they cou'd never have so immediately forgot them."[32]

The four judges also noted that because free blacks were not mentioned in Section 17, they could only be "punishable for an attempt to raise an Insurrection, in a like manner as white men." Moreover, the judges argued, "a bare attempt to raise an Insurrection evidenced *only by words without any overt Act in consequence of them*" could not be construed as "a levying of War within the meaning of the Act of Parliament passed in the 25th year of King Edward the 3rd and consequently" did not "amount to Treason." The royal authorities concluded that the patriot "Justices and Freeholders in the present case" had indeed "mistaken the Law" and that the sentence of death passed by them upon Jeremiah was "illegal."[33] A similar line of argument would later be made by George Milligen, who claimed that because Jeremiah was "free and a Christian and possessed of property to the amount of six or seven hundred pounds sterling, ... he ought to have been tried by the King's court and a jury."[34]

That evening, Justice Charles Matthew Coslett put forth a very different interpretation on the legality of Jeremiah's trial. The justice began by stating that although Coram did accede to Campbell's command by laying "before the Judges and His Majestie's Attorney General the Evidence," he "very incorrectly declared that the Witnesses were examined at different times and always confirmed what they had said on their first examination." Coslett recollected that barristers in England "could not make any report *viva voce* Evidence which we ourselves had not heard, and that it was always the Judge who heard and saw the Witness examined who reported to his Majesty." Yet, despite Coslett's stance against the Committee's faulty use of evidence and improper procedure, the justice agreed with Coram's report.[35]

Coslett argued that the Negro Act was indeed applicable to "free Negroes." He grounded his opinion entirely on the Section 14 of the statute, specifically the section that enacted that "the evidence of any free Indian or Slave with Oath shall be allowed and admitted in all cases against any free Negroes, shall be proceeded in, heard, tried and adjudged by the Justices and Freeholders appointed by this Act for the trial of slaves in a like manner as is hereby directed for the trial of Crimes committed by Slaves any Law &c to the Contrary."[36] The construction Coslett put on the clause was that the Whig justices and freeholders were in their rights "to try and convict all free Negroes for any crime which a slave under this Act can be tried or convicted for except in the 29th section where free Negroes are fined only for harboring slaves."[37]

Coslett conceded that Section 17 only used the term "slave" and never actually referred to free blacks, but he stated that "if it is not to be construed that free Negroes are liable to the same punishment for this same offense, they will not be punishable at all under this Law or any that I know of." Coslett rested his decision primarily on South Carolina's unique racial demography. Surely, he must have had the black majority in mind when he argued that "the peculiar circumstances of this Province would never permit the Legislature to make any difference in the punishment of a slave and a free Negroe in an offense of so enormous a nature," especially when one was "at least as equally dangerous as the other." Coslett conceded that that Negro Act was indeed a penal statute, which ought to be taken strictly, but noted that in "the 53rd section: it is enacted that all Clauses therein contained shall be construed most largely for the promoting and carrying into Execution this Act." Coslett concluded his report to Campbell by making an explicit reference to the black majority: "Besides, I could not help reflecting, that there was a vast multitude of slaves and free Negroes, Mullatoes &c in the Province, and that it might be of the most fatal consequence to the lives and properties of the white Inhabitants, if these fellows once got into their heads that free Negroes &c were not punishable under this Act for such an enormous crime."[38]

Lord Campbell eventually received a third opinion from his divided legal panel. The opinion submitted by Justice John Fewtrell can only be described as neutral. Not only was the report strikingly evasive, but it was also submitted two days late and after the execution had already taken place.[39] Fewtrell began by stating the obvious, namely that "the Legislature of the Province" based its opinion on the Negro Act of 1740.[40] According to Fewtrell, the act gave the justices and freeholders the power to "examine Witnesses and other evidence & *finally* hear and determine the matter brought before them." According to the justice, "another section" of the Negro Act gave the colonial authorities "power in Cases Capital to mitigate the Sentence, except for the homicide of a white person, to corporal punishment in such discretion as they see fit." Invoking *stare decisis*, Fewtrell cited a precedent from 1751, which provided "Justices and Freeholders" with the power to mitigate punishment, and concluded that "such full power being placed in the Justices & Freeholders in Criminal Matters . . . takes away all jurisdiction from the Judges & that they cannot anyways interfere."[41]

It is unclear what Campbell thought of Coslett's and Fewtrell's opinions, but when the governor spoke with Gordon, Savage, Simpson, and Gregory on the evening of Thursday, August 17, he became disheartened. Despite the favorable opinion given by the four judges, the men informed Campbell that "they were well assured his death was determined on" and told the governor that it might be improper for him to interpose. In his letter to Dartmouth, Campbell remarked, "I leave your Lordship to conceive of the poignancy of my agony and distress on this occasion. I was almost distracted, and wished to have been able to fly to the remotest corner of the Earth from a set of Barbarians who are worse than the most cruel Savages any history described."[42]

Henry Laurens's description of the royal judges' reports was somewhat caustic. The merchant-planter later told his son that the law by which Jeremiah "was tried was called into question, the Judges & Attorney General were called on for their opinions, & for a while those Sages were pleased to aver that a Free Negro was not amenable to that Act." He added that one of the judges even "threw the Magna Charta in the faces of the people—but loose opinions would not pass & the Gentleman dared not venture to Subscribe to a declaration which must have called something more valuable than their Law knowledge into question."[43]

At six o'clock that evening, Governor Campbell pardoned Jemmy according to Smith's request[44] and ordered Reverend Smith "to attend the [patriot] Committee then sitting." The governor would later tell Lord Dartmouth that he believed Smith's reputation as a virulent patriot would have some influence on the Council of Safety and cause its members to change their minds. At precisely seven o'clock, Campbell sent Smith's report (entitled "After Some conversation with Jemmy, I put forth the following Questions") to both John Coram and Henry Laurens and scripted personal letters to each asking them to rethink the sentence of execution (figure 3.1).[45]

Campbell deliberately "wrote in such terms" as he "hoped might rouse their consciences."[46] In his letter to John Coram, Campbell declared: "In Case of Blood I wave <u>Ceremony</u>, I would even give up <u>Dignity</u> to Save the Life of an Innocent Man. Consider it Seriously Sir, lay it before your Brother Justice, & the Freeholders, between God & your own consciences be it, I take every Holy Power to witness I am innocent of this Mans death, upon your heads be it, for without your interposition, I find I cannot Save him."[47]

In the letter to Laurens, Governor Campbell openly informed the merchant that he was trying to appeal to his feelings for "the Representative of Majesty in this unhappy Province."[48] In a further effort to rouse the patriot leader's conscience, the governor called on Laurens to think of "the weight of Blood," and—apparently protesting the recent letter of warning that may have come from Laurens—concluded, "I am told I cannot attempt to save this Man without bringing greater Guilt on this Country than I can even bear to even think of."

Laurens received the letter at nine P.M. on Thursday, August 17, while "Sitting in the Chair of the Committee" and "offered it immediately as a matter proposed." The governor's letter and Smith's report were then read aloud, but when the members of the Committee "had heard the Contents, they utterly refused to take them under Consideration." Laurens would later claim:

> the retraction by Jemmy could have no weight with Men who would give themselves time to consider that his first Evidence was corroborated by two other witnesses, that a Sambo who was the main Witness would not retract & that Jerry when he was first confronted by Jemmy, possitively [sic] denied that he knew his person—that he knew the Man—although upon enquiry it clearly appeared that they were old acquaintance[s] & nearly allied by Jerry's connection as a husband to the other Man's sister.[49]

Although Henry Laurens refused to intervene on Jeremiah's behalf, out of "good manners" and a "Love of plain dealing," he drafted a response to the governor shortly after the hearing drew to a close at ten-thirty. Laurens later told his son that the rebuttal to Lord Campbell was "done in haste & very late at night," claiming that he failed to express "his thoughts so clearly as he might have done at a little more leisure." This rebuttal, coming on the eve of Jeremiah's execution, touched off a set of harsh exchanges between the merchant-planter and Campbell's private secretary, Alexander Innes, which, according to Laurens himself, reportedly "gave" the patriot leader "Some pain."[50]

In his first letter to the governor, Laurens claimed that he had not "heard the Evidence fully against Jerry" and would not declare the man innocent or guilty. Laurens implied that a sort of underhanded plea bargain had been made to the detriment of justice: "If the retraction of Evidence by one who had been

FIGURE 3.1 (LEFT). A handwritten pardon for Thomas Jeremiah's accuser and ostensible accomplice, a slave named Jemmy, from August 17, 1775. Jemmy, as the trial would later reveal, turned out to be Jeremiah's brother-in-law. It was on that basis that our protagonist was finally found guilty. *South Carolina Department of Archives and History*

FIGURE 3.1 (RIGHT). A handwritten pardon for Thomas Jeremiah for assaulting a white ship captain, from July 17, 1771. The judge, like several twentieth-century historians, had trouble pinning down Jeremiah's name. Given the location of the hearing described in the document, Jeremiah may have had ties to Berkeley County (upriver from Charles Town). *South Carolina Department of Archives and History* admitted an accomplice & after he had secured his own pardon and Reward, was to be admitted at the Old Bailey many Rogues would escape Punishment and many of his Majesty[']s Proclamations [would] prove worse than Nugatory, but such a retraction I also presume would not even be listen'd to in a case where there had been another firm Evidence."[51]

The patriot leader declared that "the unhappy Man in Question was found Guilty after a fair Legal trial, that the Justices and freeholders were unanimous in their opinion of his Guilt." He argued that alarm of "the people" was justified, given the "Calamitious Situation of this Colony under the threats of Insurrection" and "the strong proofs" which the people had in their possession.[52] In an effort to make the governor "know that" he had "some feeling for the Majesty of the People—as well as for the 'Representative of Majesty,'" Laurens alluded to the July incident involving John Tollmache, captain of the HMS *Scorpion*. Tollmache had brought the governor to Charles Town in June, and whether or not he also brought arms, it was clear that when he departed for Boston, he had, perhaps with the governor's approval, "illegally carried away" one of "the people's" valuable "Negro Pilots."[53]

Lord Campbell offered no direct response. However, in the early hours of the morning on Friday, August 18 (the day Jeremiah was to be executed), Alexander Innes scripted a quick riposte to Laurens's allegations. Campbell's secretary informed Laurens that the "Confession of the Wretch Jemmy" was voluntary and "made to Mr. Smith before His Lordship knew such a person was even under Confinement."[54] Innes informed Laurens: "No application was made to the Governor in his [Jemmy's] behalf till past 12. Yesterday. his Excellency signed the Pardon at 6 O Clock & by desire of Mr. Smith, Jemmy is now ignorant of it, unless Mr. Coram to whom Mr. Nesbitt[55] was obliged to apply for such information as was necessary to enable him to draw the Pardon has acquainted him with it."[56] Noting that Laurens had "omitted inclosing Mr. Smiths Conversation with the wretched Creature," which the governor had previously asked him to return, the secretary requested that he enclose the reverend's report in his next letter.

Later that morning, at seven-thirty, Laurens responded by sending an envelope to Innes containing Smith's account of Jemmy's recantation, along with a hostile retort. He accused Campbell of threatening Coram during the meeting on Wednesday, August 16. The merchant-planter concluded by informing Innes that Jemmy was "a liar of the most abominable order of Liars" and that his testimony was not to be given much credit.[57]

That afternoon, Innes sent a response, noting that Laurens had "mistaken Jemmy for Jerry." Innes repeated that "no application was made for Jemmy till 12 Yesterday" and "that till that time his Excellency did not know Jemmy was under Confinement." Changing his tone somewhat, the secretary declared, "How cruel then that Suggestion in Mr. Laurens Letter of last Night, that either pardon or reward was offered to procure his recantation." Innes then told Laurens that if he still doubted the point, he should consult Smith, whose testimony would surely "satisfy." Innes conceded that he thought Jemmy was "the most Abominable of Liars" and informed Laurens that the "persons of both wretches" were unknown to him. Addressing the alleged statement that Campbell made to Coram regarding what might happen to "the people" should the times change, Innes claimed that "his Excellency...never made use of that expression." The secretary defended Campbell by asserting that his attempt to intervene on Jeremiah's behalf was rooted only in "what proceeded from Humanity Justice and Mercy." The governor's assistant was quick to point out, however, that had Campbell been convinced of Jeremiah's guilt, "his Lordship would have been the last Man...to save him from the Punishment due to a Crime of so *Black* a dye." The secretary's concluding remarks were no doubt designed to elicit guilt. Begging Laurens's pardon, Campbell's assistant declared, "the horrid Scene will soon be closed and this Matter decided by that Eternal God to whom all hearts are open & before whom the most Secret thoughts cannot be hid."[58]

In spite of Campbell's best efforts, between 11 and noon, Thomas Jeremiah was brought before the gallows, strung up by a noose, and "burned to ashes" for all to see. While there are no eyewitness accounts of the spectacle, the rain-soaked crowd must have harbored conflicting emotions.[59] Jeremiah reportedly "asserted his innocence to the last, behaved with the greatest intrepidity as well as decency, and told his implacable, and ungrateful Persecutors, God's judgement[sic] would one day overtake them for shedding his innocent blood."[60] Milligen, who may have been in attendance or learned about the event after the fact, recalled, "Jerry met death like a man and a Christian, avowing his innocence to the last moment of his life." "Surely," the doctor would conclude, "there is no murder so cruel and dangerous as that committed under the appearance of law and justice."[61]

Shortly after Jeremiah was executed, Laurens sent a final letter to Innes.[62] It was somewhat apologetic in tone and began with a concession by the patriot leader. Laurens admitted that in his last letter to the secretary, he had indeed "mistaken the name of Jemmy for Jerry." The patriot leader claimed that he now understood that "no application was made in favor of the former till Yesterday Noon" and solemnly declared that he never intended to "Complain of a Want of Candour" on Innes's part. Laurens informed Innes that he did not mean "an unkind Suggestion" when referring to "the inefficacy of retracted Evidence after a fair trial." He conceded that at "a Court of Oyer and Terminer in Great Britain," there are cases where "His Majestys Proclamations not only Pardon but Rewards are offered to accomplices for discovering their Confederates." Laurens argued that such practices were common, citing what he called a proverb—" 'the greatest rogue turns Kings Evidence.' " He then denied that he "by any means intended to Infer from thence that Pardon and Reward had been offered to Jemmy by the Governor or by his authority directly or indirectly."[63]

Changing his tone somewhat, Laurens broached the subject of Coram and the alleged tête-à-têtes that occurred back-to-back on the 16th and the 17th: "I am sorry the Magistrate has been so criminal as to misinform the people in that important declaration which his Excellency says is not warranted by his expressions—he [Coram] must have taken pains to be wicked in this point by averring a falsehood in writing one day and deliberately Confirming it upon the day following."[64]

Laurens again denied that Campbell had ulterior motives for attempting to "save the Life of Jerry," but at the same time declared, "I now believe Jerry was Guilty and I am fully persuaded that the Governor and you are so open to Conviction that I should have no difficulty in bringing you both to be of my opinion on this [head]." Laurens admitted that he "was till this morning unacquainted with particular circumstances" and "had avoided the knowledge of the whole of this horrible Insurrection Report as much as possible." Laurens concluded the letter and the correspondence by claiming that he was "in hopes of having steered clear of an affair which in the sequel has given me some uneasiness. but I learn the Scene is closed! Justice is satisfied! I beg our correspondence on this disagreeable Subject may here end."[65]

The next day—Saturday, August 19—an anonymous patriot wrote to Philadelphia, "we are putting the town in a posture of defense, and all are determined to oppose whatever troops may come here. Yesterday a negro was hanged and burned for intended sedition, and burning the town, & c."[66] The same day, Governor Campbell, wrote to British secretary of state William Legge, second Earl of Dartmouth, in a state of frenzy:

> Your Lordship will I am sure excuse my warmth when I acquaint
> you, that yesterday under the colour of the Law they hanged &
> burned, an unfortunate wretch, a Free Negroe of considerable
> property, one of the most valuable & useful men in his way in the
> Province, on suspicion of instigating an Insurrection, for which I am
> convinced there was not the least ground. I could not save him my
> Lord! the very reflection Harrows my Soul! I have only the comfort to
> think I left no means untried to preserve him. They have now dipt
> their hands in Blood, God Almighty knows where it will end.[67]

4

Charles Town Harbor

September 1775–October 1775

By September 1775, the British naval presence in Charles Town Harbor was feeble. The affairs of South Carolina had, in the words of Lord Campbell, been left to the care of a "poor solitary worm-eaten sloop," the HMS *Tamar*. This ship, named for the river that pours into the harbor at Plymouth, England, was described in admiralty records of the time as unsafe for active service. It had remained on station in the waters off Charles Town for months as its tiny crew attempted to strengthen its foremast and make other repairs. On Saturday, July 29, the man-of-war's captain, Edward Thornbrough, made a less than optimistic assessment, which he related to Admiral Samuel Graves: "Her sheathing is dropping off forward and as the Worms bite so much am fearful that her Plank will soon eat thro' as my Anchor Stocks are all eat to a honey Comb, and a foot of the Ends dropped off although it is not a month since summoned last." To make matters worse, Thornbrough himself was, by Campbell's and Alexander Innes's estimation, as unfit for the naval service as his vessel. Captain Innes referred to the skipper as "a poor, helpless, lame, bedridden old Man," who had served nearly fifty years in the Royal Navy.[1]

The *Tamar* did have one thing going for it, however: a battery of sixteen guns. This alone was cause for consternation among the white revolutionaries of Charles Town, prompting Henry Laurens to remark that the ship was "as well prepared as such a Crazy Bark can be." Lingering by itself in Rebellion Road, the anchorage ground between Shute's Folly and Sullivan's Island, the sloop was desperately in need of naval reinforcements.[2]

Help for the British would arrive fortuitously on Thursday, September 7, in the form of the HMS *Cherokee*. Originally called the *Codrington*, the armed sloop was most likely renamed by British surveyor general William Gerard De Brahm, who had lived briefly among the Cherokee Indians during the construction of Fort Loudoun in 1756. In September 1774, the ship had been personally selected by De Brahm to carry out a surveying expedition of the southern district of North America. The engineer and his geographic research vessel had come to Charles Town Harbor not for anything having to do with the Anglo-American conflict but for the sole purpose of drawing up a report for the lords commissioners of the admiralty. Unfortunately for De Brahm, conditions in the Carolina capital had deteriorated to such an extent that Lord Campbell insisted that the sloop be detained and that the surveyor general's orders be countermanded. Although Campbell and Innes would receive a great deal of cooperation from Lieutenant John Fergusson, the vessel's commanding officer, De Brahm protested, demanding to know why his ship was diverted to a purpose for which it was ill suited. Innes quickly grew tired of De Brahm's incessant complaints and remarked to the royal governor of East Florida, Patrick Tonyn, that it was "A fine time to talk of his surveys of a Country that we are in doubt to whom it may belong."[3]

The HMS *Cherokee* had been in harbor for less than a week when the situation with the governor began to unravel. On the evening of Monday, September 11, 1775, in the black of night, disguised backcountry leader Moses Kirkland made his way into Charles Town flanked by two bodyguards. When the trio arrived in the heart of the city, the men split up, and Kirkland took refuge at the governor's residence, where he spent the remainder of the night. The next morning, continuing to evade patriot authorities, Kirkland stole away to the *Tamar*. The next day, one of Kirkland's traveling companions, a loyalist by the name of Bailey Cheney, was seized by the Council of Safety. After a lengthy interrogation, Cheney divulged that Campbell had secret plans to encourage resistance in the backcountry. The Council promised to set Cheney at liberty, but not until he first participated in a ruse against the governor. Captain Adam McDonald of the First Provincial Regiment was called in and ordered to accompany Cheney on a mission to see Lord Campbell. To effect this plan, as Charles Drayton recalled, McDonald donned a backcountry disguise and was made up to look like "a cracker." Cheney's participation was ensured by dint of the fact that McDonald was carrying two pocket pistols, with the threat "that if he hinted or made any signs to the Governor,...he would blow his brains immediately."[4]

At ten o'clock that evening, Cheney appeared before the governor as planned and introduced the patriot captain as backcountry loyalist "Dick Williams." As the meeting ran its course, "Williams" portrayed himself as an anxious yet dutiful Tory, eager to serve the Crown but frightened of being tarred and feathered. Pretending to dread the wrath of the Council of Safety for his "active" support of the king, the impostor repeatedly tricked the governor into making condemnatory remarks about the Association. At one stage in the conversation, Campbell blithely dismissed the Whig committee as "a parcel of profligates." To make matters worse, McDonald managed to draw a confirmation from Campbell that Kirkland was onboard the *Tamar* and would soon be receiving a fresh shipment of supplies.[5]

To extract more information, McDonald queried the governor repeatedly about the situation in the backcountry. At one point, McDonald/"Williams" even boasted that he was a sergeant to Moses Kirkland and would be glad to relay messages to Fletchall, Brown, or Cunningham. According to John Drayton, Campbell told the disguised patriot that he had "nothing to send them" but ordered him to inform the ringleaders that they should "keep all the men in good order."[6] When pressed by McDonald about whether His Majesty would send troops to South Carolina, Campbell replied that the province would indeed "be a place of settled soldiers; and a seat of war shortly."[7]

Later that night, McDonald transcribed the entire exchange. The next day, when the transcript was read aloud before the Committee, the details reportedly "excited universal indignation." A motion was made by Arthur Middleton to seize Lord Campbell and take him into custody immediately. Middleton further suggested that the Committee confine Campbell until an exchange could be worked out for Kirkland. This plan was vehemently opposed by Rawlins Lowndes and other conservatives, who prevented the measure from being passed. As a compromise, the Council of Safety decided that eight of its leading members (those most exasperated by Campbell) would accompany an undisguised Captain McDonald and confront the governor to his face. From that point on, according to John Ball, the patriot party labeled Campbell "an old Traitor."[8]

As John Drayton recalled, McDonald and the band of eight Committee members flagged Campbell down while he was "going to the riverside." They escorted Campbell to his residence and presented him with a set of McDonald's accusations. According to John Ball, when Campbell flatly denied that he was corresponding with the backcountry insurgents and that he was harboring Moses Kirkland, "McD went up to him and told he was the man...he had spoken with last night."[9] Nonplussed, Campbell refused to comply with the committee, but, according to Henry Laurens, he "acknowledged that Ships & Troops were to be sent from England to all the Colonies & might be shortly expected."[10] In frustration, the Committee members returned to their chambers and took a second vote on seizing Lord Campbell, which was reportedly voted down, twenty-three to sixteen.[11]

Around the same time that Whigs were grappling with the Campbell situation, the *Swallow* packet, captained by William Copeland, arrived in Charles Town, carrying news from England that the king and his administration were "determined to reinforce Gen[eral] Gage" and "throw Troops into all the Colonies." Rumors of an impending British invasion swirled throughout the city. Ten transports and two frigates were reportedly en route to Charles Town. To prepare for a full-scale naval assault, the Council unanimously decided to take control of Fort Johnson, but Campbell anticipated the seizure. On the evening of Thursday, September 14, the governor gave orders to Captain Alexander Innes and several crew members of the *Tamar* to systematically dismantle Fort Johnson. As John Drayton recalled:

> During that night, his Secretary, Mr. Innis, with part of the Tamer's
> crew, landed at Fort Johnson; and entering the room of the person
> who there commanded, made him a prisoner. After this, they
> proceeded to dismantle the fort, by dismounting all the cannon
> therein; consisting of seven twenty-six pounders, twelve eighteen
> pounders, one twelve pounder, and one nine pounder; throwing
> them down from the platform, so as to be rendered useless for
> immediate service; but they did not spike their touch holes, nor break
> any of their trunnions.[12]

After ransacking the fortress and shielding the commanding officer from any blame for the disruption through his "arrest," Innes and his men quietly slipped away just before dawn, completing their mission with little time to spare. Three or four hours after the loyalist party's departure, Colonel Moultrie and 150 provincial troops met little opposition when they took possession of the fortress. The unfortunate gunner, George Walker, was taken prisoner along with four others.[13] Although temporarily in shambles after the Innes raid, Fort Johnson still represented a strategic location overlooking Charles Town Harbor, coveted by both sides.[14]

The seizure of Fort Johnson, coupled with the successful ruse of Captain McDonald, convinced Lord Campbell that he needed to take action. Realizing that he was now completely powerless and that he and his family were in jeopardy, the governor issued an official proclamation dissolving the Commons House of Assembly. In the cover of darkness on Friday, September 15, Campbell took the Great Seal of the Province and privately withdrew from Charles Town to the *Tamar*. Lord William's escape was made easy by Vanderhorst Creek, a small rivulet, linking the Cooper River along what is now Water Street to the rear entrance of his residence at 34 Meeting Street.[15]

The absconding of Lord Campbell to a boat in Charles Town Harbor was a crucial moment, marking the official end of royal government in South Carolina. Campbell had officially joined the ranks of other royal governors who had abandoned their capitals earlier that summer, including Lord Dunmore of Virginia, who had taken refuge aboard the HMS *Fowey* on Thursday, June 8, and North Carolina's Josiah Martin, who had escaped to HMS *Cruizer* on Saturday, July 15.[16] Patriots, quick to interpret Campbell's move, likened the governor's actions to those of King James II, who had fled in 1689 with the Great Seal of England. James II had long symbolized weak and unfit rule and was regarded as a traitor in the eyes of Whigs—who took delight in the fact that he pusillanimously "abdicated" the British throne to William of Orange.[17] Campbell was now in a precarious position. His dilapidated vessel, along with the *Cherokee* and the *Swallow* packet (both of which had arrived in Rebellion Road only a few days earlier), represented the last vestiges of the king's authority in the province.[18]

As soon as the governor reached the *Tamar*, he dispatched his secretary, Alexander Innes, to return to Fort Johnson and inquire about its seizure. Innes sailed out to the base of the fortress, and a heated exchange quickly ensued between the secretary and Captain Charles Pinckney. The governor's assistant demanded to know which troops were in the fort. Pinckney responded, "American Troops." Innes then asked, "Who commands them?" Averting a direct response, the patriot leader answered, "By what authority do you ask it?" The secretary informed Pinckney, "By the Governor's. The Governor desires to know by what Authority you took possession of this Fort." The answer given by the Whig captain was, "By the express Command of the Council of Safety." As Drayton related, Innes then made his bow and was promptly taken away in a boat back to the *Tamar*.[19]

The next day, Colonel Motte, presiding over Fort Johnson, ordered his men to repair the damaged armaments. To reinforce the patriot garrison, 250 additional troops were called in. The Council of Safety commissioned Colonel William Moultrie to design a flag to be placed atop the fortress. Inspired by the uniforms of the Whig soldiers, Moultrie's design, which consisted of a blue background with a silver crescent moon in the dexter corner, would ultimately evolve into the official flag of the independent state of South Carolina.[20]

On the morning of Sunday, September 17, enraged by the Whig party's success and its insolence to Captain Innes, Campbell commanded all three of His Majesty's armed ships in the harbor to sail within firing range of Fort Johnson. For a brief moment, it appeared as if a military engagement was about to take place. Yet, as John Drayton remembered, before any altercation ensued, the three Tory vessels "very peaceably" returned to the former anchorage ground.[21] Perhaps a shift of wind prompted the retreat, or it may have been because Campbell became violently ill. In a letter to Henry Laurens, Dr. Alexander Garden described Campbell's condition and asked whether visiting the governor onboard the man-of-war would give "offence to the Community."[22]

That day, the Council of Safety issued orders to Colonel Motte "to prevent people from going on board the ships of war in the Road...without a permission from the Council, or their giving a good account of their intended business." With access limited, tensions quickly arose over how and when the British vessels in the harbor would be supplied. When the Council of Safety learned of Campbell's departure, it immediately gave orders to "the Agent Victualler," Fenwicke Bull, "not to supply the King's ships with provisions" until further notice. This was partially rescinded when the Council decided that the vessels *would* be allowed provisions but only on a day-to-day basis, a policy that prevented the ships from laying in supplies and kept them steadily dependent on onshore providers, thus helping to force a compliant posture.[23]

Despite the easing of the Council's position, the governor and his entourage were irate. On Monday, September 18, the captain of the *Tamar*, Edward Thornbrough, penned a hostile letter to the patriot committee.[24] The document itself is not extant, but the Council's response survives. Henry Laurens, the author of the Council's retort, began by stating definitively that the patriots had not cut off water and food to the king's ships. Laurens justified the Council's decision to ration the provisions by providing a litany of the elderly captain's offensive actions:

> The hostile Dispositions which the Commander of those Ships has
> for some Time past shewn towards this Colony, by imprisoning its
> Pilots, affording sanctuary to a Traitor, Seizing its Seamen, disman-
> tling its principal Fortification, stopping private property, and firing
> upon the Persons of its Inhabitants who were not only peaceable but
> unarmed, and driven from the Shore, do make it necessary, in their
> Opinion, to alter the Mode of Supply. And as you have declared, that
> you do not mean to leave the Station, it can be no Disadvantage to
> His Majesty's Ships to receive their Provisions from Day to Day in
> this warm Climate.[25]

Laurens proceeded to deny Thornbrough's charge that the committee had taken "the absolute Government" of the province into its hands. "But," he assured the captain, "you may depend we shall notwithstanding any Threats take every necessary step in our Power for securing our Property and preserving Peace and good Order in this His Majesty's Government."[26]

Within hours, Thornbrough responded to the Council of Safety. In his riposte, the captain refused to address the Committee's allegations, declaring that reasons for his conduct "must be obvious."[27] He did, however, make an overt threat regarding the harbor pilots of Charles Town. "You may be Assured," Thornbrough wrote, "that whilst I have the Honor of Commanding one of his Majesty's Ships. I am determined to have the Assistance of a Pilot, and every necessary Supply, *by force*, if I cannot obtain them in an *Amicable* way."[28]

While Laurens and Thornbrough exchanged barbs, patriots learned that a boat was loading in Charles Town with liquors and provisions for the men-of-war. They alerted Isaac Motte to keep a watchful eye from his station at Fort Johnson. At 1:30 P.M., a suspicious vessel appeared in the harbor. Motte ordered his men to fire a musket and a cannon. Heeding the warning shots, the boat abruptly dropped anchor. Aboard the craft were Campbell's wife and Dr. Garden. Garden, who must have received permission from the Council to treat the governor, produced a letter from Henry Laurens, and Motte "suffered them to pass."[29]

A half an hour later, when a second suspicious boat appeared in the distance, Motte fired two muskets. When the oarsmen did not alter their stroke, the captain fired a cannon. To Motte's dismay, the vessel still eked its way toward His Majesty's ships, so the patriot leader ordered his men to fire "a 6 pounder." When the boatmen again paid the shot scant attention, Motte manned a vessel with a party of well-armed volunteers and set them in pursuit. As the captain recalled, when "they had got a considerable distance from the Fort & our boat could not over take them," patriot pursuers fired again, "upon which they lay upon their Oars & surrendered."[30]

When finally overtaken, the small harbor boat proved to be manned by several blacks and three white sailors. They were carrying with them "21 Casks, 1 Case & 2 Bottles of Liquor & some brown Sugar." Motte began to question all of them "very closely," but to his dismay, the motley crew refused to reveal anything. When pressed further, the men claimed they did not know where they were going, but they were sure that they did not "intend to go to the Man of War." A frustrated Motte wrote in his letter to the Council of Safety, "this is suspicious." Not sure what to make of the incident, the Whig captain decided to retain the men and await further orders from the patriot committee.[31]

That evening, Motte interrogated the three white sailors.[32] He determined that they belonged to the crew of the *Swallow* packet and that their names were John Jeffries, Patrick Murray, and Elias Painter.[33] Motte was able to get the sailors to admit that they had received the alcohol, the slaves, and the boat itself from a woman named Eleanor Jones, who ran a tavern on Elliot Street.[34] Two of the prisoners—Jeffries and Murray—disclosed that Lieutenant John

Fergusson of the *Cherokee* and Captain Arthur Clarke of the packet *Diligence* came aboard the *Swallow* looking to recruit sailors for the men-of-war. According to the testimony of the prisoners, when Fergusson and Clarke approached Jeffries and Murray to board the *Tamar*, the two shipmen adamantly refused. Because they were unwilling to switch stations, they were reportedly "damned for Rascals" by their superiors. Jeffries and Murray further added that "the Man of War had weigh'd twice to attack the Fort [Johnson], but the Wind failing them, was oblig'd to drop thoughts of it."[35]

Elias Painter, the boatswain of the *Swallow*, provided a bit more detail. He claimed that "Capt. Clarke & the Governor's Secretary were the most forward for Attacking the Fort [but] Capt. Thornbrough was very much against making the Attack." According to Painter, Clarke had come aboard the *Swallow* and said to the men, "What are you Men that object [to] fighting for the King, You Dogs—the Americans are in Rebellion." Painter recalled that Clarke then took ten crew members from the packet and brought them aboard the *Tamar*. The captain reportedly returned "with the Governor's Secretary and 22 men to press them." When they refused to submit to any intimidation, "they were severally[*sic*] abused and not [brought] out of the Swallow packet." According to Painter, the abuse even extended to Captain Copeland, the commander of the *Swallow*. As the boatswain recalled, Captain Fergusson of the *Cherokee* "took Capt. Copeland by the Nose & wrung it, calling he a Bouger because he wou'd not consent to come to Attack the Fort." When this tactic failed, Clarke and Alexander Innes delivered a letter from the governor to Copeland, "desiring he wou'd persuade his Crew to come on bo[ar]d of the Man of War & that they wou'd be well rewarded." When Campbell's secretary "found it had not the desired effect," he "pressed" the hands of the *Swallow's* entire crew, sans Jeffries, Murray, and Painter.[36]

During the course of Motte's interrogation of Painter, it was revealed that the crew of the *Tamar* had begun to clear away the woods on Sullivan's Island. Establishing a new base of operations, the loyalist forces were reportedly building a strategic entrenchment "on point of the Island." To make matters worse, the boatswain reported that the Tories were expecting "3 [additional] Men of War and a Bomb Ketch" to destroy Fort Johnson and set fire to Charles Town.[37]

This last bit of information was taken seriously by Whig authorities. The next day, Laurens wrote to William Henry Drayton (who was then on his conversion mission in the backcountry): "We are called together by an alarming account which threatens the destruction of this Town by three Frigates & a Bomb Ketch we hope it may prove a groundless report, but it becomes us to act instantly as if it was real."[38] Frightened by the prospect of a royal fleet invading

Charles Town, for several days, the Council of Safety deliberated. According to John Drayton, the patriots considered a number of measures, some of them extreme. The first proposal was to thwart the governor's plans by taking Sullivan's Island for themselves. The second was to seize the *Prosper*, which was then at port, and equip it with several guns to drive out His Majesty's ships of war. The third and most drastic was to revive the old plan to blockade the entrances through the bar at the mouth of the harbor in the event of a necessary patriot retreat.[39]

On Friday, September 22, Laurens wrote to his brother James in London and informed him about all of these competing plans: "We have lately been busy in talking & Some attempts to fortify Sullivants Island, to equip Armed Vessels & to make places for retreat from Charles Town." With some chagrin, the shipping magnate told his brother that "at present the Scheme for Stopping up the Channels to this Harbour is revived & intended for debate to morrow." He reminded James that "this was reprobated by the Representatives of the whole Colony in June last, & I counted mySelf happy in being Instrumental in procuring its overthrow." However, he concluded, "now the Same destructive measure" to seal two key entryways—Lawford's Channel and the Ship Channel—"is introduced by a Committee & I have some fears of their Success.[40]

The next day, as planned, the Committee considered the subject of the blockade.[41] Two white harbor pilots (Bryan Foskey and Alexander Elsinore) and two white ship captains (Edward Blake and Thomas Tucker) were brought before the Council and asked to provide a feasibility report. According to John Drayton, the boatmen informed patriot authorities that the Ship Channel was 2,700 feet wide, having thirteen feet of water on the south side twelve feet of water on the north side at low tide. Lawford's Channel, the other principal entrance, was reportedly a mile wide, carrying twelve feet of water from side to side at an hour's flood. In addition to this information, the four men claimed that it would require eleven schooners to obstruct the passage of the Ship Channel and twenty schooners to stem Lawford's Channel.[42]

After the pilots and captains made their report, the Committee voted thirty-two to fourteen "to proceed in making such entanglements."[43] Laurens was outraged. As soon as the vote was read, the patriot leader denounced the decision. In a lengthy oration, Laurens explained that he remained in his former opinion and had heard nothing new that could induce him to alter his sentiments. He declared that "if the Bars should be effectually stoped up, this Town & the most valuable part of the Country would be ruined." Besides "vastly depreciating the value of our Lands," Laurens asserted, "the effectual stopping [of] the Bar...would not protect us against the Arm of England if she was seriously disposed to stretch it over us." The Whig leader stated in reference to his opponents that "many of those who Voted for the Measure had judged as blind Men do of Colours." Laurens wanted to get it on record for posterity and for his children that he was against the act and thought it would permanently destroy the harbor. Concluding his speech, the merchant-planter averred that he hoped he was wrong and that despite his feelings on the issue, he "would not oppose the execution of the project since it had been Resolved upon by a Majority" but "could not believe the People at large would be pleased with it."[44]

Despite Laurens's strong objections, a subcommittee was immediately formed to put the blockade into effect.[45] Seven men volunteered to find the thirty-one schooners necessary to span the channels leading in (and out of) the harbor.[46]

Realizing that a blockade would be futile if the king's armed vessels continued to remain within striking distance of Charles Town, on Wednesday, September 27, radicals within the Committee (including Reverend William Tennant) put forth a motion that the men-of-war should first be "secured, destroyed or removed." A tally was taken, and the measure was struck down by a vote of twenty-three to seventeen. Adherents of the plan continued to press the issue, however, and on the next day, a new vote was carried in the affirmative, twenty-nine to twenty-one. Unsure of how to proceed, the members of the General Committee decided to let the Council of Safety settle the matter. Yet the Council had an equally difficult time reaching a decision. It was therefore decided that Henry Laurens, the acting president, should cast the deciding vote. After taking a day to reflect on the measure, Laurens appeared before his fellow members of the Council. Reiterating his objections to the blockade, the merchant-planter nevertheless voted in favor of driving out His Majesty's ships from Rebellion Road. According to John Drayton, Laurens made his decision "in the hope that the public impulse should not be checked and cooled—while a better measure might be devised."[47]

In a last-ditch effort to avoid armed confrontation, Laurens penned an address to Lord Campbell the same day and implored him to return to Charles Town:

> We submit to your Excellency's Consideration, whether the
> Retirement of our Governor to a King's Ship, in this general
> Disquietude, when the Minds of the People are filled with the
> greatest Apprehensions for their Safety, may not increase their
> Alarm, and excite Jealousies of some premeditated Design against
> them. We therefore entreat, that your Excellency will be pleased to
> return to Charles-Town, the accustomed Place of Residence of the
> Governor of South Carolina.[48]

Laurens informed the governor that his safety would be ensured as long as he refused to take an active part "against the good People of this Colony, in the present arduous Struggle for the preservation of their Civil Liberties."[49]

The next day, Campbell issued a hostile retort. In addition to informing the General Committee that it was an illegitimate body with no legal authority, the governor averred that he considered the patriots to be "in actual and open Rebelion [against] their Sovereign." His Excellency claimed that the Committee's request that he return to the seat of government deserved "no answer." However, he asserted, "I will never return to Charles-Town till I can support the King's authority and proteck [sic] his faithful and Loyal Subjects."[50]

In the wake of Lord Campbell's declaration, tensions continued to mount within the patriot party. On Tuesday, October 3, Thomas Ferguson wrote to the radical leader Christopher Gadsden:

> I never was for stopping the bar and fortifying the town till I found
> we could not get nine-tenths of the people to leave the town. We have
> had strange delays. In business and in other affairs there's a party of
> men who strive to put back every measure, that we have nothing
> ready when the King's ships arrive, that they may have a pretence to
> lay down their arms and save their houses. I hope I may be mistaken.
> I have stated my suspicions to the General Committee, and there
> declared that if there were men base and mean enough to act so, and
> if any persons would join me, I would burn the town over their
> heads.[51]

The proposals of the radicals had a divisive effect and, as John Drayton recalled, "created a great alarm" among the moderate men of Charles Town. During the first week of October, Council of Safety member Thomas Bee—a wealthy conservative who also led the slave insurrection committee—drafted a petition against the blockade and the proposed assault against the governor's entourage. According to one observer, the petition "was industriously carried about the town." Seemingly within no time, the moderates were able to obtain 368 signatures.[52]

On Wednesday, October 4, while the document was circulating, Colonel Powell, one of the commissioners to obstruct the bar, approached the Council of Safety and requested a detachment of troops.[53] His request was granted, and, as Thomas Ferguson noted, he soon became "very busy preparing to attack the Ships of War."[54] However, shortly after Powell departed from the Council chamber, a Mr. M——t [possibly Gabriel Manigault] entered the room and presented the moderates' petition.[55] The text itself was essentially condemnatory. Although Bee's draft is not extant, it is clear from Drayton's memoir that it inveighed against the fortification of Charles Town and the obstruction of the bar—both of which, Bee argued (echoing Laurens), were "altogether impracticable. And if persisted in, would bring on the inevitable destruction of this now flourishing town." The petitioner claimed that no attack would be attempted by the king's forces, "unless hostilities were begun by firing on the British navy." The author suggested that a land defense "was their only security" and recommended placing a deep entrenchment across Charles Town Neck to prevent the British from proceeding upcountry.[56] Bee requested that a stop might be put to the measures in hand until "the sense of all the inhabitants of Charles Town should be fully known."[57]

When Colonel Powell learned that the petition had been presented, he immediately returned to the Council chamber. Fearing that his mission had been jeopardized by the moderates, he made a request for a supply of gunpowder. The measure was put to a question by the Executive Committee, and Powell's application was refused by vote of five to four. Shortly thereafter, the moderates' petition was brought before the General Committee. After a lengthy debate, the petition was confirmed, twenty-two to eleven, thus ending plans to blockade the harbor and attack men-of-war (at least temporarily). Henry Laurens had gotten his wish, at least for the time being.[58]

The next day, the seven members who made up the Committee to Obstruct the Passages over the Bar applied to the Council of Safety for permission to disband.[59] In the wake of the Committee's decision, the radical faction lamented the failure of its proposals and the fact that they had been outmaneuvered by Laurens and Bee. On Thursday, October 5, Thomas Ferguson wrote to Christopher Gadsden, who was then representing South Carolina at the Continental Congress in Philadelphia: "We last night determined to lay aside all fortifications of the place and harbor, I am sorry to say many of our people seem more inclined to lay down their arms than defend their country. I shall make a motion to-day to move all the goods out of Charleston; we are full of making lines across the neck, but I fear this has only been agreed to frustrate the other matter."[60] Ferguson's motion to "move all the goods out of Charleston" was approved.[61] According to John Drayton, "on the 5th of October, it was recommended to the merchants, to remove their merchandizes from Charlestown to places of security in the country." During the same meeting, the moderate or more conservative Council members ordered plans to be drawn up for the intended entrenchment on Charles Town Neck. Not to be deterred, members of the radical faction—William Henry Drayton, Thomas Ferguson, Colonel Charles Pinckney, and Arthur Middleton—decided to draft their own plan of defense for the entire colony.[62]

While the radicals were conferring, the sloop *Polly*, captained by John Wanton, sailed into Charles Town Harbor "on or about the twelfth of October" and was intercepted by Captain Thornbrough. When brought before Governor Campbell, Wanton claimed that he and his crew, originally from Newport, Rhode Island, had gotten lost en route to Nantucket when a "hard gale of wind" drove them southward without the benefit of a "chart or quadrant." Believing the story to be suspicious, Campbell allegedly directed George Walker, who had been freed since his capture on September 15, to take command of the vessel and sail it to St. Augustine, where it would be "condemned." The poor and decrepit Walker was reportedly given a pistol to carry out the mission, as well as letter to the governor of East Florida, Patrick Tonyn, requesting "that soldiers should be sent to Charlestown from St. Augustine."[63]

As Campbell was deciding the fate of the *Polly*, William Henry Drayton presented the radicals' plan of defense on Friday, October 13, to the remaining members of the Council of Safety.[64] In addition to recommending against the entrenchment on Charles Town Neck, Drayton and his fellow radicals called for cutting off all "communication between the town and the backcountry," as well as the removal of every person of color from the surrounding coastline. A chain of slave patrols would be set up in order to prevent loyalists from relaying messages to blacks in the interior of the province:

> All the negroes between the sea, and a line drawn from North Edisto Inlet to Tugaloo, thence along the river to Stono, thence to Dorchester, thence to Goose Creek Bridge, thence to the mouth of Back river, thence to Cain Hoy, and thence to the sea, should be removed upon the approach of the enemy; and the militia within those lines, and upon the outward borders of them, should form a constant and continued chain of patrols along those lines, by which all communication will be cut off between the enemy in town, and the negroes in the country. Orders should be immediately issued, so that this plan should be executed when it may be necessary.[65]

The next day, the Council of Safety began to consider the radicals' proposals. A long and heated debate followed over the rejection of the plan to draw lines across Charles Town peninsula. Eventually, a compromise was reached. Drayton, Heyward, and Motte were authorized to build a strong redoubt west of Fort Johnson, while Lowndes, Powell, Cannon, and Moultrie were appointed to erect an entrenchment five miles north of Charles Town between the Ashley and Cooper Rivers.[66]

One item that was not up for discussion, however, was the removal of African-Americans from the seacoast. Memories of the Thomas Jeremiah affair were still fresh in the minds of Whig authorities, and the last thing that any patriot wanted (radical or conservative) was for the black majority to join forces with His Majesty's ships. In a further effort to suppress insurgency among blacks, Captain Samuel Boykin was ordered to bring down the Catawba Indians from their native territory. On Monday, October 16, Boykin wrote that he was "sorry" he could not comply with the Council of Safety's demands because the Indians had taken "very Sick." According to Boykin, three of his twenty-five Catawba mercenaries had died when they came down with a strange fever. Boykin reassured the Council, however, that the Catawbas, who were now healthy, had been paid a sum of "ten pounds Each man" and would be "willing to come down at any time."[67]

In mid-October, as the Council was busy trying to maintain the Catawbas' allegiance, several hundred families began to evacuate Charles Town with their furniture and personal effects. In fact, so many began to leave that patriot authorities had difficulty finding enough men to defend the colony.[68] A number of enlisted soldiers deserted, and things began to look grim for the Whig military effort.[69] An irascible Henry Laurens wrote to brother James:

> At length we have driven our selves into a labyrinth—rash Men have
> devised means for affronting the King's Government in many
> instances too grossly to be borne—ignorant & timid men have been
> persuaded to join them & to make up a Majority; they have gone too
> far to retreat, know not how to get out, & are at their wits end to find
> out Men & means for defending the Powers which we are told are on
> their way to destroy or to keep quiet under this menace—hundreds of
> families have already sent their household goods & valuables into the
> Country & have followed & are following their effects, hundreds more
> stand ready to take the same course upon the first account of Men of
> War & Troops upon our Coast—some have Quitted the Colony.[70]

As Charles Town's inhabitants were busy escaping to the backcountry, on Thursday, October 19, *Diligence*, "the Pensicola Packet" captained by Arthur Clarke, was spotted at the mouth of the harbor "between Morris Island and the Bar." That day, a report was sent to the Council of Safety that Clarke intended to seize "all the Vessels" entering Charles Town.[71] Desperate to defend the harbor, the patriots decided to organize a naval force. The operation was hampered by a lack of available sailors, however. The Council of Safety therefore ordered William Moultrie to inquire "how many Seamen" were enlisted as foot soldiers. According to the directive, Colonel Moultrie was to see if members of the regiments would be "willing to change service by acting on board the Colony Schooners," where their pay would "be considerably advanced."[72]

In addition to raising a naval force, the Council of Safety made the critical decision to revise its ruling on the moderates' petition. On the same day that the packet *Diligence* was seen lurking off the bar, William Henry Drayton and Thomas Heyward Jr. were authorized to obstruct the passages of Marsh Channel and Hog-Island Creek.[73] Before Drayton and Heyward could take action, however, they had to wait several days for Moultrie to woo a sufficient number of militia into the naval service. On October 27, thirty seamen from the provincial regiments that had been armed with two nine-pound guns the previous month joined Captain William Tufts and began to board the schooner *Defence*.[74]

As the Whigs were busy forming a navy, enslaved Afro-Carolinians began once again to assert themselves overtly. In the third week of October, the Council of Safety received word from Little River, South Carolina, of a slave conspiracy near George Town. The evidence surrounding the affair is sparse, but it is clear that blacks and whites were both involved. According to a letter from the Little River Committee, a Mr. Robert Bell (presumed of Scottish origin) had been charged with "Carrying [off] a Negroe [and was] to be heard before the Geo. Town Committee on Accusation of being Concerned in an Insurrection."[75]

That week, a "Negro Fellow" named Shadwell escaped from a schooner "lying near Lamboll's bridge." According to the runaway notice placed by his owner, John Alleyne Walter, Shadwell was a "stout and squat" slave who stood five feet eight inches tall and spoke remarkably "good English." The bondman, an experienced "patroon," used to guiding supply boats known as pettiaugers along local waterways, was reportedly "well acquainted with all the rivers and inlets to the southward of Charlestown." His owner, vexed by the loss of such a valuable pilot, offered a reward of twenty pounds sterling to anyone who would "apprehend and deliver the said fellow" to himself or the warden of the workhouse, Michael Kalteisen.[76]

On Saturday, October 28, the day after Walter scripted his runaway advertisement, the Council of Safety ordered local brewer and bookkeeper John Calvert to deliver a letter to the captain of the *Tamar*, Edward Thornbrough. The document began by informing the elderly captain that the Council had learned that Shadwell, "the property of John Allen Walters Esqr.," was onboard the *Tamar* and employed under his command. Remembering Thornbrough's threat to take a pilot by force if necessary, the Council declared that Shadwell was indeed a runaway slave and that harboring him or carrying him off was "highly penal" and would constitute a "Felony" under South Carolina law. The carefully crafted letter steered clear of an outright accusation by suggesting that Thornbrough was probably unapprised of the subtleties of the province's legal code. In a further effort to avoid pointing the finger at the captain, the Council made it clear that it was not "insinuating" that Thornbrough gave "any encouragement for Slaves to leave their Masters." "If he is on board the Tamar," the Council added, he "has imposed himself upon you as a Freeman: & therefore we doubt not if our information is true—but that you will cause him to be delivered up to Mr. J C the bearer of this Letter."[77]

When Thornbrough was done reading, he reportedly "appeared angry at the contents of the letter, declared his astonishment & concern that any Gentleman could Suspect that any runaway Negro could be on board his Sloop." Assuring Calvert that Shadwell was not hidden somewhere on the *Tamar*, Thornbrough gave the patriot messenger a tour of his ship. The captain demonstrated that he did in fact have a black man onboard, but the man was someone else and not the property of John Alleyne Walter. After escorting Calvert above and below deck on his vessel, Thornbrough ordered the letter bearer to stay put while he boarded the *Cherokee* and shared the contents of the document with the governor. After a brief period, Thornbrough returned and discharged Calvert, saying that "when he should have fully considered the letter he would send an answer" to the Council of Safety. Several days would pass without a word from the captain.[78]

5

Low Country/Backcountry: The Volatile Geopolitics of Revolutionary South Carolina

November 1775–December 1775

The spatial zone between Low Country and backcountry was the foremost geo-political reality in Revolutionary South Carolina (see map 3). Low Country meant concentrated economic wealth and political power and the reality of a black majority. Backcountry meant inclusion into "Greater Pennsylvania"—the region stretching from south-central Pennsylvania, the valley of Virginia, the Carolina piedmont and upcountry, and the west bank of the Savannah River in Georgia. Backcountry also meant Regulator politics—periodic uprisings by white settlers against remote and incompetent coastal authority. And back-country meant a spirit of resistance by maroon communities of runaway slaves, by native peoples, and by white settlers from the North as yet unfettered by an economic stake in export agriculture.

While the economic base of the Low Country was heavily dependent on slave labor, in the upcountry or backcountry, the situation was markedly differ-ent. In order to reduce the discrepancy between the black majority and the white minority in South Carolina, the settlement of whites was encouraged in the piedmont. Far different from the Low Country planters, these new arrivals owned fewer slaves and bitterly resented having to come to Charles Town to do their business or to have legal matters settled. The situation became so volatile that in 1769, a circuit court was established to help maintain law and order in the upper reaches of the province.[1] During the same decade, Charles Woodmason, an Anglican preacher living in the backcountry, lamented the lawless ruffians he encountered there who often had little regard for his beloved heterodox style of worship.[2] These frontiersmen in the upcountry were poorer than the Charleston nabobs and preferred what would come to be called new

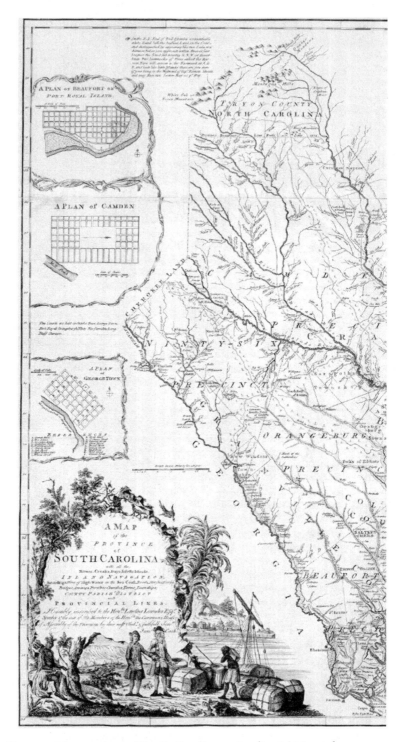

MAP 3. "A map of the province of South Carolina.... Lawlins [*sic*] Lowndes, Esqr.... by their most obedt. & faithful servt. Jams. Cook. Thos. Bowen, sculpt. 1773." Note the scene in the lower left-hand corner. Two white merchants observe a black slave unloading cargo from a ship. An Indian headman lurks ominously in the distance. *Courtesy of David Rumsey Map Collection*

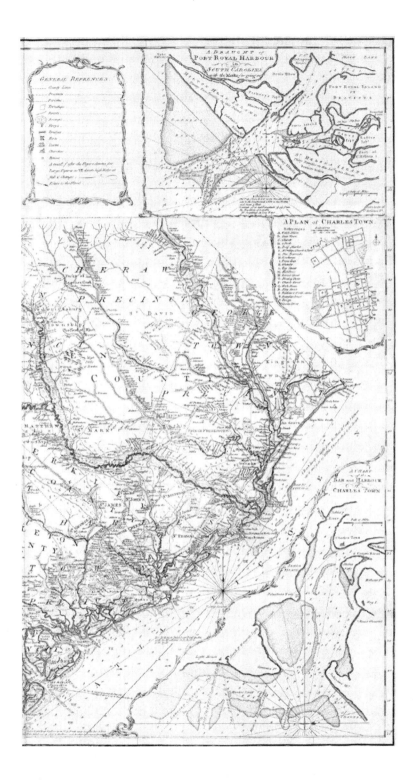

light or itinerant preaching, largely associated with the Great Awakening. Many of the men living in this region had recently made their way down from farther north—from places such as Virginia, North Carolina, or Pennsylvania. Often, they were of Scots-Irish extraction and were the hardy sort of men such as Andrew Jackson, John C. Calhoun, or Sam Houston. Along with them was a sizable contingent of German immigrants who had settled in and around the area known as Dutch Fork.[3]

In the years leading up to the Revolution, several of these men had become Regulators. By the mid-1770s, when relations between colonists and the Crown neared their breaking point, the Low Country leaders realized that these new arrivals, whom they frequently dismissed as rubes or bumpkins, would have to be onboard with their agenda. To accomplish this, these men would have to be wooed. Indeed, some convincing would be required if these men were to support the measures about to be adopted by the statesmen-planters of Charles Town. In addition to inviting some of the backcountry leaders to the capital to participate in the provisional government, there would have to be some effort made to unite them to the Whig cause. This would be more difficult than Low Country leaders first imagined. To win friends and influence people beyond the haunting swamps and busy waterways of greater Charles Town, the Whig elite would have to cast their gaze westward and persuade the new arrivals that their interests were one and the same.[4]

As Robert Weir noted, at the outbreak of the Revolution, the backcountry became "something like a diplomatic prize as imperial and local authorities contended for the allegiance of its inhabitants."[5] Indeed, in what amounted to a crisis of allegiance in South Carolina, both the Crown and patriots themselves were in the business of convincing or coercing individuals to join their respective sides. Although the British would later base their Southern strategy on the shoulders of backcountry loyalists who they believed would rally to the Red Ensign the moment the redcoats arrived, in the wake of Lexington and Concord, none of this was readily apparent. In the case of African-Americans, brutality and spectacles of violence would be used to deter them from joining or assisting Britannia. In the case of Indians, presents in the form of gunpowder and shot would used to pacify the Cherokee and keep them either out of the conflict altogether or firmly tied to the Whig cause. This had to be done carefully. Enough was needed to keep the Indians happy and at bay, but give them too much, and they might become incredibly dangerous. The backcountry whites were different. Although seen as rustics by the Low Country elite, they were still of European decent and were perceived as being on more of an equal footing than blacks or Indians. These individuals might just be swayed by allowing them to participate in the break with England or by grafting them into the political process.[6]

In July 1775, before Drayton, Tennant, and Hart embarked on their diplomatic mission to the backcountry, Henry Laurens sent a letter to the prominent loyalist Thomas Fletchall, asking him to help persuade others to unite with the Low Country planters in their fight against Britain. In an incredibly revealing document, Laurens asked Fletchall (who happened to own a number of slaves) to think of the welfare of their province, considering how South Carolina was "alarmed by threats of Invasions by British Soldiery, of instigated Insurrections by our Negroes, of inroads by Neighboring tribes of Indians." Fletchall responded that he would not take up arms against the king and later issued a document stating that anyone who assisted the Low Country grandees against their slaves would be "a Fool." As someone familiar with the demography of the Low Country, Fletchall understandably did not want to take part in a race war.[7]

As the scenario worsened during the summer, it looked as though war was imminent on the frontier. By gathering 1,100 rebel militia near the Ninety-Six District, William Henry Drayton nipped the situation in the bud. Fletchall, who was then out of ammunition, sensed defeat and decided it was better simply to negotiate a truce. In mid-September, the First Treaty of Ninety-Six was signed, bringing a temporary peace to the troubled region. The other ringleaders of the backcountry opposition—Thomas Brown, Moses Kirkland, and Robert Cunningham—each had a price on his head. For a time, they managed to escape, but Drayton knew that if the influence of these men was to be attenuated, Lord William Campbell would have to be forced out of the colony or taken into custody.[8]

The situation in the backcountry was seemingly neutralized in the early fall. However, on November 1, 1775, that all changed. During the opening of the second session of the Provincial Congress at the State House in Charles Town, patriot leaders elected William Henry Drayton to the presidency and Peter Timothy to the position of secretary.[9] Although intended to pacify the hotheaded radicals, the move, as we shall see, had the opposite of its intended effect.

Henry Laurens, no longer the body's president, returned that evening to his home at Rattray Green. There he found a letter addressed to him from Captain Thornbrough of the HMS *Tamar*. In this document, the captain denounced "the many unprovoked Insults the King's Servants" had received in South Carolina "from those *Assemblies* who have had the Hardiness to assume the Reins of Government." Enraged by the patriot seizure of power, the skipper ignored Laurens's previous request to return Shadwell, the runaway slave who had earlier caused so much controversy. Thornbrough went on to inform the planter that "if his Majesty's Agents in Charles-Town" were not "permitted regularly, and without Molestation" to supply the *Tamar* and the *Cherokee* with adequate provisions, he would henceforth "not suffer any Vessel to enter into, or depart from Charles-Town."[10]

At around the same time, Captain John Wanton had returned to Charles Town aboard the *Polly*. Apparently, during the voyage to St. Augustine, Wanton and his men had overpowered the gunner of Fort Johnson and forced him to disembark at Savannah. Despite knowing this information, Thornbrough claimed that Walker was still in the custody of patriot authorities. In his letter to Laurens, he threatened to detain Wanton and his ship until Walker was delivered in person to the *Tamar*. The Tory captain concluded by demanding "an immediate and explicit answer."[11]

On Thursday, November 2, Laurens brought Thornbrough's letter before the Provincial Congress. Captain Wanton was immediately summoned and asked to provide an account of the events that took place aboard the *Polly*. The next day, William Henry Drayton penned a response to Thornbrough's letter. He began by reminding the captain that he "promised a written answer" to the accusation that was harboring Shadwell aboard the *Tamar*. The newly elected president declared that Thornbrough's "unexpected silence" was not only "a breach of the rules of propriety" but also "a negative confession, that the negro, if not on board the Tamer," was "actually harbored on board the Cherokee, the residence of Lord Campbell, or some other vessel" under the captain's command.[12]

Drayton attempted to shift blame away from the elderly captain and onto Alexander Innes. He argued that "the public" was "too well acquainted with the arbitrary and irritating stile peculiar to Lord William Campbell's Secretary" to imagine that Captain Thornbrough was "the framer of the letter" sent to Henry Laurens on the "1st instant." The president of the Provincial Congress further added that he knew of no "'unprovoked insults'" to the king's servants "received from any assembly by authority of the people." Drayton went on to declare that the patriots wished that they could say "that the conduct of the King's *principal servant* hath not made him an object of the just resentment of the public." However, he hinted to Thornbrough that the Whigs were "not destitute of means" to take vengeance against crown officials "for any violence" they might "perpetrate against the shipping bound to, or out from this port."[13]

Addressing the issue of George Walker, Drayton flatly denied that the gunner was in "confinement at the barracks." He claimed that the patriot party had indeed paroled Walker several weeks before and that the man was no longer in South Carolina. Drayton then declared that the Whigs were well aware that Campbell had dispatched Walker to St. Augustine with a letter designed to bring about a military assault "against the good people of the colony" and that

Thornbrough was "privy" to this occurrence, despite the captain's claims to the contrary. "Walker was landed at Savannah," the patriot leader wrote "and we have not heard of him since."[14]

Moving on to the subject of the *Polly*, Drayton informed Thornbrough that he had "been deceived into a belief, that Lord Campbell [had] shewed great humanity to Captain Wanton" and that it was in his "interest to employ Walker, on board his vessel." The radical Whig notified the Tory that the patriot party had "strictly inquired of Captain Wanton" and found that he was vehemently opposed to the governor's decision to have Walker pilot his vessel to St. Augustine. Wanton was fully within his rights, Drayton argued, to dispose of the armed gunner of Fort Johnson "as soon as he could by landing him at Savannah."[15]

While Drayton was busy writing a response to Thornbrough, events quickly took a turn in the backcountry. On Friday, November 3, a wagon loaded with 1,000 pounds of gunpowder was suddenly seized by a contingent of about sixty loyalists.[16] The powder, slated for the Cherokee Indians, was designed to secure the tribe's allegiance to the patriot cause. When the wagon reached a place called "the Ridge" in the Ninety-Six District, the Tories, led by Patrick Cunningham (brother of Robert Cunningham), "did, by force of arms," descend upon the shipment and carry off "a quantity of lead and sundry kegs of gunpowder." According to a report later commissioned by patriot authorities, the theft of the powder and lead came at a "great loss and damage" to the public, "thereby exposing the frontier inhabitants of the colony to the depredations and horrors of an Indian war."

Later that evening, back in the Low Country, Drayton's letter was rowed out to the *Tamar*. According to the messenger, when he appeared before Thornbrough between eleven and twelve o'clock, the captain said "it was too late to send an answer; but he would send one when he had a proper opportunity." That opportunity arose the next day, Saturday, November 4, when the elderly skipper sat down and scripted a response to William Henry Drayton. He began by denying that Alexander Innes had written the letter of November 1 to Henry Laurens. Thornbrough claimed that, armed with "the truth," he could easily thwart Drayton's "weapons" of "sophistry, falsehood," and gross "misrepresentation." Finally addressing the issue of Shadwell, Thornbrough wrote: "On after consideration, I did not think Mr. Laurens's letter worthy a written answer, as I never directly or indirectly harboured the run-away slave of any person, and I will answer for the gentleman who commands the Cherokee, that his conduct has been exactly similar to mine in these matters."

In reference to Wanton and his crew, the captain informed the Congress that he had enclosed an extract of the controversial letter that Campbell had written to Governor Tonyn. The purpose of this, Thornbrough argued, was to refute the "candour and veracity" of the patriots' claims, while at the same time enabling "the people" of South Carolina "to form a judgment of Capt. Wanton's worth and gratitude." Thornbrough's enclosure provided a markedly different portrayal of the exchange between Lord Campbell and the captain of the *Polly*. According to Campbell's version of events, Wanton was a willing participant, and Walker was only onboard "to assist in navigating" the vessel and to "prevent any attempt to run her into any of the little harbours" along the southern coastline. As far as soliciting troops and military assistance from Patrick Tonyn were concerned, Campbell's letter contained no mention of these whatsoever.

In addition to providing an enclosure that would cast events in a pro-Tory light, Captain Thornbrough alerted patriot authorities to the fact that he intended "to procure provisions by every means" in his power, even those that included subjecting "his Majesty's faithful and loyal people" to any "inconveniency." He acknowledged that Walker was not lately a prisoner of the Whigs and that "in that point" he was "misinformed." Thornbrough concluded by stating: "I shall only add, that I am here determined to drop this correspondence, which is a very disagreeable one to me, and I shall only expect a speedy and explicit answer."

After the letter and its enclosure were read before Congress, it was decided that the entire correspondence between Whig authorities and Captain Thornbrough "be printed and made public." That day, patriot leaders ordered that all boats and vessels passing in front of Fort Johnson first receive special permits from the chairman of the Committee of Observation. Furthermore, it was resolved that "the two pilot-boats lately taken into public service by the Council of Safety, be continued in the service, armed and manned as heretofore; and that they be employed in cruizing along the coast, to the northward of the bar, to warn vessels against coming into the harbour of Charles-Town, and to advise them to go into other ports or inlets in this colony."[17]

In furtherance of this plan, Colonel William Moultrie was directed to send a detachment of nine privates and a sergeant onboard the pilot-boat captained by Joseph Vesey and another detachment of nine privates and a sergeant onboard the pilot-boat captained by Thomas Smith. All of the troops in this service were to receive the "necessary arms and accoutrements," as well as double their usual pay. Vesey and Smith received personal letters from William Henry Drayton ordering them to command the armed pilot-boats "and cruize for ten days on the coast, to the northward of Charles-Town bar, in order to speak with and warn all vessels bound for Charles-Town, not to come over that bar, as the man of war is resolved to detain all such vessels as shall come within her reach; but that they do proceed to some other port or inlet in this colony."

At the same time that these orders were being issued, a slave named Limus "absented himself" from his owner, Joshua Eden, a chair maker in King Street. Limus, who was likely biracial by dint of his "yellow Complexion," was "well known in Charles Town for his saucy and impudent Tongue." According to the runaway advertisement his owner placed in the *South Carolina Gazette*, the slave had three fingers missing from his left hand (possibly a result of previous infractions). Eden apparently had a history of violence.[18] Yet it is unclear whether such aggression was directed at his slave. A more plausible motive for Limus's escape is that he wished, as Shadwell had, to join an increasing number of slaves aboard the governor's flotilla. Eden may have sensed this, as he took special care to "forwarn Masters of Vessels from carrying him off the Province." Before Limus left, he reportedly told his owner that he would "be free," that he would "serve no Man," and that he would "be conquered or governed by no Man." Clearly, Charles Town's white elite did not have a monopoly on the idea of liberty.[19]

Two days after Limus escaped, on Monday, November 6, Captain Wanton appeared before Justice of the Peace Peter Bounetheau and gave a sworn affidavit that "Lord William Campbell, against the consent of deponent, caused an armed force to be put on board his vessel, to conduct her to St. Augustine." Refuting the version of events provided by Thornbrough, Wanton further claimed that Walker did indeed have a letter to give to Tonyn, which called for the sending of an armed force from St. Augustine to Charles Town. According to Wanton's deposition, the gunner of Fort Johnson was under "strict orders, that if he was in any danger of being taken by the Americans, he should sink the said letter in the sea, with two swivel bullets."

Later that day, Wanton's affidavit was "laid before the Congress." Afterward, it was resolved that Thornbrough's letter of Saturday, November 4, contained "*unmerited*" expressions "unbecoming the pen of a gentleman." Members of Congress were told to keep in mind "not to credit anything" from the governor, especially that which was "not supported by absolute proof." Patriot authorities opined that although Campbell provided Captain Thornbrough with "an extract of his letter to Governor Tonyn," it did not mean "that the extract was faithfully made," nor did it preclude the existence of "*another letter*" to the East Florida governor. There was sufficient evidence to conclude, Whig officials reasoned, that Lord William Campbell did actually write to Governor Tonyn to procure troops and to cause Captain Wanton's sloop to be condemned. Despite the fact that the "important letter" never appeared in public, patriots concluded, it was "not improbable" that Tonyn had "received it" or that Walker had "destroyed it." "The extract in question," Congress members decided, was "from a letter written only as a mask to the other, and with intention, if necessary, to be delivered up to the public." In an effort to sway the opinion of the people themselves, Whig leaders ordered Wanton's affidavit and the congressional resolution to be printed in the local gazettes.

After dealing with the Wanton issue, members of Congress heard evidence against an alleged Tory named John Dunn. He had previously violated the patriot Association and had recently been paroled from the Charles Town jail for good behavior. Now accused of violating his oath of neutrality, Dunn was brought up on charges for denouncing the patriot movement in public. Two men, a Mr. Lang and a Dr. Redman Burke, were called in and asked to provide sworn testimony. In his deposition, Lang claimed that he was drinking in Hatfield's Tavern on Halloween, when he overheard a stranger "arguing warmly in favour of ministerial measures." Although Lang conceded that he could not remember the entirety of the conversation, he informed Congress that he specifically recalled that Dunn openly declared that the Americans "had no right to prescribe to Prince and Parliament." In addition, Lang testified that Dunn was a loyalist who even "called his stray dog *Tory*."

Dr. Burke's testimony varied somewhat from Lang's. Burke told Whig authorities that when he saw Dunn in the tavern, he appeared to be "much in liquor" and alternated between speaking "in favor of the American cause" and condemning it outright. According to Burke, "nothing but drunkenness could excuse him." As a result of Burke's deposition, the Congress found that Dunn's "impudent conduct was, in a great degree, the result of intoxication" and recommended that he "be admonished to be more cautious for the future." Dunn was ordered to appear before the Congress the next day.

Later that afternoon, members of Congress learned that Patrick Cunningham and his men had seized the gunpowder that had been sent by the Council of Safety to satisfy the demands of the Cherokee. When Whig authorities discovered that an individual who witnessed the seizure was now somewhere inside the city limits of Charles Town, they immediately sent a messenger to find the person and bring him before the legislature. An ad hoc committee consisting of William Henry Drayton, Henry Laurens, and Colonel James Parsons was established "to inquire and examine touching the conduct of Patrick Cunningham, in seizing the public gun-powder."[20]

At the same time that Congress was learning of the purloined powder, Andrew Williamson, a major in the Whig service, penned a letter to South Carolina's newly appointed Indian commissioner, Edward Wilkinson. Writing from his camp near Long Cane, Williamson related the details of the incident to the patriot commissioner, stressing how important it was to let the Indians know exactly what had transpired:

I have thought it necessary to acquaint you of this by express, that you may be able to explain this matter properly to the warriors and head men, and I am confident they will be able to prevent this affair being productive of any breach of comity between them and this Province, as I think the people who committed this act, were led on to it, by two rash inconsiderate men. And, indeed, it appears to me that by getting this ammunition into their hands, they thought to rule this Province, but I flatter myself they will soon be fully convinced to the contrary.[21]

To prevent the young, pro-war Cherokee led by Dragging Canoe from exacting revenge on backcountry whites, Williamson intended to march a portion of his regiment to Ninety-Six in the hopes of commandeering the stolen ammunition and bringing Cunningham and his men to justice. If his plan to retake the powder failed, the major emphasized, the Council of Safety would send "a like quantity for the Cherokees immediately."[22]

On Tuesday, November 7, when Wilkinson received word of the robbery from Williamson, he was already in the company of the Cherokee. When he tried to explain what had occurred, the headmen took it badly. According to Wilkinson's November 7 response to Williamson, the Indians accused the Whigs of telling "a great many Lies about giving them ammunition." Although they reportedly did not wish to end their friendship with the Americans, they were determined to "go now & hunt for their father Capt. Stuart" to see if powder could be obtained by him.[23]

Maintaining the allegiance of the divided Cherokee was now the Provincial Congress's first priority. The patriot leaders reacted quickly. First, they ordered the arrest of Lieutenant Charlton, the man charged with transporting the initial shipment to the Indians. Second, an order was immediately issued calling for the backcountry ringleaders to be apprehended and brought to Charles Town "under a strong guard." To carry out the latter command, the next day, Colonel Richard Richardson was instructed to assemble a motley crew of rangers, militia, and volunteers. Their mission was ostensibly simple: to recover the stolen ammunition and crush what the Whigs perceived as a vile and "dangerous insurrection."

That day, Drayton wrote to Captain Richard Pearis (the man charged with distributing the ammunition) and requested that he inform the Cherokee about Cunningham's seizure of powder and shot. Drayton made it clear that he wanted Pearis to tell the Cherokee that "the King's mad people concerned in this daring act" would be swiftly and severely dealt with. The Whig leader gave strict instructions to Pearis to spread the "particulars" of the incident by publication as well as by word of mouth, so that Indians might see that "the Headmen of South-Carolina" were "faithful to their engagements" and would not allow their "lawful authority to be trampled upon with impunity." In the postscript, Pearis was explicitly told to assure the Indians that as soon as the powder and lead or any part of it was retaken, it would be "forwarded to them without delay."[24]

But Pearis had different plans. Passed over for a promotion in favor of Edward Wilkinson, he had become irate over his failure to secure an appointment as an Indian commissioner for the Provincial Congress.[25] On the basis of this perceived effrontery, Pearis began to discredit both William Henry Drayton (who had allegedly promised him the position) and Wilkinson himself. His own personal crisis of allegiance had begun in June, when he first learned of Wilkinson's appointment.[26] In mid-October, he secretly wrote to the Council of Safety and, employing an age-old tactic, began to question his colleague's patriotism. When the Council swiftly dismissed the captain's allegations, Pearis decided that the time had come to switch sides.

On Saturday, November 11, in the presence of several loyalists, including Patrick Cunningham, Richard Pearis formally aligned himself with the Crown. He did so by appearing before Justice of the Peace Evan McLaurin in Ninety-Six District and signing an affidavit in which he declared that "Mr. Wilkinson was a Roague" and that the Cherokee "Desir'd he Should be taken out of the Nation." To make matters worse for the patriot cause, Pearis attempted to vitiate William Henry Drayton's efforts to win the hearts and minds of the backcountry settlers. After blatantly denigrating the patriot leader and accusing him of attempting to swindle Indian lands for himself, Pearis alleged that the Whigs had hatched a plot to bring down the Cherokee against all who had refused to sign their Association. To give credence to this design, Captain Pearis averred that the ammunition intercepted by Cunningham was on its way to the Cherokee Nation for that specific purpose.[27]

Pearis's actions inflamed the Tory insurgency. The ranks of the backcountry opposition began to swell. One of the ringleaders, an associate of the Cunningham brothers by the name of Joseph Robinson, drafted a "test oath" designed to encourage support for the Crown. According to Andrew Williamson, the growing band of loyalists began to administer the oath to everyone they came across. Those who were approached were first asked to swear that they would be "faithful" and bear "true allegiance" to His Majesty, King George III. They were then asked to swear that they would "observe, obey and abide by all the laws of England," as well as the "Acts of General Assembly" that applied to the province of South Carolina. All who agreed to take the oath were incorporated into Cunningham's party. All who refused to swear allegiance to the "red ensign" were forcibly disarmed.[28]

As hostility toward provincial authority spread throughout the back-country, events quickly took a turn in Charles Town Harbor. For months, radicals such as Drayton had been pushing for a blockade. Fearing that their fortunes would be dashed, conservatives such as Henry Laurens, Thomas Bee, and Gabriel Manigault repeatedly overruled the measure. When the execution of Thomas Jeremiah failed to quiet fears about the security of the harbor, Thomus Bee, and its vulnerability to British attack, the radicals continued to push for obstructions in the Charles Town Bar. To placate and silence the firebrands, Drayton was chosen to be president. However, the scheme failed miserably. On Thursday, November 9, a mere nine days after his selection, the patriot leader began making preparations for the two things he wanted most: a blockade and war with Britain.

By the second week of November, news had arrived that the British had mounted an assault on Bristol, Rhode Island. Dispatches from England told of large naval forces headed to the colonies. Word had also reached the province that the king had issued a proclamation on Wednesday, August 23, declaring the Americans to be in open and avowed rebellion.[29] No one could be certain when or where the British might attack.

Charles Town had become a city gripped by fear. Scores of people had evacuated. Resplendent domiciles that had bustled with activity only weeks earlier were now completely empty.[30] The citizens who did remain were on high alert.[31] It was in this atmosphere that Drayton made his move. First, he ordered Captain Simon Tufts to take command of the schooner *Defence*. Second, he instructed Colonel Moultrie to take thirty-five men and board the vessel the next day. In an effort to provoke the governor, Drayton ordered the commander of Fort Johnson to "oppose the passage of any British naval armament."

That evening, Drayton drafted yet another letter to Captain Thornbrough. Citing a litany of grievances against the Crown, the president warned that if any of His Majesty's ships happened to pass in front of Fort Johnson, blood would be shed. Before sending out his letter, however, Drayton presented his draft to Congress, where it was openly discussed and amended. When a revised message was finally approved, it was promptly rowed out to the elderly captain, who was still lurking in Rebellion Road.

While this was transpiring, members of Congress tried to allay fears about contact between fishermen and the British men-of-war. Although evidence on the matter is scant, it is possible that a certain black boatman's name cropped up during efforts to pass a resolution. After finally making a motion, it was decided that "all the boats and canoes employed in fishing, be obliged to pass Fort Johnson, and call at the said fort." In addition, Congress resolved that the commander of the fort had to "strictly examine all fishing and other boats" passing in front of him, "in order that no improper correspondence be carried on, which might prove injurious to the colony in its present state."

On top of these measures, Congress appointed a "Commissary of Stores" to provide and supply the naval armaments of the colony "with every requisite." Orders were issued to Isaac Motte, David Oliphant, Thomas Ferguson, William Gibbes, and John Joyner to survey the city and report back as soon as possible on "works of defence" that were immediately necessary for the "most effectual security against hostile attacks by ships of war." In an effort to rally slaves to the patriot cause, Benjamin Stone and Isaac Rivers were given a directive "to hire a sufficient number of negroes" to finish a redoubt that was being erected on James Island just west of Fort Johnson.

The next evening, Friday, November 10, an unknown messenger arrived at the State House. He informed Congress that Captain Thornbrough had read the contents of the president's warning and when he was finished had simply replied, "it is very well." With that news, the die was cast. Immediately, Captain Tufts was given the go-ahead to "sink certain schooners in Hog Island channel." Were Drayton and the radicals about to have their hopes realized?[32]

The next morning, the *Defence* was armed with two nine-pounders, six six-pounders, and two four-pounders. It was boarded by Moultrie's regiment of thirty-five men, along with an additional thirty-five "marines" under the command of Captain William Scott. Directing the operation were Captain Tufts and a very determined William Henry Drayton. At two o'clock that afternoon, the crew sailed out on the ebb tide to Hog Island Creek. Behind them were four hulks, which they intended to load with sand and sink in the channels of the bar in full view of the *Tamar* and the *Cherokee*. As the *Defence* and the four dilapidated schooners neared their destination, the *Tamar* fired six shots from among its sixteen guns. This, as John Drayton remembered, played right into his father's hands, for it would (pursuant William Henry Drayton's wishes) galvanize the patriot movement in South Carolina and embolden the Whig leadership into declaring independence. Now that the British had fired the opening salvo (and missed), Tufts and Drayton felt free to retaliate. After dropping anchor between two soundings, the *Defence* fired two nine-pounders directly at the governor's entourage. The *Tamar* then returned with three or four shots. Not to be deterred, Tufts ordered his men to fire one more cannon.

Relieved that no blood had been shed, Tufts proceeded to sink three schooners in the channel. Before the fourth dropped below the water, however, the flood tide swirled in and temporarily prevented the Whigs from achieving their objective. A decision was made to stay and wait for the ebb tide to come at dawn the next morning.

During the night, as the *Defence* lay still in the channel, the *Tamar* and the *Cherokee* maneuvered their way into Hog Island Cove. Now in close proximity to the patriot schooner, Thornbrough and Lord Campbell ordered their men to begin firing at a quarter past four. As John Drayton recalled, the volley lasted approximately three hours, during which nearly 130 shots were exchanged.

As the sun rose over Charles Town, the sound of an alarm resounded throughout the city. An anxious and excited crowd quickly formed along Bay Street to witness the events as they unfolded in the harbor. The second regiment of infantry left the barracks and began to assemble. The militia sprang out of their beds and took their positions at the various alarm posts scattered around the mostly vacant metropolis.

As the frenetic horde looked on, the *Defence* towed the last of the four hulks into position. Having weighed down the remaining schooner with sand and convinced that their mission was accomplished, Tufts, Drayton, and the crew of marines decided to retreat. Before the deed was finalized, however, a small armed boat was lowered from the *Tamar*. As the *Defence* sailed back to Charles Town, the small British vessel fired on the slowly sinking hulk and dragged it away from the bar and into the shallows. Witnessing this occurrence, Tufts decided to fire one last shot, this time at the armed schooner. When the shot missed its target, several more cannons were fired at the British, not from the *Defence* but from Fort Johnson.

According to John Drayton's memoir, the patriots at the fort had fired a total of three twenty-six-pounders at the men-of-war, all at an elevation of ten degrees. One of the shots reportedly fell within a few yards of the *Tamar's* bowsprit, while another had passed through its sprit sail. The third, Drayton claimed, went through the "mizen sail," but none of them did much damage.

As for the *Defence*, it had sustained three direct hits: one below the deck, one in the broadside, and a third that tore through the "forestarboard" shroud. By all accounts, no one was harmed in the Battle of Hog Island Creek. When it was all over, between seven and eight o'clock in the morning, the *Defence* made its way toward Beale's Wharf along the Cooper and dropped anchor. As Tufts, Drayton, and the seventy-man crew stepped onto dry land, they were greeted with a formal salute by Colonel Charles Pinckney and three huzzahs from the Charles Town mob. After the excitement had waned, the people queried Drayton about how many shots the patriot schooner had incurred. He stretched the truth a bit when he replied, "None, excepting one shot, that struck her between the wind and the water."

Now that armed action against the crown had been taken, many of the wavering residents of Charles Town began to attach themselves firmly to the patriot cause (as Drayton had intended). That very same morning, Congress called for a divine service to be performed by one of its members, Reverend Paul Turquand. As the Whigs gathered to pray, Captain Tufts related the details of his battle with the British. Afterward, he and William Scott were singled out for their "spirited and prudent conduct." Both men were ordered to return the thanks of Congress "to all the officers and men who acted under their respective commands."

When the religious ceremonies ended, the radicals, spurred on by what had taken place in the harbor, called for the formation of a committee to consider arming and manning the ship *Prosper* "for the purpose of taking or sinking the men of war." William Gibbes informed the Congress about the state of Charles Town's defenses against an attack by the *Tamar* and the *Cherokee*. After taking the matter under advisement, the radicals decided to increase security in and around the city.

First, they called for a battery of six cannons to be placed on or near the property of Christopher Gadsden. Second, they determined that "some proper cannon" needed to be mounted on the wharves near the center of the bay. Third, they declared that Granville's Bastion had to "be put into a better posture of defence." Fourth, they averred that the platform in the north face of Lyttleton's Bastion should be extended. Fifth, they pushed for a battery of three or four guns to be erected near Cummins's Point. And sixth, they called for an additional battery to be placed at "some proper spot at Wappoo, to prevent vessels of force [from] lying in Ashley-River."

Later that evening, Congress decided that the *Prosper* would "be immediately impressed and taken into the service of the colony." Captain Edward Blake and Captain Robert Cochran were charged with arming it, while Colonel Moultrie was given the responsibility of finding its crew. When the issue of ammunition cropped up once again, the need of patriots in the interior had to be taken into account in the interests of building a broad coalition. Whig leaders resolved that "five thousand pounds weight of gun-powder" be reserved for the defense of the backcountry. Sensing that they lacked the necessary amount, members of the Provincial Congress decided that Drayton would notify patriot leaders in Savannah of the Battle of Hog Island Creek and request a supply of "gun-powder, arms, and other military stores."

The next day, Congress members allocated 1,000 pounds to Robert William Powell and Daniel De Saussure to recruit Georgians for the South Carolina navy and "to purchase all the sulphur, salt-petre and lead" they could obtain from the neighboring colony. Powell and De Saussure were also ordered to deliver William Henry Drayton's letter to the Georgia Council of Safety. In self-aggrandizing fashion, Drayton celebrated his ostensible victory over the conservatives by proclaiming the Battle of Hog Island Creek to be "an event of the highest moment to the southern part of the United Colonies."

The president of the Provincial Congress may have been exuberant over the events of the weekend of November II–I2, but there were many who were not. On the same day that Drayton's letter to the Georgia Council of Safety was laid before the Congress, a second private letter authored by Drayton was considered as well. This secret communiqué (also addressed to Georgia patriots) claimed that the powder South Carolina was requesting would be used to assail the governor's entourage. According to John Drayton, one sentence in particular raised the ire of more conservative Whigs such as Rawlins Lowndes and James Parsons: "We are with all possible expedition fitting out a ship, with which, aided by the schooner Defence we mean forthwith to attack the men of war."

A heated debate ensued. Parsons and Lowndes sensed that many members of the House had "cooled on the subject" and made a direct attempt to frustrate the measure. The conservatives argued that Drayton had no right to use such wording and that his entire scheme was too "rash." For hours, conservative and radical Whigs clashed over phrasing that seemed to indicate that the body was aggressively anti-British rather than cautious and respectful in its opposition. Eventually, the president won out, and a resolution was passed ordering the *Defence* and the *Prosper* to cruise outside the mouth of Charles Town Harbor, warning all incoming vessels to steer for some other port.[33] The next day, Henry Laurens wrote to his London business associate William Manning and lamented: "those who would have plunged us into desperate measures...have Step by Step, by ways & means which are too mighty for me, gained the ground which they had in view."[34]

As conservatives became increasingly despondent over what they perceived as a rush to arms, members of Congress learned that the alleged backcountry opposition leader, Moses Kirkland, had been spotted somewhere inside Charles Town. They promptly issued orders to apprehend the suspect and bring him before the assembly. A "committee of intelligence" was formed for the purposes of communicating with "the inhabitants of the interior parts" of the colony. The stated goal of the committee was to obtain "every kind of necessary information" in order to seize and secure "all such persons, who being at large, may endanger the public safety, or prove injurious to the common cause of America."

Returning their attention to the harbor, Whig leaders made Clement Lempriere the commander of the *Prosper* and appointed Thomas Sherman to serve as his first lieutenant. The next day (Wednesday, November 15), information was laid before the Congress that Robert McKeown, a local customs official, had boarded the *Tamar*. Fearing that McKeown had interacted with or assisted Lord Campbell, the Congress summoned him immediately. During the course of his examination, McKeown pleaded ignorance and claimed that he did not know that going onboard the men-of-war was prohibited. He explained to patriot authorities that the reason he sailed out to the governor's vessel was to transport a son of the collector of customs, who happened to be a midshipman in the British navy. McKeown was not punished for his actions but was "enjoined and required" to "strictly confine himself in the limits of Charles-Town; and to have no further communication with the men of war."

Dreading the possibility that others, perhaps even slaves, might try to aid Lord William and his flotilla, the Congress authorized and empowered commissioners to fit out the *Prosper* so that vessel could interdict all correspondence with the ships in Rebellion Road. As they had in September, patriots fretted over the quantity of provisions that the governor's entourage received.

That day, the House mulled over a report on the preparedness of the colony to face additional threats. Patriot leaders requested information on "the present state of the Treasury," and members voted 120,000 pounds for artillery and other "incidental charges." In a stunning move, representatives from the backcountry put forth a motion to hold future meetings of the Provincial Congress "at Camden, or some other more centrical and convenient place." Although coastal members managed to reject the plan, this was the first of several attempts to shift the political center of South Carolina from Charles Town to the interior, and it illuminated long-standing regional differences and tensions.[35]

Just as Whigs were grappling with the Low Country/backcountry divide, things began to heat up in the inner part of the province. Since receiving his directive from Congress to recapture the powder and shot from Cunningham, Williamson's force had begun to march toward the courthouse at Ninety-Six. At some point during the evening of Friday, November 17, one of Williamson's scouts returned with news that more than 1,500 loyalists were steadily advancing toward their camp. The next evening, Williamson learned that the loyalists were advancing across the Saluda. Before the band of loyalists arrived, however, Major James Mayson appeared with a total of thirty-seven rangers. Mayson and Williamson conferred with their captains and decided to march from Ninety-Six to "the Cleared Ground" of James Savage's plantation, where they hoped to rendezvous with additional troops under Colonel William Thomson.

Early the next morning, Sunday, November 19, the patriot force marched back to Ninety-Six and began to erect a fortification made of "old Fence Rails Join'd to a Barn and Some out-Houses." Before they could complete their hastily fashioned stockade, Cunningham's posse surrounded them.[36] Severely outnumbered, Williamson sent one of his officers to demand the enemy's intentions.[37] But Joseph Robinson and Patrick Cunningham refused to negotiate, insisting that they talk to a superior officer. Andrew Williamson then sent out Major Mayson and fellow Indian commissioner John Bowie. After conferring with Justice of the Peace Evan McLaurin for fifteen minutes, Mayson and Bowie informed Williamson that the Tories insisted that his troops deliver up their arms and disperse. In the confusion of the moment, the loyalists captured two patriot soldiers and made them prisoners. When patriot leaders commanded their men to retake the hostages, a skirmish ensued.[38]

That day, William Henry Drayton, enraged over Richard Pearis's affidavit of Saturday, November 11, sat down and penned a declaration "to the misguided people in the Back Country." The president of the Provincial Congress began by explaining the complexities of the relationship between the colonists and the Native Americans. He claimed that it had always been "the policy of America in general, and of this Colony in particular, to endeavour to cultivate a good correspondence with the neighboring Indians." This policy originated, Drayton asserted, "from a view of preserving, at the cheapest rate," the borders of South Carolina "from savage inroads, pushed on by French or Spanish management or Indian avidity or ferocity." Now that the British administration intended to bring down the Indians on the backcountry settlers, the politician argued, it was especially important to supply the various tribes with "occasional presents" to secure their friendship. Unless the Native Americans "were furnished with some small supplies of ammunition, to enable them to procure deer skins for their support and maintenance," Drayton declared, "a general Indian War" would be "inevitable."

The Whig leader went on to explain that provincial authorities were in a tight spot. Drayton insisted that some powder for the Indians was necessary to secure peace with them, but giving them too much could be dangerous to the welfare of the colony. Claiming that the Indians' demands for powder were unquenchable, Drayton cited the precedent of Georgia and attempted to demonstrate how patriots there "resolved to supply the Creeks with such a quantity as might, in some degree, satisfy their urgent wants, but could not incite, by enabling, them to commit hostilities." It was the Georgians, the president asserted, who "strongly pressed the late Council of Safety [in Charles Town] to supply the Cherokees." Drayton told how, in keeping with the neighboring colony's request, he had met with several of the Cherokee leaders at the Congarees in September. During the course of their negotiations, Drayton professed, "Nothing could in the least degree satisfy them but a promise of some ammunition."[39]

Downplaying the fact that the Cherokee were given 1,000 pounds weight of powder and 2,000 pounds weight of lead, the president claimed that this was "the only probable means of preserving the frontiers from the inroads of the Indians." Because Council of Safety members "almost daily expected that the British arms would attack the Colony in front on the sea coast," Drayton wrote, "they thought they would be inexcusable, if they did not, as much as in them lay, remove every cause to apprehend an attack at the same time from the Indians upon the Back Settlements." Contrary to Pearis's claims, Drayton stated that the decision to send the powder to the Indians was based on the soundest policy "of Christianity" and was intended to breathe "equal benevolence to the associators and non-associators" alike:

> These wicked men, to the astonishment of common sense, have
> made many of their deluded followers believe, that this ammunition
> was sent to the Indians, with orders for them to fall upon the fron-
> tiers and to massacre the non-associators; and taking advantage from
> the scarcity of ammunition among individuals, arising from the
> necessity of filling the public magazines they have invidiously
> represented, that, ammunition ought not to be sent to the Indians,
> while the Inhabitants of the Colony, individually, are in a great
> degree destitute of that article; industriously endeavouring to incul-
> cate this doctrine even in the minds of associators.[40]

After outlining the rationale for providing the Cherokee with ammunition, Drayton used all of his legal prowess to poke holes in each one of Pearis's assertions. Maintaining that Pearis's allegations were absurd, the president argued that the whole tenor of the Council of Safety demonstrated that the body was incapable of "such inhumanity." His own conduct at Ninety-Six, Drayton claimed, was enough to show that shedding the blood of the nonassociators "was not the object of his policy."

Drayton's second refutation was that if the Indians were let loose upon the frontiers, they would be unable to distinguish between "associators" and "non-associators." Since there was no mark to distinguish either to the Cherokee, the patriot leader contended, "no associator, of but common sense, could think of promoting the interest of his party, by executing a measure which must equally ruin friend and foe."

Having made a determined effort to dispel these divisive ideas, Drayton offered a solemn oath that no individual or body associated with the provincial government ever authorized "the Indians to commence hostilities upon the frontiers." Instead of being hostile to the nonassociators, the Whig leader avowed, patriot authorities had made an effort "to inculcate in the Indians, sentiments friendly to the inhabitants without any distinction." The president concluded by discounting charges that the Congress was giving away the entire supply of public ammunition. Contrary to his assertion to the Georgia Council of Safety that all of the powder was going to be used to destroy the men-of-war, Drayton announced that South Carolina would "make an allotment [of] five thousand pounds weight [of gunpowder] for the defence of the interior parts of the colony."[41]

Even as Congress made preparations to distribute printed copies of Drayton's declaration to the inhabitants of the backcountry, a battle was commencing at Ninety-Six on the afternoon of Sunday, November 19. By sunset on Tuesday, thirty-two men were wounded, and five had been killed.[42] When night began to fall on November 21, the Tories unfurled a white flag out of one of the windows of the Ninety-Six Jail. The firing stopped, and a voice cried out from among the loyalists, requesting to speak to one of the Whig commanding officers. Williamson shouted back to his opponents that if they wanted to send a messenger, the individual would in no way be harmed. Minutes later, a Tory soldier appeared, carrying a lighted candle and a note from Joseph Robinson to James Mayson demanding that the patriots deliver up their arms and disperse. Mayson and Williamson conferred and, after two hours, sent John Bowie to deliver news that the Whigs refused to surrender. Bowie returned to the patriot camp, carrying another letter demanding once again that the Whigs give up. Williamson could see Patrick Cunningham in the distance and, realizing that his soldiers were about to run out of gunpowder, agreed to meet him in between the two encampments. After conversing for some time, both men decided to meet at eight o'clock the next morning. When the appointed time came, Whig commanders James Mayson, Andrew Williamson, John Bowie, and Andrew Pickens convened with Joseph Robinson, Patrick Cunningham, Evan McLaurin, and Richard Pearis. Together, they agreed to a cessation of hostilities and drafted what became known as the Second Treaty of Ninety-Six.[43]

The treaty called for release of all prisoners, cessation of hostilities, dismantling of the patriot fort, and withdrawal of both sets of troops. In addition, it was agreed that any grievances related to the state of affairs in the backcountry henceforth be addressed by both Lord Campbell on one hand and the Council of Safety on the other. To ensure that this precarious balancing act took place, two delegates—one from the loyalists and one from the patriots—were to be sent out to the governor and the provincial authorities, respectively. Each delegate was to be given twenty days to appear before the designated authority, and both sides promised not to molest the messenger from the rival party.[44]

As the two delegates began to make their way toward Charles Town, trepidation continued to spread in the provincial capital. On Saturday, November 25, William Moore, Esq., a representative from the Ninety-Six district, related news of the skirmish in the backcountry to the assembly. Moore did not yet know all of the details of the battle, and for a brief period, Whig officials feared the worst.[45] Congress declared the colony to be in "a state of actual alarm" and ordered 1,350 additional soldiers to proceed upcountry.[46] The next day, Henry Laurens wrote to his London business associate William Manning:

> The people in America generally are reduced to unhappy circum-
> stances, but no Colony in the Union, has before it so dreadful a
> prospect as this of So. Carolina, we have been precipitated into
> measures which in all probability will work to our destruction & the
> dreadful day is hastening—yet those who Struggled hardest against
> the prosecution of Such ruinous measures (I am one of them) are
> Still Striving to Struggle against the prosecution of more diabolical
> measures by the British Administration, & prefer poverty & death to
> a tame Submission.[47]

Still apprehensive that the *Tamar* and the *Cherokee* might attack the city, Whig leaders banded together and formed a second Council of Safety.[48] The militia was ordered to patrol day and night,[49] and wagons hastily brought 2,000 pounds of gunpowder from Dorchester to the metropolis. Fearful that more of His Majesty's ships might link up with Lord Campbell's entourage, Congress ordered the Commissioners of the Pilotage to cut down and demolish "the leading marks over Charles Town Bar."[50] Patriot fears were well founded, for on that very same day (Monday, November 27), two British ships from North Carolina approached the bar: the transport vessel *Palliser* and the armed HMS *Scorpion*. Aboard the *Scorpion* were Royal Governor Josiah Martin of North Carolina and Captain John Tollemache, both of whom had a reputation for tampering with black slaves.[51]

A directive from the Continental Congress, which called for local patriots to defend Charles Town to "the last extremity," put mounting pressure on Whig officials. In keeping with this order, on Tuesday, November 28, the Provincial Congress ordered all residents of the city able to bear arms to return immediately. The next day, the Provincial Congress adjourned until February 1, 1776,[52] and on Thursday, the second Council of Safety met for the first time.

At the opening of the session on Thursday, November 30, the Council members reelected Henry Laurens to the presidency and made Peter Timothy secretary. Whig leaders were relieved to learn the full details of the fighting in the backcountry and of the Second Treaty of Ninety-Six.[53] Having received an actual copy of the Pearis affidavit, the Council declared the document to be "a groundless and malicious libel, calculated to deceive the people; and to prejudice their minds against the Hon. Mr. Drayton; because, of the active part which he had taken in favor of American liberty."

In an address to the Council of Safety, Drayton attempted to "apply an antidote" to the "poison" that Pearis had spilled on November 11. Describing the first encounter he had with Pearis, Drayton concluded that "the man of no principal" [sic] had been offended with him on four points. First, he did not indulge Pearis by "endeavoring to rid him of Mr. Wilkinson"; second, he "did not purchase a part of Pearis's land"; third, Drayton had not assumed a debt the agent had owed; and, finally, the Council member did not see to it that Pearis was "made a commissioner of Indian affairs."[54] On Saturday, December 2, Henry Laurens wrote to Andrew Williamson in reference to Pearis and requested that he take steps to seize "the grand offender" and bring him to Charles Town. "We need not urge," the president wrote, "the necessity of keeping this a profound secret."[55]

Two days later, Laurens wrote to Richard Richardson, reminding him that his mission was not to reinforce Williamson's fort at Ninety-Six but to "seize and apprehend persons who had committed an atrocious robbery, to suppress effectually an insurrection, and to deter all persons from attempting insurrections in [the] future." After chastising Richardson and referring him to his "original instructions," Laurens suggested that "a proper declaration, inculcated among the *lower classes* [emphasis mine] of those misguided people under the enemies to liberty, may have the good effect of inducing many of them to come in to you, and to lay down their arms."[56]

In keeping with the Ninety-Six treaty, that week, Matthew Floyd,[57] the delegate sent to Charles Town by Robinson and the backcountry Tories, entreated the Whig leadership for permission to speak with the governor.[58] The Council viewed Floyd with suspicion because he claimed that he had lost his dispatches while drunk in Orangeburg.[59] On Monday, December 4, the thirteen patriot leaders decided to allow the agent to speak to Lord Campbell on the condition that a witness be brought along to transcribe the entirety of the conversation. The next day, Benjamin Lewis Merchant accompanied Floyd aboard the *Cherokee*. After an awkward conversation with the governor, Merchant was ordered by Alexander Innes to leave the ship. He was also told that Floyd was "a friend to government" and that Campbell needed to detain him privately "until he determined on a proper answer."

On Wednesday, December 6, Merchant appeared before the Council and reported what had transpired. In addition to telling the patriots that he had not been privy to the governor's communication with Floyd, the envoy claimed that "four pieces of cannon, six-pounders, with *Bermuda* marked on the carriages," had been brought onboard the *Cherokee* from the *Palliser*. When Whig leaders learned of this troubling information, they decided to violate the Second Treaty of Ninety-Six by calling for the seizure of Matthew Floyd upon his return from the man-of-war.

The next evening, Floyd rowed out from the *Cherokee* and was captured by a patriot officer as soon as he reached his home in Charles Town. The envoy was carrying with him a certificate (signed by Captain John Fergusson, commander of the *Cherokee*) claiming that he had been detained for two days and two nights because the governor found it highly suspicious that Floyd did not have "any message from His Majesty's faithful subjects in the back part of the Province." When the Council summoned Matthew Floyd the next day, he claimed that Lord William had told him that the backcountry Tories should try to "obtain a good and beneficial peace...if not, they should make war." Dissatisfied with the delegate's testimony, patriot officials deemed Floyd a "spy" and consigned him to the common jail in Charles Town the next day.[60]

Later that December, the Treaty of Ninety-Six would be violated once again, as Thomas Fletchall raised 1,500 men and crossed over the Saluda into Dutch Fork. This last-ditch attempt to revolt against provincial authorities was quickly put down by Colonel Andrew Williamson. In what became known as the Snow Campaign because of the inclement weather conditions, the Tory ringleaders who stole the precious gunpowder were rounded up and thrown in the Charles Town jail.[61] Ironically, about thirty of the captured insurgents were subsequently put to work on Sullivan's Island. At this important strategic location, during the late winter and spring of '76, the lower-class Tories were forced to labor alongside slaves in an effort to fortify the harbor against an impending British attack. In February, an anonymous Whig "volunteer," relieved by the cheerful cooperation of these men, wrote to a gentleman at Philadelphia:

> The troubles in the back parts are entirely subsided. Their ringleaders, with about one hundred and thirty others, were taken. All to about twenty have been dismissed, and sent safe to their own houses, being convinced of their mistake, and well satisfied with the treatment they received when taken.... About thirty of the prisoners work at a battery six miles from town, on *Sullivan's Island*, at the mouth of the harbour. I did myself the honour of going down as a volunteer with the detachment. Here I got acquainted with several of the insurgents, who were plain, honest, sensible fellows; and as I assumed no character above a digger or spadesman, in which, without vanity, I excelled the whole corps, they looked upon me as their brother, and heard me gladly. I gave them a full and proper

account of every thing concerning the ground of the war. This, with three or four gallons of rum, was of infinite service to our cause.[62]

Although the backcountry uprising had been subdued, other threats lingered. The same anonymous author fretted about the harrowing sight across the harbor of slaves congregating near Campbell's ships on Sullivan's Island. He told his Philadelphia confidant that he should be "happy, my dear friend, in not being exposed to the more than diabolical machinations of Government tools, and the dread of insurrections from your Slaves." Echoing previous sentiments, the patriot described such practices as "hellish" and argued that even the "*Devil* would blush at the impudence of the man who would have the effrontery to recommend a re-union with so barbarous a Government."[63]

6

The Greatest Hope and the Deepest Fear

December 1775–January 1776

On Tuesday, November 7, the royal governor of Virginia, Lord Dunmore, penned an offer of freedom for slaves and indentured servants (in the service of patriots) who would take up arms in defense of the Crown.[1] He published the proclamation a week later, on November 14, and word of the provocative move quickly spread to other colonies by land and sea. Although it is difficult to gauge the precise moment, it was probably during the last week of November that black and white South Carolinians learned of this event. If the royal government in Virginia offered freedom to enslaved blacks, what would become of the 107,000 African-Americans in South Carolina?[2] Would Lord William Campbell make a similar proclamation? And if so, would the rigid fabric of South Carolina society begin to unravel? Charlestonians of all races must have pondered these and similar questions during the late fall of 1775.

Three months earlier, Thomas Jeremiah had been hanged and burned by white patriots fearful that the British would enlist the services of South Carolina blacks. In the winter of 1775, that fear would become a reality. Inspired by news of Dunmore's proclamation, and perhaps recalling that Governor Campbell had attempted to intervene on behalf of Jeremiah, Afro-Carolinians started to make their way toward Sullivan's Island in droves by early December. This thin strip of sand, jutting into the harbor between Rebellion Road and North Channel, provided a sheltered anchorage for British men-of-war. In addition, the tiny landmass, in the shape of a check mark, was well known to eighteenth-century slaves.[3] Since 1707, this had been the place where hundreds of enslaved Africans who had endured the Middle Passage first set foot on American soil. They were quarantined in and around the well-guarded pesthouse at the southwest end of the island before being sold at public auction in Charles Town. Since mid-September, the crews of the *Tamar* and the *Cherokee* had worked to clear away most of the trees on the island for strategic purposes.[4] By the late fall, approximately 500 refugee slaves—almost a tenth of the population of black Charles Town—had absconded to the island in hopes of receiving aid from the British. Members of this maroon community had begun to construct crude thatched huts and living quarters in the area surrounding the pesthouse, a location that many must have recalled all too well from the first days of their arrival in America.[5]

To make matters even more nightmarish for the slaveholding Whig elite, a mixed band of Tories and bondsmen began to conduct nightly raids on outlying plantations.[6] The number of incidents seems to have escalated on Tuesday, December 5, when notary public Fenwick Bull, a loyalist who had earlier been harassed by the Charles Town mob during the tarring and feathering of George Walker, applied to the Council of Safety for "no less than five hundred pounds of fresh beef to be sent on board the *Scorpion* sloop of war lately arrived." In addition to the victuals, Bull requested that patriot authorities provide a pass for the departure of the ship *Betsey*, which had been seized along with the *Polly* by the governor just two days before.

When the patriot leaders refused to take either matter into consideration, Lord Campbell decided to take action. On Wednesday, December 6, he instructed Captain John Tollemache of the *Scorpion* to seize two more sloops that were about to make their way into the harbor. The *Hetty*, captained by Jacob Milligan, had arrived from Jamaica carrying a cargo of rum and sugar. The other craft, the *Thomas and Stafford*, captained by Solomon Gibbes, had come from Saint Kitts bearing a sizable sum of money in specie.[7] Tollemache reportedly plundered the money, rum, and sugar from the two vessels and handed the ill-gotten gains to the governor.

In need of more supplies, Campbell commanded the crews of the *Tamar* and the *Cherokee* to reconnoiter the same day, searching the nearby estates for additional provisions.[8] Later that evening, Lord William ordered "a number of armed men, blacks as well as whites," to storm the plantation of John Ashe near Haddrell's Point in Christ Church parish, across the cove from the pesthouse on Sullivan's Island. The next morning, Michael Bates, the overseer of Ashe's plantation, identified two men in connection with the incident: "Robinson, who has the care of the post-house [sic] on Sullivan's Island," and "one Swan, a mulatto [John Swann]; both of whom he declared he perfectly knew."

That very same day (Thursday, December 7), Samuel Butler informed the Council of a conversation he had overheard the night of the incursion "between a mulatto fellow [possibly Swann] and some slaves belonging to the inhabitants of this town, inticing them to go on board the King's ships." He reported that one of these slaves, a man belonging to William Logan, had since almost immediately gone missing. Later that day, Captain Jacob Milligan of the *Hetty* confirmed that "there were a considerable number of slaves upon Sullivan's Island, and he learnt huts were building for them in the woods."

Whig authorities did not take this information lightly. After hearing the depositions of Bates, Butler, and Milligan, Henry Laurens penned a letter to Colonel William Moultrie in which he ordered the Scotsman to take 200 of his best soldiers "to seize and apprehend a number of negroes, who are said to have deserted to the enemy, together with every person who may be found upon that island." The president of the Council of Safety specifically instructed Moultrie to burn down the pesthouse and destroy all of the livestock that the marooned slaves were using for sustenance.[9]

Moultrie delegated the task to Major Charles Cotesworth Pinckney. But the junior officer's initial effort proved futile. On the evening of Saturday, December 9, Pinckney and his men (four captains, eight lieutenants, twelve sergeants, and 150 rank and file) stealthily marched over to Haddrell's Point. His orders were to find a proper fording place from which to mount an assault on the slaves who had begun to congregate near the cove behind the tip of Sullivan's Island. When none could be found, Pinckney relayed a message "setting forth the disappointments he had met with" to Moultrie, who, after conferring with the Council, ordered him to return immediately with the detachment to Charles Town, "the expedition being entirely frustrated."[10]

That night, Samuel and Benjamin Legare, hearing that Captain Tollemache and the governor had seized 160 half-johannes from their sloop *Thomas and Stafford*, approached Lord Campbell's home at 34 Meeting Street and proceeded to steal his chariot and four horses. The next day (December 10), when the two brothers appeared before the Council of Safety, Whig leaders declared the seizure to be "unauthorized, illegal and irregular" and ordered the carriage and horses to be immediately restored and replaced. When a Mr. Winyard, one of the messengers of the Council, attempted to return the property to Lady William Campbell, who was still in Charles Town, she adamantly refused to accept the items "without her lord's orders."[11]

Meanwhile, that day, Fenwick Bull appeared once again before the patriot leadership and reported the details of a conversation he had with Lord Campbell and the three commanders of the British sloops in Rebellion Road: Edward Thornbrough (*Tamar*), John Tollemache (*Scorpion*), and John Fergusson (*Cherokee*). According to Bull, Captain Tollemache "did not deny having some of our negroes on board [the *Scorpion*], but said they came as freemen, and demanding protection; that he could have had near five hundred, who had offered." Citing George III's inflammatory proclamation of August 23, the captain told Bull that the Carolinians "were all in actual rebellion" and that "he had orders to distress America by every means in his power." Moreover, Tollemache reportedly boasted that Charles Town "would surely be destroyed" and swore "upon his honor, [that] he soon expected two frigates and a bomb to arrive." The ship captain had also allegedly bragged that he had indeed stolen the money from the Legare brothers, had given it over to Campbell, and could even produce a receipt from the governor as proof. Despite his obvious sanction of the depredations, Lord William reportedly denied that he had anything to do with the purloined money, the recent seizures of property, or "the affairs of negroes."

In response to Bull's testimony, the Council of Safety ordered the companies of militia in Christ Church parish to secure Haddrell's Point, "in order to prevent landing from the men of war, and every attempt by the enemy to commit further robberies and depredations upon that neighborhood." Two days later, on December 12, the Council of Safety decided to allow the Legare brothers to sell Campbell's effects at public auction after giving the governor ten days' notice to restore their money.

On Wednesday, December 13, Captain Simon Tufts, who was now in command of the Whig vessel *Prosper*, was ordered to retake the ship *Betsey*, which was then lying near William Gibbes's Wharf on the Ashley River. In addition, Tufts was given explicit instructions to "be very attentive to prevent negroes going on board the said ship" and to remain keenly alert to "every irregular correspondence with the shore."[12]

The next day, the Council summoned one Alexander Wylly, who is described in the documents as "a master of a coasting scooner." Wylly testified that he had been detained as a pilot by Lord Campbell for five weeks after the seizure of his coastal vessel, the *George Town* packet, on Wednesday, November 8, 1775.[13] The captain reported that he had seen a number of slaves (several of whom he knew personally) belonging to the inhabitants of Charles Town aboard the men-of-war and on the shores of Sullivan's Island. According to the schooner master, when a report prevailed several days earlier that the black refugees were to be attacked by Moultrie's men, the slaves were "taken off shore in boats sent from the ships." Moreover, the captain reportedly witnessed about twenty bondsmen being carried off in his packet boat, including two of his own slaves. In October 1775, Wylly complained that one of his slaves, a carpenter named Ishmael, was "daily employed by Masters of vessels [although] he has no ticket or licence to work out." Especially vexing to Wylly was the fact that in the evenings, the bondsman had been "often seen playing fiddle at tippling houses." It is possible that Ishmael was one of the slaves who was taken away by the British.[14] As a result of his experiences with Campbell, Wylly made the decision to sign the Whig Association and promptly declare his allegiance to the patriot cause.

The same day, Jonathan Scott informed the Council that at moonrise the night before, John Ashe's plantation had been robbed yet again of "sundry livestock, by armed men landed from the men-of-war's boats." Upon hearing this information, Henry Laurens penned a letter to Colonel John Allston, requesting that he secretly lead his men back to Charles Town to receive further instructions from the Council. Colonel Moultrie was immediately ordered to procure five "proper boats" to cruise across the channels of the bar from James Island to the marsh of Shute's Folly. The vessels were to be used to "cut off all irregular correspondence with the men of war and other ships in Rebellion Road."

On Friday, December 15, the council voted 7.70 pounds sterling to a Mr. Loveday "for guarding Hog Island creek, and apprehending negroes." The payment was apparently well timed. That evening, as Lady William Campbell (figure 6.1) and her four children were secretly whisked away to the governor's flotilla, a canoe loaded with five slaves was intercepted by the provincial guard in Hog Island Creek. Ferrying mail along with "sundry quantities of provisions and other articles," including her ladyship's accoutrements, the bondsmen were attempting to row from Christopher Gadsden's Wharf to the *Cherokee*. According to the report later made by William Moultrie, two of the domestics belonged to Lord Campbell, while the other three were the property of local patriots.[15]

As the night progressed, another canoe carrying urgent letters to the governor was captured en route to the men-of-war. Onboard was a free black man named Scipio Handley. Handley, who was one of two dozen free African-Americans in Charles Town, had no doubt been well acquainted with Thomas Jeremiah. Both men were employed in the local market, worked as fishermen, and earned a living by piloting ships to and from their moorings. Handley, obviously undeterred by Jeremiah's execution, had decided at some point after September 15 (when Campbell absconded to the *Tamar*) that his interests would be best served by siding with the British.

According to testimony he would later file with the Loyalist Claims Commission in London on January 13, 1784, Handley had carried dispatches for the governor several times before the night in mid-December when he "was at last discovered and fired on by the Rebels." While endeavoring to make his escape this last time, the boatman was reportedly "run on Shore" and was "dangerously wounded." The injured Handley was promptly thrown in jail. His boat and personal effects were then seized by the Council of Safety.[16]

FIGURE 6.1. Lady William Campbell (174?–1784), before 1776, by Nathaniel Hone. The lovely Lady William Campbell, formerly Sarah Izard, came from one of South Carolina's most important and well-connected families. Portrayed here in full splendor with her trusty greyhound, Lady William could not bear the cold of Nova Scotia. She urged her husband to return to the Low Country, where they had met and fallen in love during the early 1760s. As the situation worsened in Charles Town, her husband fretted that she might become a target for mob violence. *The Campbell-Johnston Family, care of Historical Portraits Limited, London*

On Saturday, December 16, John Allston and his men appeared before Whig authorities. Arthur Middleton, who would be a signer of the Declaration of Independence six months later, was in the room, along with Henry Laurens, Dr. David Oliphant, and William Moultrie. They conferred with Lieutenant William R. Withers about how to find a way to frighten into submission the blacks who had sought freedom with Campbell.[17] The "problem" had obviously grown out of control. As Moultrie recalled in his own memoirs, the matter "was very alarming, and looked on as dangerous to the province at large...it was absolutely necessary at all events to dislodge them." But how would it be done? What kind of action would it take to maintain the position of the slaveholding patriots while at the same time preventing the unraveling of the social order?[18]

A public execution might work. After all, the Council had just captured Scipio Handley and had a perfect candidate on their hands for a spectacle of violence that would recall what happened to Thomas Jeremiah on August 18. Would hanging and burning another free black boatman be enough to scare rebellious slaves away from the royal governor? Perhaps not. What about Native Americans? Would a band of Catawba Indians friendly to the American cause be able to deter runaways from collaborating with the British?

There were earlier precedents for such thinking. On Christmas Day, 1765, Charles Town had teetered on the brink of a slave rebellion. South Carolina's highest authority at the time, Lieutenant Governor William Bull, frantically wrote to his Council and suggested that they employ the services of the Catawba Indians. Revealing the logic behind the white strategy of using Indians to suppress African-American insurgency, Bull explained, "I thought it very Advisable to call down some of the Catawbas, as Indians strike Terrour into the Negroes, and the Indian manner of hunting render them more sagacious in tracking and expert in finding out the hidden recesses where the runaways conceal themselves from the usual searches of the English."[19] In 1755, when Indians posed a greater threat to the colony, the strategy of "divide and conquer" had been suggested in the reverse. On March 7, 1755, the Commons House of Assembly urged the South Carolina Council that "If Indian Enemies should appear in our settlements, as they too often do, we thought it might be necessary to Arm some of the most Trusty of our Slaves to defend their masters' Lives and Property and to destroy such Enemies; we thought it good Policy in this way to keep up and increase that natural aversion which happily subsists between Negroes and Indians."[20]

Ultimately, another answer would be determined upon. After running through all of the possibilities, patriot officials decided that Henry Laurens should pen a personal letter to Edward Thornbrough. Before the letter could be written, however, the Council of Safety summoned "the domesticks" of Lord Campbell who had been apprehended the night before. During the course of their examination, the slaves testified that "some of his Lordship's effects had been put on board the sloop—, Alexander Mills, master, bound for Georgia." Dismayed by the news, Whig leaders ordered the vessel to "be immediately stopt; that no goods whatever be taken out; and that all letters in possession of the master be demanded." Although the documents are silent on the issue, it may have been at this point that Scipio Handley received a sentence of death under the Negro Act of 1740.

When the examination of the domestics was over, the Council of Safety ordered that a guard be placed immediately at Campbell's home at 34 Meeting Street to prevent other attempts by black boatmen to remove the governor's effects. The rationale given for this measure was that valuable items still in the dwelling might be sold to repay those who had been "injured by his Lordship's seizure and detention of their property, and [by his] encouraging, harbouring and protecting their runaway slaves."[21]

Royal Governor Josiah Martin of North Carolina had been in Charles Town Harbor since Wednesday, November 29. At Campbell's and Thornbrough's request, he had fled from his untenable position in the Cape Fear River in order to "concert some plan of operations for restoration of his Majesty's Government" in the two colonies.[22] When it became obvious that Martin was desperately needed in his own province, he promptly told Lord Campbell that it was time for him to depart. Immediately, the South Carolina governor became incensed, telling Martin that it was unlikely that the British men-of-war could maintain their position in Charles Town Harbor without the presence of the HMS *Scorpion*. Without intending to, the elderly Thornbrough quickly became embroiled in a crossfire between the two royal governors. As Campbell and Martin exchanged barbs, Thornbrough began to side with the North Carolina governor. Lord William became hostile and accused the captain of failing to recognize the strategic import of Charles Town and the necessity of keeping the waterway open to His Majesty's vessels. Thornbrough, who was at a loss for how to proceed, was given strict instructions by Campbell to answer a series of pointed questions and to justify his decision in writing.[23] After a delay of two weeks caused by unfavorable wind conditions, on Monday, December 18, Governor Martin and Captain John Tollemache cleared Charles Town Harbor in the *Scorpion* with "thirty or forty negroes." The small breakaway fleet included the transport vessel *Palliser*, two Bermuda sloops, and a schooner bound for Cape Fear River.[24]

That day, Henry Laurens wrote to Edward Thornbrough and explained that because of the recent seizures of "negroes," the supply of provisions to the men-of-war would be cut off immediately:

> We would have wished, if it had been possible, to have continued the
> permission which lately subsisted for supplying his majesty's ships
> with provision for a longer term, even until a happy reconciliation
> with our parent country had taken place; but the measures adopted in
> Rebellion-Road, which we do not impute to you, sir, of harbouring

and protecting negroes who fly from their masters to Sullivan's
Island, and on board the vessels in the road, oblige us to determine to
cut off all communication, until justice is done to the inhabitants, by
a restitution of those negroes. There is the less reason, too, for
supplying provisions at this time, when we have daily complaints
from the inhabitants on the [seacoast] of robberies and depredations
committed on them by white and black armed men, from on board
some of the ships under your command.[25]

Whether or not this message reached Thornbrough is unclear. But that
night, the plan to dislodge the slaves was finally put into effect. Instead of
bringing down the wrath of Catawbas, it was decided that a portion of John
Allston's foot rangers (occasionally referred to by contemporaries as the
Raccoon Company or the Indian Company), made up of fifty-four men under
the command of Lieutenant William Withers, would dress and paint themselves to look like Native Americans. This alternative to a Catawba-led slave
patrol would be cheaper, easier to execute, and easier to control. In the dark of
night and in the commotion of a violent attack, it would be difficult, if not
impossible, to distinguish a patriot foot-soldier disguised as an Indian from an
actual Catawba scout.[26]

Although the evidence is sketchy, it appears that Charles Cotesworth
Pinckney and William Moultrie led a detachment of more than 200 men over
to Haddrell's Point and quietly began to erect a fascine battery of four eighteen-
pounders. Early the next morning, when the "regular" soldiers were finished
mounting the cannon, the men who made up the "Indian Company" of rangers descended on the runaway blacks and Tories while they were still asleep.
Withers's men reportedly made a deafening war whoop as they torched the
huts and set fire to the pesthouse. From reports of the assault, it is clear that in
the midst of the fighting and the scattering of slaves and livestock, the men-of-
war began to fire shots at the patriots from Rebellion Road. A number of invaluable freshwater casks were destroyed, hampering the ability of the loyalist
seamen to sustain themselves while onboard His Majesty's ships. The "Indians"
mortally wounded between three and five runaways, took four slaves as prisoners, and captured three sailors belonging to the *Cherokee.* Four white women
and three children were also seized. It is unclear what happened to the approximately 460 slaves who were on the island at the time of the attack.[27] According
to Josiah Smith, at least twenty bondsmen were carried offshore by Campbell's
entourage.[28] Apparently, there were no patriot casualties.

On Wednesday, December 20, the day after the Sullivan's Island incident,
Henry Laurens wrote to Colonel Richard Richardson, who was then in the

backcountry. The merchant-planter notified Richardson of the Battle of Kemp's Landing involving Lord Dunmore, which had taken place in the days leading up to the important British defeat at Great Bridge near Currituck, North Carolina.[29] According to Laurens, the Virginia governor "armed all the negroes who would come in to him" and "skirmished with some of the Virginia troops, without any considerable effect on either side." In the same letter, the merchant-planter noted that Campbell "had gone [to] great lengths in harbouring & protecting Negroes on Sullivants [sic] Island" and that "those Villians [sic] made nightly Sallies and committed roberies [sic] & depredations on the Sea Coast of Christ Church." Laurens concluded that "this alarming evil received such a Check" the previous morning as would serve to humble Charles Town's "Negroes in general & perhaps to mortify his Lordship not a little."[30] The same day, a Mr. Clegg from the Indian Company of rangers reported to the Council of Safety that his fellow soldiers took fifteen prisoners, including two slaves belonging to Sarah Mitchell, the free mulatto John Swann, and a bondsman named Peter, the property of shipwright George Powell.

In the late afternoon, a petition of Sarah Mitchell was read, "praying for the discharge of two negroes belonging to her, which had been taken going to the Cherokee armed ship." The matter was put to a question, and the Council decided that the warden of the workhouse, Michael Kalteisen, was to release the two slaves from his custody as soon as Mitchell paid the requisite fees.

At five o'clock, Peter and Swann were brought from their cells at the workhouse to the Council chamber, where they were promptly examined by Whig officials. After interrogating the men at length, Council members decided that John Coram (the same justice of the peace who had been in charge of the Thomas Jeremiah hearings) would summon another magistrate and five freeholders to preside over the trial of Swann in accordance with the Negro Act of 1740. Michael Bates, overseer to John Ashe; William Coates; Mrs. Robinson, the wife of Robinson who ran the pesthouse; and Mrs. Walker, the wife of the hapless George Walker (the gunner of Fort Johnson who was tarred and feathered on August 12) were ordered to appear as witnesses against Swann "in relation to some robberies lately committed upon Haddrell's Point." When the examination was over, Swann and Peter were both remanded to the workhouse.

Later that evening, the white prisoners taken at Sullivan's Island were also brought before the Council and cross-examined. Mrs. Walker; Mrs. Robinson; Mrs. Farrow, wife of William Farrow (a harbor pilot); and young William Carrington, the son of the carpenter of the *Tamar*, gave accounts of their experiences on Sullivan's Island and were promptly discharged.

Although it is difficult to assess the fate of the slaves who fled from the Indian Company on December 19, a number of them evidently went over to

Morris Island (site of the Charles Town Harbor lighthouse directly south across the harbor from Sullivan's Island). On Thursday, December 21, patriot councilmen called for the removal of all livestock and "negroes" not belonging to John Morris (the owner of the island). They ordered Captain Benjamin Stone to "employ proper persons" to apprehend all bondsmen on the landmass and to drive the animals to neighboring James Island, where an extensive inventory would be made.[31]

The next day, the *South Carolina and American General Gazette* contained a report designed to terrify blacks into staying put. The front-page story, unconfirmed by any other sources, told readers that Lord Dunmore had sold to the French or Spanish West Indies "two Sloops full of Negroes, who had gone on board the men of war, with the Foolish Expectation of gaining their Freedom."[32] The obvious intent of such rumors was to discourage additional slaves who might try to flee from their masters and seek refuge with Crown officials. It is uncertain whether this blatant attempt to deceive the majority population of South Carolina functioned as intended. However, it does seem that the number of slaves stealing away temporarily ceased around the time that this bit of apparent propaganda was published.

With the ostensible easing of tensions, Whig leaders began to loosen restrictions on some of their prisoners. On Christmas Day, the Council of Safety convened and decided to release one of the captives taken on Sullivan's Island from the workhouse, a female slave belonging to Mrs. Farrow. Three days later, Mrs. Walker was allowed to board the *Tamar* along with her son. On Friday, December 29, a slave aptly named Adventure was released into the custody of his master, William Tweed (whose other slave, Dewar, was implicated in the alleged Jeremiah plot) after having been "taken up at sea by one of the armed pilot boats." The next day, the Council of Safety ordered that "Mr. Easton's wench, taken by the Foot-Rangers upon Sullivan's Island, be discharged, he paying the fees."

On Saturday, December 30, Henry Laurens sent a communiqué to Lieutenant Withers thanking him for the services that his "Indian Company" had rendered during the Sullivan's Island raid. The Council of Safety president informed Withers that he and his men could now "return to their respective habitations" and private affairs. However, Laurens also cautioned the Indian Company leader that his soldiers might have "to take the field again, when the service of the colony shall render it necessary to call upon them."[33]

As 1775 changed into 1776, rumors swirled that His Majesty's ships (which at this point consisted of the *Tamar*, the *Cherokee*, the *Sandwich* packet, a brigantine, a pilot boat, and an armed schooner) would soon depart from Charles Town Harbor. With only a few water casks and a limited supply of provisions, the flotilla would have to go somewhere else. But where? In a letter to the Provincial Council at Wilmington, North Carolina, Laurens speculated that Governor Campbell and his retinue were up to something sinister: "We are told they are bound to the river Savannah—and we fear they have more mischievous schemes a foot then merely to obtain bread and beef—probably to protect ships loading there in violation of the General Association, and to over awe the friends of liberty."[34]

Would Lord Campbell actually go to Savannah? And if so, would he try, with help of Royal Governor James Wright, to encourage Georgians to load ships with cargoes bound for Britain in an effort to undermine the Continental Association?[35] Would there be a mass exodus of slaves from Savannah and the outlying plantations, as there was in Charles Town? People up and down the Low Country coastline must have wondered how it would all play out.

On Tuesday, January 2, five freeholders and two magistrates appealed to the Council of Safety for mercy in the case of Jupiter, a slave belonging to Captain Benjamin Stone. While it is unclear what the bondsman allegedly did to receive his sentence of death, it is likely that he was involved in the nightly marauding that took place in late November and early December. It is also plausible that he was one of the runaways who fled to Morris Island in the wake of the Sullivan's Island attack. After hearing the plea for clemency, the Whig planters decided to postpone Jupiter's death sentence until the opening of the Provincial Congress in February. Acting in the capacity of president, Henry Laurens ordered Jupiter to be placed under safe custody. He also called for a report be made on the state of the case and on the evidence presented against him.

The same day, the British vessels lurking near the port attempted to navigate across the bar. When the wind failed to comply, the ships were forced to return to their former positions in Rebellion Road. Less than twenty-four hours later, the armed schooner that Campbell's men had commandeered cleared Charles Town Harbor on the strength of a favorable wind and began to make its way north up the coastline. Suspecting that the ship was bound for the Santee River, the Council of Safety issued an order to the Committee for St. James Santee "to land the cargo if possible—or even to scuttle and sink the vessel."

After issuing this directive, John Calvert, one of the messengers of the Council of Safety, reported on the status of John Swann and affirmed that the free mulatto was still in safe custody and was being closely watched by the warden of the workhouse, Michael Kalteisen. Whether Bates, Coates, Robinson, and Walker refused to testify regarding Swann is unclear. However, it seems that patriot officials had a difficult time procuring evidence against the free "mulatto." That day, presiding justice of the peace John Coram appeared before the Council and conceded that he was unable to shed new light on the case against Swann. Dismayed by the magistrate's ostensible inability to gather proof, Whig leaders ordered him to present his arguments the next day. But when the appointed time came, Coram failed to appear.[36]

While waiting for Coram to materialize, patriot councilmen decided that John Rutledge should pen a letter to Colonel Richard Richardson. Rutledge urged Richardson to discharge the volunteer companies under his command, because it looked as though Tollemache's warning that two frigates and a bomb ketch would soon attack Charles Town was unfounded.

On Saturday, January 6, after waiting four days for the right wind conditions, the *Tamar*, the *Cherokee*, and the *Sandwich*, along with a brigantine and a Georgia pilot boat, were finally able to set sail. Campbell, who had been confined to his flotilla since September 15, 1775, had finally abandoned South Carolina. Because of fresh intelligence, patriots suspected that the *Tamar* was bound for North Carolina to be careened and that the remainder of the fleet was headed for Tybee Island at the mouth of the Savannah. On the day the vessels departed, Henry Laurens wrote to Colonel Stephen Bull at Beaufort, South Carolina, and informed him that he wanted the Beaufort committee to send a boat immediately to wait at Cockspur Island (next to Tybee) in order to provide South Carolinians with intelligence regarding the activities of Lord Campbell in Georgia. In particular, Laurens was concerned with the timing of Campbell's arrival because of a report that a vessel in the Savannah River was nearly loaded with a cargo of indigo bound for England. Whigs in Charles Town feared that Georgia might turn on the other colonies and, with the help of the South Carolina's royal governor, thwart the efforts of patriots up and down the eastern seaboard to enforce the Continental Association.[37]

Three days later, members of the Council of Safety were relieved to learn from messenger John Halsal that the committee at Beaufort had seized John Mercier's brigantine *William* from Cockspur Island, Georgia, for loading an illegal cargo of South Carolina indigo intended for London.[38] According to the report, the Beaufort committee had incurred an expense of about 275 pounds for transporting the boat from the Savannah River to Beaufort Harbor. On January 10, the Council of Safety agreed to pay the amount requested along with an additional twenty pounds to Halsal for delivering a response by express and fifteen pounds for a notice prohibiting exportation to be drawn up and posted in St. Helena parish.[39]

Although Charlestonians were still unsure whether to believe Captain Tollemache's warning that British ships were en route to their harbor with the intent to attack, patriot leaders decided that day to erect fortifications using forced black labor on the freshly cleared ground of Sullivan's Island.[40] Before the slaves could finish, however, between nine and ten o'clock on the morning of Thursday, January 11, the outlines of two large ships and a sloop began to appear through the fog. Was this the beginning of the attack that patriots had been dreading since the spring of 1775?

At first, no one knew what to make of the vessels. As John Drayton remembered, the weather was extremely hazy, and the only thing that could be discerned was that three craft were descried at anchor to the northward of the bar, making signals for a pilot. After approximately three hours, patriots sent a boat from Fort Johnson to discover what they were. But because the atmosphere was so thick, these scouts could not distinguish whether the ships were armed. The next day, a ten-oared barge was lowered from one of the three mysterious vessels. At eleven o'clock, the barge exchanged fire with the *Hibernia*, under Captain Thomas Smith, which had been patrolling the harbor in accordance with the Council of Safety's instructions of November 4 to warn all vessels headed for Charles Town not to come over the bar.[41]

In an attempt to procure intelligence, the barge approached the Spanish snow *San Miguel*, under Don Joachim de Laraquebel, which was then lying at anchor in Five Fathom Hole, waiting for a pilot to guide it out of the harbor. The men from the barge boarded the snow and conversed with Bartholomew Rilliet, one of the few men on the ship who could speak English. Wishing to obtain more information, the men in the barge began to make their way toward Fort Johnson. The fort consequently fired on the tiny boat, and the oarsmen began to retreat. Before the barge could make its way back to the three vessels, however, it was intercepted by patriot spies pretending to be fishermen.

According to testimony later provided by two of the spies, a Sergeant Redman and a Mr. Ellis, the barge and the fishing boat lay next to each other for fifteen minutes, during which time the oarsmen asked the "fishermen" why they were fired on by Fort Johnson. The bargemen then reportedly asked where the *Tamar* and the *Cherokee* were. When they learned that the patriots were in possession of the fort and that the men-of-war had departed, they immediately threatened to attack Charles Town at "the first fair wind and tide." As Ellis and Redman related the story, the bargemen allegedly told them that "there was a 50 gun ship in the offing, and a frigate of 28 guns... together with a sloop to lighten the large ship, that she might come over the bar." To make matters worse, the sailors claimed that the warships "had a black and six white pilots on board." As it turned out, the bargemen were exaggerating slightly. In actuality, the ships in the offing were the HMS *Syren*, captained by Tobias Furneaux, of twenty-eight guns, and the HMS *Raven*, commanded by John Stanhope, of fourteen guns.[42]

An attack seemed imminent. It was widely believed at the time that the *Tamar* and the *Cherokee* were on their way back to Rebellion Road with the intent of mounting a full-scale assault. Recalling the charges leveled against Thomas Jeremiah seven months earlier, white Charlestonians became panic-stricken that "domestic enemies" would set fire to the city while patriot forces were engaged with the men-of-war.[43] In an effort to secure control over black Carolinians during this time of uncertainty, the Council of Safety ordered Captain Benjamin Stone to recruit as many "trusty, able-bodied slaves" as necessary to march to the new battery that had been erected just west of Fort Johnson. The Council gave Stone strict assurance that it would indemnify the owners of "all such slaves...as shall happen to be killed, maimed or lost, by means of the enemy."

The fear of a concerted slave insurrection with the attack of the British ships was so great that the Council of Safety commanded John Allston to bring down his "Indian Company" once again and instructed Captain Samuel Boykin to collect fifty Catawba Indians and march them to a position "at some convenient distance" fifteen miles from the Carolina capital. In addition to these measures, Whig councilmen demanded that Colonel Richard Richardson immediately send between 500 and 1,000 men armed with rifles to Charles Town. Henry Laurens, the author of the letter, urged Richardson to appeal to the backcountry militia's sense of patriotism in an effort to garner more support: "We hope the friends of liberty and lovers of their country will shew their zeal and attachment in this hour, when their services are really wanted. Time will not permit us to add, nor do we think it needful, that men who are in earnest require no more to induce them to the service of their country, than to be told she is in danger."[44] Similar letters requesting militia volunteers were sent out to Colonel Joseph Glover, Colonel Benjamin Singleton, Colonel Job Rothmaler, and Major Alexander McIntosh.

Concerned about the vulnerability of the Continental Association, that day, the Council of Safety warned the committee at Georgetown "to guard against tricks, which...may be attempted to carry off any vessels loaded contrary to resolutions." In a separate letter, South Carolina Whig leaders advised their Georgia counterparts not to "relax in their zeal" but to be animated as "open danger" approached.

At precisely eight o'clock on the morning of Sunday, January 14, Charles Cotesworth Pinckney commanded the soldiers stationed in Fort Johnson to fire a warning of "Six Guns—two at a time, at three minutes distance." As Charles Town reeled from sound of the alarms, the slaves must have anticipated that their liberation was close at hand. As the apprehensions of white Charles Town deepened, the hopes of black Charles Town became ever greater.[45]

As patriots and African-Americans wondered about the outcome of an impending British attack, hundreds of militia volunteers rushed to the aid of

Charles Town. On January 16, Henry Laurens wrote to his son John and observed that men in the city "appear to be animated. God only knows what will be the event." The Whig leader added that if "the people are cool in Action," a conquest by the Royal Navy would not come easily. However, he lamented that "a Manly defence against British Ships of War will cost a valuable Life and Limb...Heads of Families, Brothers[,] Sons, friends & good fellow Citizens. Not the Canaille of Soldiery will fall." He concluded despondently: "Who can dry eyed reflect upon this picture?"[46]

That week, local merchant Josiah Smith Jr. described the bleak and deserted state of the metropolis:

> Charles Town always heretofore lively & busy at this Season of the Year, is now Melancholy to behold, houses Shut up, Wharves & Stores all empty, Trade not carried on, Places of worship almost deserted, Scarce a woman to be seen in the Streets, Men continually on Military Duty, and no other Musick but Drum & Fife daily Sounding. Our trust I hope is ultimately on the Great Ruler of the Universe, whose Just Providence hath hitherto been favorable to our cause, & through his Strength hope we shall yet come off conquerors.[47]

As it turned out, the huge buildup of anticipation was all for naught. What Charles Town residents did not know at the time (because of fog and poor visibility) was that the crews of the *Syren* and the *Raven* had quietly and uneventfully sailed off to Georgia in the hopes of finding the *Tamar* and the *Cherokee*. For the time being, white patriots could breathe a sigh of relief. For those Afro-Carolinians who pinned their hopes on the kind of British liberty promised by Lord Dunmore or the kind described in the landmark *Sommersett* decision, a profound sense of disappointment and frustration undoubtedly set in.

As the commotion over the potential naval assault quieted down, controversy soon arose over the departure of the *San Miguel*. On Tuesday evening, January 16, John Coram Jr. (whose father was still gathering evidence against John Swann) asked permission from the Council of Safety to allow a Mr. Pharaoh to pilot the Spanish snow in Rebellion Road over the bar. Additionally, Coram requested that he be allowed to accompany Pharaoh onboard the ship. The Council of Safety granted the request but with the proviso that the pilot "take especial care not to fall into the enemy's hands." Before Coram and Pharaoh had a chance to depart, however, the Council of Safety zeroed in on a passenger named Francisco Morelli.

Morelli, an Italian immigrant, had resided in Charles Town since at least October 1772, when he married Honora Feltman, a widowed tavernkeeper.

In the three years between 1772 and 1775, Morelli worked as an innkeeper and pastry chef. At some point during that period, he fell deeply into debt and was subsequently taken to court for his failure to meet five bond obligations.[48] Suspecting that he was attempting to flee the colony and escape his creditors and that he was harboring a number of Charles Town slaves, Whig leaders the next day issued an order to Captain Thomas Smith of the *Hibernia* to board the *San Miguel:* "If Morelli himself, or any inhabitant of this colony who has not been permitted to depart, or any negro, shall be found on board, you are to bring on shore such inhabitant or negro, and if the Spanish commander shall offer any violence or opposition, the pilot is to be taken from on board."[49]

Apparently, when Smith set foot on the snow, he discovered that Morelli was indeed hidden below deck, along with five runaway slaves. For reasons that are unclear, Smith disobeyed his superiors and left Morelli and the slaves alone. Not to be deterred, however, on Thursday, January 18, the Council of Safety tried once again to address the issue. This time, they sent Captain Simon Tufts to "demand Morelli, and all the negroes" hidden in the *San Miguel*. If the ship's captain, Don Joachim de Laraquebel, refused to relinquish Morelli or the bondsmen, then Tufts was to pilot the ship to the wharf district.

Tufts searched the vessel following the Council's instructions and that evening delivered to the militia guard Morelli and five slaves: Daniel and Richard, belonging to Justice Charles Mathews Coslett [who reviewed the legality of Jerry's trial]; Jack, belonging to the wealthy slave merchant Miles Brewton; Polydore, belonging to a Mr. Donoven; and Sambo, belonging to John Gaillard. Whig leaders summoned the slaves to appear in their chambers. According to the report, the men were separately examined, but each declared that "he had been seduced from his owner—secreted on board the said vessel—promised £100 a month wages, good usage, clothing and living." Morelli, "who had been concealed with them a whole week, in the same part of the vessel," had made another promise as well: "on their arrival in Spain, freedom."

When the slaves were finished providing their depositions to the Council, Morelli was brought before the board. In the course of his interrogation, the Italian conceded that he "knew all the negroes, that he had conversed with them, and that they were secreted with him on board the Spanish snow." The reason that the debtor cited for not restoring the slaves to their masters was that they reportedly told him "they would rather die than return to their owners." With that, Henry Laurens issued a warrant for Morelli's arrest and had him consigned to the common jail in Charles Town.

The next day, Friday, January 19, when the master of the *San Miguel* appeared before the Council of Safety, he reportedly told patriot leaders that he thought the stowaway slaves belonged to Morelli. The documents indicate that during his cross-examination, the ship captain produced a ticket dated January 2, authorizing him to carry off Morelli and his family. Much to the vexation of Whig authorities, the document was signed by Lord William Campbell.[50]

Although Campbell had departed from Charles Town thirteen days earlier on January 6, patriots were still very much concerned about his actions. That day, Laurens wrote to Colonel Stephen Bull in Beaufort and warned him that Lord William might try to "plunder or export provision for the Tamar and Cherokee" from the South Carolina side of the Savannah River. The merchant-planter was particularly concerned that Campbell would land at Inverary, the governor's own 750-acre plantation along the banks of the Savannah, named for the Campbell family's ancestral estate in Scotland. To prevent this from happening, Laurens recommended that Bull enlist the aid of approximately 200 men along the Georgia-South Carolina border. The Whig leader told the colonel to have his men "in constant readiness" to heed the call of the Provincial Congress or the Council of Safety, so that they might "at all times" be able to prevent robberies and illicit exportations from being committed from the many islands and rivers along the Low Country coastline.[51]

After he was finished with this letter, Laurens penned a message to the Georgia Council of Safety in which he praised his neighbors for taking preemptive action with respect to the slaves who resided near the Georgia capital: "It was a wise Step to Strip the Negroe Houses on both Sides of the Savannah of Arms and Ammunition, we highly applaud it & are now taking measures in concert with Col. Bull for having an Armed force of 200 men in readiness to guard against Seizures or clandestine exportation of provisions from our Side & also to March to the assistance of our friends in Savannah if required."[52]

Explaining why it was necessary to keep blacks away from the British, on January 20, Henry Laurens wrote once again to Bull and told him that every ship in Campbell's flotilla had "carried off some of our negroes, in the whole amounting to a considerable number." The patriot politician warned that this was "sufficient to alarm every man in the colony, and put those on the sea-coast and river-sides more particularly on their guard." He concluded that such "robberies and depredations" warranted Whigs to fire "upon any of the men-of-war, their boats and men, in attempting to land."

Later that day, the Council of Safety learned from Justice of the Peace John Coram that John Swann had been acquitted of all charges. Although the documents are silent about why he was found innocent, it was most likely the result of a lack of hard evidence.

Four days later, on January 24, South Carolina Whigs learned that the *Syren* and the *Raven* had rendezvoused with the *Tamar* and the *Cherokee* at Cockspur Island at the mouth of the Savannah. It was around this same time that patriots in Charles Town discovered that Georgia Governor James Wright and his council had been taken hostage by Savannah patriots under the direction of Joseph Habersham. Wright had raised the ire of Georgia Whigs when he declared that "inhabitants who should refuse to supply provision" to His Majesty's ships or attempt hostilities against them "should be deemed and treated as rebels [and would have] their houses burnt, &c." South Carolinians were pleased to find out that Georgia patriots had reacted swiftly to Wright's threats, taking him prisoner, beginning to fortify Savannah, cutting off all intercourse with the men-of-war, and starting to blockade the Savannah River in order "to hinder an ascent to the town."

On January 30, Reverend Henry Purcell and William Hort, two members of the Christ Church committee, notified the South Carolina Council of Safety that "it might be dangerous to the community, to permit Tom, a negro lately tried...for inticing other slaves to desert on board the men-of-war to be at large."[53] Tom had been indicted for his actions in December, and the committee was at a loss about what to do with him. Having heard Purcell and Hort's petition as well as numerous accounts of Tom's attempts to persuade his fellow blacks to seek freedom with the British, the Council recommended that the Christ Church committee take steps to apprehend the man and place him in the Charles Town workhouse.

Lord William Campbell never made an emancipation proclamation as the Earl of Dunmore had done. But the actions of South Carolina's colonial governor in the winter of 1775–76 played on the deepest fear of local Whigs and the greatest hope of the region's African-Americans. The crisis of allegiance that typified the summer and fall of 1775 intensified in December and January and became further complicated by patriot efforts to reimpose an environment of strict racial hierarchy and subordination. Clearly, South Carolina Whig leaders did not hesitate to use violence. Nor did they show any reluctance to play Africans and Native Americans off against each other. Yet despite the machinations of patriot authorities, the deeply held fear that the British and the black majority would collaborate came to fruition. There may have only been 500 or so blacks who made it to Sullivan's Island in December 1775, but their actions and those of men such as Scipio Handley helped forge an irreparable rift between provincial elites and the Crown.

7

The Masters Were Still
in Charge

January 1776–August 1776

Unlike their South Carolina neighbors, white Georgians never experienced an organized slave rebellion like the one that began at Stono on the morning of Sunday, September 9, 1739. The most significant episode of African-American resistance in the Georgia colony's brief history occurred on the eve of the American Revolution in mid-November 1774. The revolt, which may have marked an attempt to capitalize on the growing divisions in the white community, began when less than a dozen bondsmen belonging to Captain Morris of St. Andrew parish murdered their overseer and his wife. In addition, the slaves maimed a carpenter named Wright and took the life of a small boy. The men proceeded to a nearby plantation, where they seriously wounded the owner, Angus McIntosh. Witnessing the commotion, one of McIntosh's slaves joined in and began to assail his master. The band then traveled to the house of Roderick McLeod. McLeod's son, perhaps alerted to their arrival, went out to confront them. In front of his father, the young McLeod broke the arm of McIntosh's slave, but he was soon killed during the altercation. The rebellious slaves were apprehended the same day, before they could get very far. According to a presentment of the grand jury, two of the participants, McIntosh's slave and the supposed ringleader, were sentenced to be burned alive.[1]

Little is known about the men involved in the St. Andrew Parish Revolt. According to historian Betty Wood, with the exception of McIntosh's slave, they were all "New Negroes." How long the participants had been in the colony remains uncertain. It is equally unclear from the report published in the *Georgia Gazette* on Wednesday, December 7, 1774, whether the event was planned ahead of time or whether the violence broke out in an impromptu fashion.

We do not know if the men involved made a conscious decision to recruit other slaves to join their ranks. It is patently obvious, however, that the bondsmen were not afraid of whites and that they did not distinguish between slaveholders and non-slaveholders. Each white person the rebels encountered, including the small boy, were subjected to the same type of violence. This played on some of the deepest apprehensions of white Georgians and confirmed reports streaming in of similar episodes of black rebellion in the West Indies. We cannot say with any certainty whether the saltwater slaves knew what was in store for them for having fomented an uprising. The bondsman belonging to Angus McIntosh must have known that punishment for such rebelling against enslavement would be swift and brutal.

Two months after the bloodshed occurred, on Thursday, January 12, 1775, a group of Scottish patriots in St. Andrew parish convened along the banks of the Altamaha River in the village of Darien and drafted a set of six resolutions. Led by Lachlan McIntosh (a protégé and friend of Henry Laurens who may well have been related to Angus), the Georgia Whigs claimed that they were making an effort to put slaves on the same footing as their masters:

> To show the world that we are not influenced by any contracted or
> interested motives, but a general philanthropy for all mankind, of
> whatever climate, language, or complexion, we hereby declare our
> disapprobation and abhorrence of the unnatural practice of Slavery in
> America (however the uncultivated state of our country, or other
> specious argument may plead for it,) a practice founded in injustice
> and cruelty, and highly dangerous to our liberties (as well as lives,)
> debasing part of our fellow creatures below men, and corrupting the
> virtue and morals of the rest, and is laying the basis of that liberty we
> contend for (and which we pray the Almighty to continue to the latest
> posterity) upon a very wrong foundation. We therefore resolve, at all
> times to use our utmost endeavors for the manumission of our
> Slaves in this Colony, for the most safe and equitable footing for the
> masters and themselves.[2]

In the end, this proved an empty promise. McIntosh, the author of the Darien resolutions, did not free his own slaves, nor was there a spate of manumissions in the Georgia countryside. This begs the question: why was the statement drawn up in the first place?

Essentially, the document functioned on two levels. The first was an attempt to silence critics who leveled charges of hypocrisy at the patriot faction for demanding liberty while denying it to their slaves. The second, as historian Harvey H. Jackson demonstrated, was that it signified an attempt on the part of the Whigs to target a black (as well as a white) audience.[3] Indeed, Georgia planters were attempting something entirely novel. Here was an effort by Southern Whigs to influence slaves and render them passive using means other than violence. The underlying message was that blacks could best support the cause of liberty by remaining as they were: enslaved. As we shall see, the tactic was ultimately unsuccessful, and the resolution failed to convince Afro-Georgians of the sincerity of their white patriot masters.

In January 1776, one year after Darien's six resolutions, Lord Campbell and the British men-of-war were on their way from Charles Town Harbor to Savannah. At some point during their voyage, the frigate HMS *Syren*, commanded by Captain Tobias Furneaux, overtook them. The *Syren*, which had made a brief appearance off Charles Town with the *Raven* on Thursday, January 11, was the advance ship of the British fleet preparing to invade America. At some point between Charles Town and Savannah, Furneaux presented Lord William with a two-month-old letter from the Earl of Dartmouth. The document described in detail British military plans for the Southern colonies. Having learned that a Royal Navy fleet was headed south from New York to Cape Fear, Governor Campbell decided that once he landed in Savannah, he and Captain Furneaux would set sail on the *Syren* for North Carolina.[4]

When the *Tamar*, the *Cherokee*, and the *Syren* arrived off Cockspur Island near the mouth of the Savannah River on Monday, January 15, 1776, the atmosphere in the fledgling capital of the Georgia colony was one of alarm. Patriots became convinced that the British warships intended to destroy the town of Savannah. As had been the case in Charles Town, His Majesty's ships were denied provisions. This further escalated tensions. The Whigs decreed that any individual caught going onboard the vessels or supplying the British crews with victuals would be imprisoned. The local Council of Safety took immediate action and attempted to put the town in a posture of defense. A two-gun battery was erected in the wharf district along the river, and another of eight to ten guns was built high above it on a bluff. Following the example of William Henry Drayton at the Battle of Hog Island Creek, partisans sank a vessel two miles below the town in the narrowest part of the channel to preclude the British warships from approaching.[5]

When the twenty-gun HMS *Scarborough* arrived on Thursday, January 18, with 200 British marines, the Council of Safety ordered Major Joseph Habersham to place Governor Sir James Wright and his council under arrest. The next day, Wright was paroled on his honor, confined to his house, and given strict instructions not to communicate with anyone without the express permission of the Council of Safety. By Sunday, February 11, Sir James had had enough. In the dark of night, the baronet attempted to escape from the governor's mansion with several members of his council and three of his children. At the rear entrance of the residence, the party met John Mulryne, a friend of the family, who saw to it that they made it safely down the Savannah to his house in the village of Bonaventure. When the family and attendants reached Mulryne's home, they were met with a separate craft and crew that had been waiting patiently for them in the darkness. The entourage crept onto the boat and was rowed hastily down to Tybee Creek. At three o'clock in the morning on Monday, February 12, Wright and his children boarded the *Scarborough*, anchored off Tybee Island. Later that morning, at nine, the commander of the ship, Andrew Barkley, ordered his men to fire a fifteen-gun salute to honor the arrival of the king's representatives.[6]

The next day, Wright penned an open letter addressed to the people of Georgia. The tone he adopted was mainly conciliatory. The governor declared that he had received fresh intelligence from London and from General Howe at Boston; he assured the citizens that the king's forces at Savannah would not commit any hostilities against them. What they really wanted, Wright claimed, was "a friendly intercourse and a supply of fresh provisions." The governor concluded by offering a final gesture of goodwill to the rebels, telling them that all would be forgiven and pardoned if they would simply desist.[7]

In March, the issue of nonexportation came to the fore. At the time, there were twenty ships in the Savannah River loaded with nearly 3,000 tierces of rice. It looked at first as though the Whig authorities would allow only three of the vessels to set sail. But the Council of Safety soon reconsidered, allowing the ships to depart when patriots learned that the king's troops were trying to procure the rice for themselves. Three hundred to 400 members of the Georgia militia and 100 men from South Carolina commanded by Stephen Bull rushed to defend the city and the harbor. Around midnight on Saturday, March 2, 300 British marines, under the direction of Commodore Andrew Barkley, Major James Grant, and John Maitland, landed on Hutchinson's Island, opposite Savannah, and boarded the rice vessels anchored above the island. The next day, a patriot coincidentally named Joseph Rice was sent to unrig the vessels. When the British forces took Rice hostage, a confrontation ensued.

Raymond Demeré and Daniel Roberts were sent by Whig authorities to demand Rice's release, but they, too, were detained by the marines. Soon, patriot forces at the bluff began to fire at the redcoats. When Whig officers determined that the vessels were out of range, they gave orders for the *Inverness*, a ship valued at 20,000 pounds sterling, to be set ablaze and cut from its moorings. This was done so that the current would push the ship into the rice vessels and destroy them. As Lachlan McIntosh recalled, the *Inverness* was so large that it grounded before reaching the others. A second boat was intentionally burned, colliding with two of the rice ships, which immediately burst into flames. The British managed to escape with the remaining vessels down the back river, on the South Carolina side of Hutchinson's Island, via a channel that the patriots believed was too shallow to be used. Yet they departed in haste, leaving behind two field pieces, which were later retrieved by several slaves belonging to the royal lieutenant governor, John Graham. The Whig prisoners were eventually set free, but the British had managed to commandeer 1,600 barrels of rice without paying so much as a "farthing" for them.[8]

As South Carolina's southern neighbor reeled from the battle of the rice ships, events came to a head in North Carolina. In the winter of 1776, Governor Josiah Martin, freshly arrived from Charles Town in late December, attempted to rouse opposition to the Whig provincials who had taken control of the colony. The royal governor was convinced that if he received immediate military assistance from London, he could nip the growing patriot movement in the bud using loyal Highland Scots and former Regulators. With that goal in mind, Martin dispatched Alexander Schaw to Whitehall to persuade Lord Dartmouth to provide reinforcements. The governor's confidence in the strategy, along with the military disasters in Massachusetts, convinced the secretary of state that he needed to send a large-scale offensive to help reconquer the Southern colonies. At the end of October 1775, a naval convoy of seven infantry regiments and two companies of artillery was sent from England to land near Cape Fear in late January or early February. Upon their arrival, they expected to be joined by thousands of Tories whom Martin was supposedly going to recruit. Once the forces united, royal government would be reestablished.[9]

Assured that redcoats were in transit, on Wednesday, January 10, 1776, Martin called upon all North Carolinians to rally to the King's Colours. The same day, the governor ordered loyalists to raise militias, seize arms and ammunition, and jail all rebels and traitors. Moreover, Martin issued a directive to Tories, telling them to march east to Brunswick along the coast, where they would be met with British troops on Thursday, February 15.

While loyalists were taking up arms in the backcountry, on Monday, February 5, the royal governor held a secret meeting at the settlement of Cross Creek (near modern-day Fayetteville) with all of the Highland chieftains in the colony and three former Regulators. The Scotsmen wanted to delay taking up arms until Friday, March 1, when they could be sure that His Majesty's soldiers would be able to offer their support. They were overruled, however, by James Hunter, a former Regulator who pushed for immediate action. With great trepidation, the Scots conceded. Captain Donald McLeod, an experienced British officer and a Scot, learned that he had 500 men already assembled and that they would be joined by 5,000 backcountry Tories waiting in the wings.

McLeod marched sixty miles south of Salem to rendezvous with the ex-Regulators. When he arrived, he found them less than enthused. The handful of former Regulators who did appear reportedly turned on McLeod, seeing him as nothing more than a foreigner. With news circulating that the Whigs were beginning to form militias, the backcountry men departed. McLeod, deserted and without allies in this strange new land, could not persuade anyone to guide him to his destination at Cross Creek. This abortive loyalist meeting would be a precursor of things to come.

On Thursday, February 15, a motley crew of Tories gathered at Cross Creek. Donald MacDonald, a British lieutenant colonel who had been recently appointed to brigadier general of the militia by Martin, assumed control. Lacking adequate training, the ragtag group began to march toward the sea to meet Martin and the promised British regulars.

Provincial authorities caught wind of the nascent Tory insurrection. Colonel James Moore mustered a group of North Carolina continentals, as well as a number of militia, and embarked on a mission to intercept the loyalists. Moore marched his men northward along the Cape Fear River and arrived at Rockfish Creek, seven miles to the south of Cross Creek. By Monday, February 19, there were more than 1,100 men eager to do battle with the Highlanders. MacDonald approached the patriot camp with a force of 1,500 men. The Tory general sent a message to Colonel Moore, requesting that he "repair to the royal standard" and surrender by noon on Tuesday, February 20. Moore rejected the offer and replied that "he and his officers were engaged in a glorious and honorable cause, the defence of the liberties of mankind." The Whig colonel added that "if M'Donald and his army would lay down their arms, they should be received as friends: but otherwise, they should only be met as enemies to public peace, and American liberty."

That evening, knowing that a battle would erupt the next day, a large number of loyalists fled their camp and headed west. MacDonald awoke to find that two companies of militia had deserted, taking their weapons with them. The elderly MacDonald mustered his strength and reportedly delivered a heated oration, denouncing the deserters and calling on the remaining troops to brace themselves for war. The Highlanders cheered, but twenty more backcountry volunteers immediately put down their weapons and left camp. At nightfall, confident that those men who remained were loyal to him, MacDonald crossed the Cape Fear River at Campbelltown, narrowly avoiding an engagement with Moore. The Scotsman then marched his men toward the coast to rendezvous with the British fleet, which he hoped had already landed.

Realizing what had transpired, Moore ordered his men to pursue the Tories and intercept them before they reached the Atlantic. Knowing that the loyalists would have to cross a key bridge southwest of the Black River on Moore's Creek, Moore ordered his men to set a trap. On Monday, February 26, MacDonald encountered a patriot force of 1,100 men, who had been eagerly awaiting the loyalists on the west side of the stream with the bridge at their backs. That night, MacDonald, exhausted from his hasty march and ill with a fever, tried to discourage his men from mounting an attack. The Highlanders, however, were impatient and voted to make a heroic charge. At first, MacDonald tried to discourage them, but he ultimately made the fateful decision to rush with them to the battle line.

At some point after midnight on the morning of Tuesday, February 27, the Highlanders positioned themselves in attack formation and marched toward the patriot camp. The Whigs, anticipating the arrival of the Tory force, left their tents erect and their campfires burning and moved to a strategic location across the bridge. Having found the patriot camp devoid of men, the Highlanders decided to cross Moore's Creek Bridge, the shortest path to the Whig troops. As the loyalists approached the bridge with trepidation, their scouts revealed that most of the planks had in fact been destroyed by the patriots. What remained were two large support logs, which had been greased with wax and soap by the Whigs. Not to be deterred, a company of Highlanders armed only with broadswords dashed across the bridge with a raging battle cry. Two companies of patriot militia had already set up their cannons to cover the bridge. The Highland Scots were ripped to shreds by a deadly fusillade as they ran across the beams of the bridge. Practically the entire company of Scots was shot to death, drowned, or wounded. The ten men who reportedly did make it across Moore's Creek were gunned down before they reached the patriot trenches. The murderous charge of the Highlanders would herald defeat at Moore's Creek and would quash any hopes for loyalists retaking North Carolina from the Whig committeemen.[10]

Back in Charles Town, the Provincial Congress reconvened on February 1 and began to consider recommendations made by the Continental Congress to form local constitutional governments. Conservatives fretted over the crucial step and argued that they had been "driven" into such measures and that their hands had been forced by the British ministry. Radicals such as Christopher Gadsden, who had just returned from Philadelphia bearing a freshly printed copy of Thomas Paine's *Common Sense*, were reportedly "wrapped up in the thought of separation & independence" and would "hear nothing in opposition." William Henry Drayton, acting in the capacity of president, seized the moment and declared to his fellow delegates that they had a choice to make: either sever ties with Britain or submit to "slavery." Drayton and Gadsden's calls for an absolute split from the mother country shocked most of the representatives, who still longed for "honorable" terms of "accommodation & Peace." As John Drayton put it, the sentiment "came like an explosion of thunder on the members of Congress." One statesman, in declaring his revulsion, stated that he would "ride post, by day and night to Philadelphia, in order to assist, in re-uniting Great Britain and America." Henry Laurens thought the notion of independence was "indecent," and John Rutledge scoffed at the idea as treasonous.[11]

With great trepidation, on Sunday, February 11, members of Congress proposed forming a special committee of eleven members to investigate the possibility of developing a new constitution. At five o'clock that evening, ballots were drawn, and the following men were elected: Charles Cotesworth Pinckney, John Rutledge, Charles Pinckney, Henry Laurens, Christopher Gadsden, Rawlins Lowndes, Arthur Middleton, Henry Middleton, Thomas Bee, Thomas Lynch Jr., and Thomas Heyward Jr. As historian Keith Krawczynski noted, to ensure that the delegates created a charter that was only temporary while the Anglo-American crisis raged on, "they stacked the panel with conservatives and moderates like Lowndes, Laurens, and Bee, and elected John Rutledge to chair it."[12] The only radicals on this new committee were Gadsden and Arthur Middleton. William Henry Drayton was conspicuously absent from the proceedings.

Little was said or done about the constitution until Tuesday, March 5, when the Provincial Congress learned about the battle over the rice ships in the Savannah. Later that day, a motion was made to prepare a form of government that would "effectually secure peace and good order in the colony." Henry Laurens and the conservative Whigs saw an opportunity to postpone what they believed was an unnatural evil. Forestalling the measure, the conservatives argued that a new and more representative body should be called before making the critical decision. Eventually, the radicals managed to convince their opponents that the Provincial Congress was indeed a "full and free representation." Despite this concession, however, conservative Whigs made a motion to delay consideration of the issue until May 1776, hoping that tensions with the Crown would by that time be ameliorated. After a lengthy debate, the measure was voted down, and the congressmen decided that they would start the process of forming a provisional government on Friday, March 8.

When the appointed time came, the Provincial Congress formed "a committee of the whole" to consider how to go about forming a constitution. The process was time-consuming and drawn out over the course of several days. Much of the debating that went on was over semantics. For example, members decided to use the term "president" in lieu of "governor," and "vice president" was substituted for "lieutenant governor." Abolishing the nomenclature of the "Provincial Congress," representatives decided to call the new body a "General Assembly." In addition to the changes, the statesmen replaced "King's Privy Council" with "Legislative Council." In terms of power, authority was vested in the General Assembly and the Legislative Council, which were to be elected every two years. Of course, all of these proposals were made with the understanding that this was to be a temporary constitution put in place "until an accommodation of the unhappy differences" could be reached with Britain. At its core, this was a conservative document that avoided change and kept power exactly where it was.[13]

While in the midst of deliberating over the new constitution in March 1776, South Carolina Whigs learned by way of an express from Savannah that Parliament had passed an act on Thursday, December 21, 1775, declaring all seizures of American property to be fully legal and that all the provinces were in a state of rebellion.[14] To make matters worse, patriots learned that they had a situation on their hands in Georgia that was reminiscent of the Sullivan's Island incident in December. With the British ships of war stationed off the mouth of the Savannah River, 200 to 300 slaves began to flock to Tybee Island (see map 4) in the hopes of obtaining their freedom. Among them were sixty-five bondsmen belonging to Arthur Middleton (a future signatory of the Declaration of Independence), who, as we saw above, was then sitting on a committee to form a provisional constitution for South Carolina.[15] Once again, the Crown represented a competing alternative to provincial authority, and once again, African-Americans responded with their feet. The blacks who sought refuge under the Union Flag had not been swayed by the Darien resolutions and refused to believe that Georgia Whigs would ever relinquish control over them as they had promised.

Unsurprisingly, the response of white patriots in Georgia was one of panic. Colonel Lachlan McIntosh, author of the Darien resolutions (who had clerked with Laurens and had spent a great deal of time in South Carolina), described the state of the province as "desperate" and in a letter to George Washington noted that "The Men of Warr at Tybee, tho' still giving out that they had no Hostile Intentions against this Colony, were encouraging our slaves to Desert to them, Pilfering our Sea Islands for Provision." President of the Georgia Council of Safety William Ewen wrote to members of the South Carolina Provincial Congress and warned them that British forces were stealing "a number of negroes," as well as livestock, from patriot plantations along the banks of the Savannah. The St. Andrew Parish Revolt was bad enough, but what would happen if 200 blacks suddenly fomented an insurrection with British assistance? Would the fledgling colony, still wavering in its commitment to the patriot cause, be brought to its

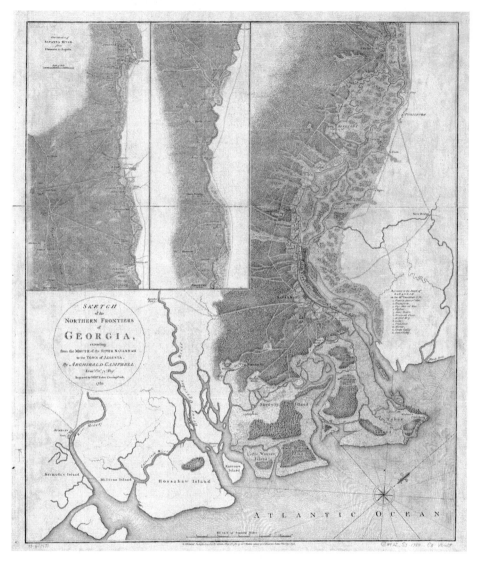

MAP 4. "Sketch of the northern frontiers of Georgia, extending from the mouth of the River Savannah to the town of Augusta, by Archibald Campbell. Engraved by Willm. Faden, 1780." This map shows Tybee Island, which today is one of Georgia's most popular vacation destinations. In the eighteenth century, it was home to a lazaretto like the pesthouse on Sullivan's Island outside Charles Town, where slaves and the infirm were quarantined before being allowed into their respective ports. In the wake of Dunmore's partial emancipation proclamation, both Tybee and Sullivan's Island became home to runaway slaves seeking British protection. *Courtesy Geography and Map Division, Library of Congress*

knees? Would patriot leaders in Georgia respond to "domestick" dangers in the same fashion as their South Carolina counterparts?[16]

Knowing full well that South Carolinians had experience in dealing with British attempts to use slaves as counterrevolutionaries, on Thursday, March 14, Stephen Bull, nephew of South Carolina's former lieutenant governor, wrote to Henry Laurens from Savannah and asked him to broach the subject of the Tybee Island runaways, stressing that he need only share the information with the members of the Council of Safety:

> This in my own hand. If the Congress is still setting [sic] no doubt my Letters will be read in Congress, if so I hope the Council will think as I do, that is *not* to have this last Paragraph read to so large a number of People, but to be known only to the Council, for no one does, at least ought not to know, anything of the following matter, but the Members of the Council of Safety of this Province and myself. The matter is this it is far better for the Public and the owners of the deserted Negroes on Tybee Island, who are on Tybee Island, to be shot if they cannot be taken, if the Public is obliged to pay for them; for if they are carried away, and converted into money, which is the Sinews of War, it will only Enable our enemy to fight us with our own money or property.[17]

Bull proceeded to inform South Carolina Whig leaders that he would rely on the time-proven strategem of using Native Americans to stamp out black insurgency; adding that all of the runaway blacks who could not be taken "had better be shot by the Creek Indians, as it perhaps may deter other Negroes from deserting, and will establish a hatred or Aversion between Indians and Negroes." Instead of using the Catawbas, Bull advocated using the Creeks, because they had been in the service of Georgia's patriot faction for some time. Just two days earlier, the colonel had reported that "One hundred Creek & Euchee Indians" were within the confines of Savannah, seventy of whom were ready to serve the province.

The plan to use the Creeks against the motley crew of Tories and blacks was quite controversial. Several members of the Georgia Council of Safety were reportedly "timid" when it came to the issue. The highly influential Benjamin Andrew of St. John parish in Sunbury was particularly hostile to the proposal. Fearing that the measure would fail to pass in the Georgia Council of Safety, Bull assured South Carolina patriots that he "had proper and certain Assurance that a good Leader and party of the Creek Indians" were "willing and desirous of going to take the runaway Negroes upon Tybee Island." The colonel concluded by stressing the necessity of keeping the matter "a profound Secret, lest the Negroes should move off, or they should ask for Arms, and so lay an

Ambuscade for the Indians."[18] Bull's message was received by Laurens two days later, on Saturday, March 16.

The statesman immediately sat down and wrote a letter to his son John, relating to him the current state of affairs. In the document, Laurens mentioned that His Majesty's ships had "taken upwards of 50 Negroes from Arthur Middleton's plantation." Fearful that Crown officials had enticed slaves away from his own agricultural estate in Georgia, known as Wright's Savannah, Laurens lamented, "What a picaroon inglorious War is the most puissant Nation in Europe engaged in. Men of War sent 1100 Leagues across the Atlantic to plunder plantations & British Troops to rob Hen Roosts. I am ashamed of them."[19]

That evening, Laurens also drafted his response to Stephen Bull. Writing diligently through the night, the patriot leader recalled how successful John Allston's "Indian Company" had been in dispersing the runaway slaves on Sullivan's Island in December and recommended that Georgia patriots now enlist the services of white men to lead the Creeks:

> Now for the grand we may say awful business contained in your
> Letter it is an awful business notwithstanding it has the sanction of
> Law to put fugitive & Rebellious Slaves to death, the prospect is
> horrible. We think the Council of Safety in Georgia ought to give that
> encouragement which is necessary to induce proper Persons to
> seize & if nothing else will do to destroy all those Rebellious Negroes
> upon Tybee Island or wherever they may be found, If Indians are the
> most proper hands let them be employed on this service but we
> would advise that some discreet white Men were incorporated with or
> joined to lead them.[20]

Feeling that the issue demanded urgent attention, Laurens immediately forwarded his letter to Samuel Grouber, a German express rider who worked for South Carolina's provincial authorities.

We have no record of when the letter reached Georgia, but Bull undoubtedly had it in less than a week and discussed the matter with the Georgia Council of Safety. On Saturday, March 23, a forty-six-year-old patriot named Archibald Bulloch began to formulate a plan of attack. Bulloch, who would later become the first governor of the state of Georgia, had served as delegate to the Second Continental Congress. He knew the black population of the Low Country well.[21] In September 1775, while at Philadelphia, the Whig leader, along with fellow delegate John Houstoun, confided to John Adams that if a British fleet appeared off the coast near Savannah, 20,000 blacks from Georgia and South Carolina would flock to the Red Duster within a fortnight. Now, Bulloch, taking the advice of Henry Laurens, made plans to use whites to lead the Creeks but would have them costumed in Native American dress with war paint on their faces.[22]

At one P.M. on Monday, March 25, the disguised Whig leader descended on Tybee Island with a detachment of seventy white soldiers (riflemen, light infantry, volunteers, and fusiliers), as well as thirty Creek mercenaries. The evidence surrounding Bulloch's raid is thin at best, but it appears that the first thing the war party did was torch three houses that may have been occupied by the maroons. Witnessing the flames rising from the buildings, the captain of the HMS *Hinchinbrook* fired two warning shots. As the raid continued, two British marines were killed, as well as "one Tory who would not surrender." According to one report, the men aboard an armed sloop and the crew members of the *Cherokee* "fire[d] Ball and Grape Shot during the whole Time of the Attack." The American account emphasized the "Zeal and Courage" that the patriots displayed during the raid. Two British accounts, on the other hand, condemned the Whigs for committing brutal atrocities. According to East Florida's governor, Patrick Tonyn, the patriots showed "signs of the most savage barbarity" that "exceeded the ferocity of the Indians." Reportedly, the two marines, just before or just after they died, were scalped by the patriots and had their legs broken "with a hatchet." Captain Thornbrough of the *Tamar* claimed that he witnessed a Tory shipwright named Nichols getting "shot through the head." Apparently, there were no casualties on the Whig side except for a Creek "Indian [that] was killed in a drunken scuffle with one of the rebels." According to Major General William Howe, "The Rebels, on the approach of [British] Troops in Boats, quitted the Spot."[23]

Just how many blacks were present at the time of the assault is a matter for conjecture.[24] Few are aware that Tybee Island was an important location, like Sullivan's Island (off Charles Town), which housed a lazaretto where slaves (and the sick) where quarantined before being brought to port. We know from the documents that 200 or 300 slaves did indeed flock to the royal governor James Wright and tell him that "they were come for the King." Whether or not those maroons were on the sea island at the time of the raid remains a mystery. Those runaway slaves who did make the journey to Tybee may have intended to align themselves with slaves hiding out at the lazaretto or to link up with a sizable force of British marines.[25] Perhaps the slaves had caught wind of the Whig attack, as Bull feared they might, and simply fled into the surrounding wetlands at the mouth of the Savannah.

Although the source material concerning this episode is frustratingly silent about the extent and the identity of the victims, one thing can be declared with absolute certainty: an exodus of Afro-Georgians did occur against extraordinary odds and despite the dubious promises of McIntosh's resolutions. This departure had the effect of further alienating those whites who were wavering in their loyalties, as well as those who already professed a love of liberty, pushing them both one step closer to independence.

Not surprisingly, the news from Georgia of the deserting blacks at Tybee Island and of the late act of Parliament silenced the moderates in South Carolina who still longed for reconciliation with Britain. Their attempts to postpone drafting a blueprint for the new government could no longer persist. The same week that Bulloch's men and the Creeks mounted their assault on Tybee Island, Whig leader John Rutledge drafted a preamble to South Carolina's new constitution. In terms that foreshadowed those used by Thomas Jefferson several months later in the Declaration of Independence, Rutledge enumerated a whole host of grievances against the administration, stretching back to the mid-1760s.[26] He took aim at "the Governors and others bearing the royal commission in the colonies" for having "excited domestic insurrections—proclaiming freedom to servants and slaves." The preamble specifically faulted the British for enticing and stealing bondsmen as well as arming them against their masters. With no small measure of irony, the statesman echoed Drayton's declaration that the British had reduced American colonists "from the rank of freemen to a state of the most abject slavery." Besides instigating rebellions among blacks, Rutledge contended that the Crown had "encouraged the Indian nations to war against the colonies" and had "dispensed with the law of the land." Referring to Lord Campbell, Josiah Martin, Lord Dunmore, and Sir James Wright, the document laid blame on the Southern royal governors for loosening the bonds of government and creating "anarchy and confusion in the colonies." Furthermore, Rutledge argued that it was necessary to form a constitution on account of the fact that William Campbell had vacated the colony. In a veiled allusion to the Sullivan's Island episode, the author asserted that the governor had "used his utmost efforts to destroy the lives, liberties, and properties of the good people" of South Carolina, instead of protecting them in accordance with the duties of his station.[27]

The remainder of the carefully drafted constitution was designed so that when the British reestablished viable direction over the province, things could return to the status quo. In keeping with this wait-and-see philosophy, the coastal elite retained control over the day-to-day workings of government. Although the Low Country only contained less than half of the white population, the area was allotted 126 delegates, as opposed to the backcountry, which only received 76. Surprisingly, white males, as Walter B. Edgar notes, enjoyed almost universal suffrage stretching back to the Election Act of 1721. The 1776 Provisional Constitution (unlike the S.C. Constitution of 1778) stipulated that voters had to be free white males and professing Christians. Moreover, they had to possess a headright of 50 acres or pay 20 schillings in taxes. South Carolina residency (for at least a year) was also mandatory. As one might suspect, however, officeholders had to meet much more stringent wealth and property requirements.[28]

As Henry Laurens put it, "in the twinkling of an eye," South Carolina's Provincial Congress metamorphosed into a new General Assembly. The first thing that this body did was to elect officers for the new government. In keeping with the desire of most elite delegates not to go too far, conservative-leaning patriots were chosen to fill most of the leadership positions. Members elected John Rutledge president and picked Henry Laurens to be vice president. Only moderates were selected to the Legislative Council. Based on his previous experience, Drayton was chosen to fill the post of chief justice, despite his open advocacy for independence.

The newly appointed officers were sworn in during a formal ceremony at the State House on Thursday, March 28. When the proceedings ended, Rutledge and Laurens led the other members of the General Assembly in a "solemn procession" through the heart of the city. Flanked by provincial troops, the delegates paraded down Broad Street and headed east toward the Cooper River. As the cavalcade marched on, the crowd of bystanders experienced conflicting emotions. According to one eyewitness, a number of people "gazed at them with a kind of rapture." Others reportedly shed "tears of joy." When the members of the new government reached the Exchange, the sheriff of Charles Town, Thomas Grimball, read the names of the officers aloud. Hundreds began to cheer as cannon from nearby battleships fired thirteen shots, one for each of the American colonies. We have no way of knowing what black Charlestonians thought of the sounds and spectacle of this elaborate ceremony, but for those who pinned their hopes on the idea of British liberation, the moment was probably fraught with a profound sense of loss. The promise of liberty so eagerly discussed in dram shops, on the wharves, and along the shores of Sullivan's Island appeared to be fading now. The masters had made sure that they were still in charge.[29]

As the colony adjusted to life under the new government, white South Carolinians enjoyed a period of calm that they had not experienced for some time. To perpetuate this newfound tranquility, on Thursday, April 11, the General Assembly passed a draconian statute designed "to Prevent Sedition, and Punish Insurgents and Disturbers of the Public Peace." The act criminalized dissent, making it a felony to speak out against the newly formed patriot government. In addition, the bill made it a capital offense to supply British forces with provisions or to correspond with enemy. The language used in part four of the law was especially revealing. In this section, Whig officials displayed their fear of racial disruption and turbulence by making it a capital offense to compel any whites, Indians, mulattos, or free blacks to flee their habitations.

Anyone found guilty of encouraging slaves to desert their masters or mistresses would suffer the death penalty "without the benefit of clergy." There was a proviso, however. Patriot legislators stipulated that nothing in the act precluded them from arming black slaves for the defense of the colony.[30] This would become the subject of much controversy in the years to come.

As patriots began to grapple with the taboo notion of putting guns in the hands of chattel slaves, on the same day, John Rutledge took the opportunity to fulminate against England's efforts to involve Native and African-Americans in the revolutionary crisis: "The endeavours, by deceit and bribery, to engage barbarous nations, to embrue their hands in the innocent blood of women and children; and attempts, by fair but false promises, to make ignorant domestics, subservient, to the most wicked purposes; are acts at which, humanity must revolt."[31] In words that were probably more applicable to black and Native Americans than they were to white patriots, Rutledge declared, "seeing, that there is no alternative, but, absolute unconditional submission, and the most abject slavery—or, a defence becoming men, born to freedom—he will not hesitate about the choice...superior force...can never eradicate from the breasts of freemen, those principles which are engrafted in their very nature."[32]

Less than two weeks later, on Tuesday, April 23, William Henry Drayton gave a fiery speech to the grand jury in which he likened the Anglo-American struggle to the Glorious Revolution of 1688. At one point in his diatribe, the Whig leader elaborated on the sentiments expressed by Rutledge, claiming that together, General Gage, the royal governors, and John Stuart had "made every attempt to *instigate the Savage Nations to War upon the Southern Colonies*, indiscriminately to massacre man, woman and child." No doubt thinking of Dunmore's proclamation, as well as the exoduses of slaves to Sullivan's and Tybee Islands, Drayton argued that "the Governors in general have demonstrated, that truth is not in them; they have inveigled Negroes from, and have armed them against their masters." Pushing the boundaries of acceptable political discourse, the patriot politician concluded that "reconcilement never can exist between Great Britain and America" as long as the latter continued to remain in subjection to the former. Casting events in a religious light, the politician boldly declared, "The Almighty created America to be independent of Britain," and proceeded to warn fellow patriots to "beware of the impiety of being backward to act as instruments in the Almighty Hand." If Drayton's assertions failed to convince wavering whites of the necessity of independence, the sight of a British armada in the waters off Charles Town soon would.[33]

In early 1776, at British headquarters in Boston, General William Howe, commander of the Crown's forces in America since October 1775, ordered his second in command, General Henry Clinton, to mount a campaign against the Southern colonies. Clearing Boston Harbor in January, Clinton sailed south with a small fleet. Meanwhile, a much larger force, under Admiral Peter Parker, departed from Cork, Ireland, with orders to rendezvous with Clinton's men off the coast of North Carolina. Encouraged by optimistic reports from the Southern royal governors, Britain hoped to establish a base of operations in the South from which to support the backcountry Tories who were supposedly jumping at the chance to overthrow patriot authorities.

Clinton sailed down the Atlantic seaboard (after stopping in New York), thinking that the loyalists were ready to fight in North Carolina. Bad news awaited him when he arrived at Cape Fear in early March, however. Learning that the Highland chieftains had been dealt a decisive blow by the Whigs at the Battle of Moore's Creek Bridge, the commander waited impatiently for Parker's fleet to arrive. On Sunday, March 10, Lord William Campbell and Captain Tobias Furneaux arrived at Cape Fear from Savannah on the HMS *Syren*. Clinton, Campbell, and Governor Martin waited patiently for the promised fleet to arrive from Ireland. After a delay of two months, Admiral Parker's expedition finally showed up on Friday, May 3.[34]

Upon the arrival of the other fleet at Cape Fear, Parker and Clinton conferred and decided that they would alter plans and advance to Charles Town. Before doing so, however, they sent two junior officers on a reconnaissance mission. When the men returned in late May, they informed their commanders that the harbor of the Carolina capital was guarded by an unfinished fortification that was being erected at the southern tip of Sullivan's Island.

For reasons that are unclear, Parker and Clinton decided to focus their assault on Sullivan's Island itself, rather than toward the actual city of Charles Town.[35] The island site, which had been stormed by patriots hunting black refugees in the winter of 1775, was now about to be attacked from sea by the British. On Friday, May 31, Rutledge learned by way of an express that a Royal Navy squadron was spotted off Dewees's Island twenty miles north of Charles Town Harbor in Christ Church parish. The next day, Parker, along with fifty sailing vessels, cast anchor a few miles north of the bar. Rutledge immediately sent out a call for the militia, and once again alarms reverberated through the city.[36] As word spread, no one knew what to expect. Was this the dreaded attack that the white patriots had feared since the spring of 1775? Was this the deliverance that black Charlestonians had been praying for? Had the war finally come "to help the poor Negroes"? We have no way of knowing for sure, but the sound of the alarms may have brought chills of anticipation to nearly 6,000 men, women, and children who made up the town's enslaved inhabitants.

The news that a British fleet was approaching threw white Charles Town into a state of disarray. Men reportedly began "running about looking for horses, carriages, and boats to send their family into the country." The women and children who had remained in the city began to evacuate and were sent up toward Goose Creek in wagons. As hundreds began their flight out of the city, they collided with militia making their way into the capital. Printers dismantled their presses and carried them to places of safety where they could continue to generate their broadsides and gazettes. William Moultrie ordered sentinels to be stationed at all exit points to prevent the desertion of provincial troops. White men throughout the port began to assemble and prepare earthworks, wielding pick axes, spades, and whatever else they could find. In addition to these measures, all remaining Crown officials were rounded up and put under lockdown.[37]

There was not enough time, though, for patriots to deal with their Achilles' heel: the black population. The last thing the white revolutionaries wanted was for the slaves to set fire to the town or foment an insurrection on the approach of the Royal Navy. The original Whig plan of defense drawn up in mid-October 1775 therefore called for the removal of all African-Americans from the Low Country coastline. The logistics of this plan proved to be too difficult. Instead, blacks were put to work. In the stifling heat of June, African-Americans sweated side-by-side with whites, building redoubts and erecting fortifications. If they could occupy slaves with hard labor, the Whigs believed, they just might be able to prevent an uprising.

During the next forty-eight hours, Charlestonians watched with awe as the armada began to assemble off the bar. From Fort Johnson, Captain Thomas Pinckney witnessed "more than 40 vessels of all sorts, sloops, schooners, etc." Transport vessels carrying more than 3,000 British troops were flanked by a plethora of supply ships and men-of-war. Two large frigates, the *Experiment* and the *Bristol* (with Lord Campbell onboard), were armed with fifty guns; the *Soleby*, the *Actaeon*, the *D'Active*, and the *Syren* (which had been in Charles Town Harbor in mid-January) carried twenty-eight guns each, while the frigate *Friendship* was equipped with twenty-six, and the *Sphynx* had twenty. These ships were supported by a bomb ketch, the *Thunder*, designed to hurl mortars.

With such a force under their command, Parker and Clinton reportedly boasted that they would have "Breakfast at Sullivan's Island, dine at Fort Johnson & sup in Charles Town." But the notoriously treacherous bar made things more difficult than they imagined. The British took five days sounding the obstacle and marking the channel with buoys.[38] "Delays of various kinds" held up the decision-making process, as Clinton would later recall, giving the patriots on land much-needed time to build their defenses.[39] Unfortunately for the redcoats, their arrival also coincided with the end of fair weather conditions and high spring tides that would have allowed easy access into the harbor. Fog, storms, and unfavorable winds began to hinder the operations of the invading fleet. To make matters worse, knowledgeable British navigators were in shorter supply than Commodore Parker realized. As a result of a bureaucratic oversight, officials within the British navy hierarchy neglected to provide Parker with a single officer familiar with Charles Town Harbor. The commodore also made a grave mistake when he failed to draw on the skills of John Fergusson and the crew of the *Cherokee*, who had firsthand knowledge of the waterway and were, at that time, only a few hours south in the waters off Savannah. As South Carolina historian Terry Lipscomb noted, "Ultimately, these omissions left the execution of the commodore's battle plan dependent upon the reliability of a handful of black pilots, who either had been seized from coastal shipping or had been spirited out of Charlestown through the ingenuity of Lord William Campbell."[40]

Thomas Jeremiah had been dead for the past ten months, but there were clearly other black navigators ready to make the British invasion of Charles Town Harbor possible, despite patriot attempts to frighten them into passivity. The "crime" that Jeremiah had been hanged and burned for—an alleged willingness to pilot the Royal Navy across the bar—was now about to be committed by an African-American named Sampson. Almost nothing is known about this man. Although his origins are obscure, he was most likely from Charles Town and well acquainted with Jeremiah and Scipio Handley. Perhaps he was one of the 500 Afro-Carolinians who sought refuge at Sullivan's Island in the wake of Dunmore's proclamation. If so, he would have been familiar with his shipmate aboard the *Bristol*, Lord Campbell, and probably declared his own independence at some point during the winter of 1775. Despite the murky details surrounding his decision to align himself with the Crown, it is quite apparent that he was given special treatment by the redcoats and was, according to several reports, "exceedingly caressed" by Commodore Parker. Despite Sampson's ostensibly privileged position among the Royal Navy crew members, he had a great deal of difficulty piloting the heavy fifty-gun flagship *Bristol* across the shoal. He finally traversed the obstacle on Monday, June 10, but inclement weather forced the ship to anchor for the next eighteen days.[41]

On the morning of Friday, June 28, white Charlestonians, who by now had gotten somewhat used to the presence of the British fleet offshore, were dismayed by the sight of warships in motion. At approximately ten-thirty, Lieutenant Thomas James of the bomb ketch *Thunder* fired a thirteen-inch mortar at Fort Sullivan—the opening shot of the battle. The patriots stationed behind the soft palmetto logs waited patiently for the *D'Active* and the *Bristol* to enter the range of their guns before they retaliated. Had the British assault gone according to plan, the men-of-war, guided by the South Carolina blacks, would have continued to move toward Fort Sullivan until the patriot gun platform came within firing range.[42] Yet, to the shock of Commodore Parker, his chief pilot, Sampson, abruptly brought the *Bristol* to a standstill, anchoring the vessel between 400 and 500 yards from the shore of Sullivan's Island. Despite numerous attempts on the part of the crew to threaten and coerce Sampson into moving the flagship closer to the fort, the pilot, perhaps fearing for his life, refused to take the ship any farther. Fed up with the navigator's obstinacy, Sir Peter Parker resigned himself to the situation, ordering the valuable pilot to secret himself below deck with the ship's physician out of harm's way.[43] At a loss about how to proceed and mired in the shallow waters of Rebellion Road, the commodore signaled the *Experiment* to sail ahead of the *Bristol*. When Captain Alexander Scott encountered a similar recalcitrance from his Afro-Carolinian pilot, the tide of the Battle of Fort Sullivan began to turn in favor of the patriots.[44] A glimmer of hope did appear for the British when the *Actaeon*, the *Sphinx*, and the *Syren* successfully attacked the patriot fort's western flank. However, those vessels, led by the black pilot aboard the *Sphinx*, reportedly took too wide a circuit, running aground on the part of the bar known as the Lower Middle Ground. When the crew was unable to extricate the *Actaeon* from the sand, the ship was promptly set on fire and abandoned.[45]

Fifty-six years after the battle, Jeremiah Harrold, a patriot war veteran, recounted a bizarre incident that may have added to the confusion of the British. The advance guard facing the redcoats at the northeast point of Sullivan's Island included a company of Catawba Indians, none of whom had ever come across a British bombshell. Whether out of curiosity or bravado, three or four scouts attempted to pick up an unexploded shell that had landed near them. The results were predictably disastrous. Thrown off by this novel method of warfare, the Catawbas, who had previously displayed great bravery under fire, could only think of escape. The Indians fled to "the bridge of boats," linking Sullivan's Island to Haddrell's Point. When a Whig guard refused to let them pass, the Catawbas threw down their weapons and swam across the cove to the shore of Christ Church parish.[46]

Further details and military particulars of the Battle of Fort Sullivan need not detain us here; suffice it to say that the British were defeated and defeated badly. The event that would come to be memorialized as "Carolina Day" was a critical triumph for the American cause. The spongy palmetto logs of the fort, despite the initial reservations of General Charles Lee, had literally absorbed most of the British cannonballs. The redcoats, on the other hand, had sustained substantial losses both in injuries and in lives. The estimate of casualties for the *Bristol* alone was seventy-one wounded and forty killed. There, according to

Terry Lipscomb, "patriot fire either killed or wounded every person on the quarterdeck, and on one occasion it cleared the deck of all except the commodore." At some point during the battle, a sliver of wood penetrated Parker's knee, rendering him immobile for some time after the battle. He was wounded by a second large splinter, which reportedly "whipt the Commodore very cleverly, tore all his breeches behind to pieces, and left his posteriors quite bare."[47]

Lord Campbell was aboard the *Bristol* throughout the encounter. Having a fair amount of naval experience, the royal governor felt that he could play an active role in retaking his port from the rebels. According to one report, he had been "very anxious for the attack; and proposed to take all the forts" with only the *Syren* and the *Solebay*.[48] Manning several guns from the *Bristol's* lower deck, Lord William was standing near a porthole when a shot penetrated the side of the vessel. The blast killed two sailors, damaged the hull, and sent a splinter into the left side of Campbell's torso. The wound was not thought to be serious, and he was able to remain at his post. However, two years later, when he died, the cause was said to be a "painful lingering consumption, which the physicians thought proceeded from the wounds he received at Sullivan's Island."[49]

In the wake of America's first decisive victory against the British, on Friday, June 28, John Bullman's former colleague, the Reverend Robert Cooper of St. Michael's, offered prayers for King George III from his pulpit. The preacher, who earlier demonstrated a great reluctance to sign the Whig Association, had been called on Saturday, June 1, to join the ranks of the patriot militia. When the minister failed to heed the summons, his captain, John Baddeley, proposed to him personally an oath of allegiance to the state of South Carolina. Cooper refused. Once again, members of the Anglican Church were up in arms. Sensing a Tory in their midst, patriot parishioners pressured the vestry to dismiss Cooper as they had Bullman. On Tuesday, July 2, after hearing the opinions of the churchgoers, the vestrymen brought the tenure of Robert Cooper to an abrupt end.[50]

As the British made their slow and clumsy retreat, they allegedly ravaged the South Carolina coastline, stealing at least fifty black slaves from outlying plantations. In early August, the last outbound ship to make it across the Charles Town Bar, the *Active*, landed at Thomas Shubrick's plantation on Bull's Island with a force of "40 White & 20 black men." After seizing livestock and provisions, the crew reportedly "augmented their black Guard by stealing Six more Negroes," slaves who no doubt were more than willing to risk their lot with the British.[51]

Conclusion

Simple Spectators?

Fueled by a powder shipment from Henry Stuart (and spurning advice both from British agents and accomodationists not to take action), on July 1, 1776, the other attack that patriots had dreaded became a reality, when Cherokee militants "poured down the frontiers of South Carolina." The assault was supposed to be coordinated with the British invasion of Charles Town Harbor. But just as the Highlanders in North Carolina had taken up arms too soon before the arrival of Parker's fleet, the young Cherokee had "as much erred," in the words of John Drayton, "by taking up the hatchet too late." A second attack came two weeks later, on the morning of Monday, July 15, when a mixed company of 88 Cherokee and 102 white backcountry loyalists, many of them painted and dressed as Indians, descended on a patriot fort near Rayborn Creek.[1] Although Dragging Canoe's warriors managed to strike fear into the hearts and minds of South Carolina Whigs, their timing could not have been worse. Having repelled the world's mightiest empire at Sullivan's Island, patriots from the four southernmost states were now free to mount a brutal retaliatory campaign.

Six thousand men from South Carolina, Georgia, Virginia, and North Carolina—already trained and mobilized for war—marched against the Cherokee late in the summer of 1776.[2] The year before, William Henry Drayton had given a friendly "talk" to the Indian tribe, promising them a coveted supply of powder and ammunition. But now, he offered the leaders of the patriot expedition "a word to the wise," urging them to devastate both the land and the people. "It is expected you make smooth work as you go," Drayton wrote; "that is, you cut up every Indian corn-field, and burn every Indian town—and that every Indian taken shall be the slave and property of the taker; that the nation be extirpated, and the lands become the property of the public."[3]

Colonel Andrew Williamson, commander of the South Carolina forces, faithfully complied with these orders. Less than a month later, he reported back to Drayton: "I have now burnt down every town, and destroyed all the corn, from the Cherokee line to the middle settlements."[4] Likewise, the North Carolina and Virginia militia also reportedly set fire to Indian villages and confiscated crops. Moreover, as historian Tom Hatley notes, 3,000 head of cattle and an unknown number of horses and mules that the patriots brought with them added "a variation on scorched earth" as they devoured the remaining forage.[5]

Ironically, at the very same moment that the Cherokee were fighting against South Carolina patriots in the backcountry, Thomas Jefferson was in Philadelphia putting the finishing touches on the Declaration of Independence. The final grievance that the Virginia Whig leader enumerated—the capstone— was that the king had "excited domestic insurrection amongst us" and had "endeavoured to bring on the inhabitants of our frontiers, the merciless Indian Savages, whose known rule of warfare, is an undistinguished destruction of all ages, sexes, and conditions."

On August 2, 1776, an express arrived in Charles Town from the Continental Congress, notifying the patriot leaders that on July 4, the united colonies had been declared free and independent states. The account was reportedly received with "the greatest joy." Three days later, on the afternoon of Monday, August 5, an official in Charles Town read out the Declaration of Independence publicly. At around one o'clock, the document was read before South Carolina's leading civil and military officials. A grand procession was made down Broad Street to the steps of the Exchange. The crowd reportedly cheered, as cannons pounded out salutes along the Cooper River. Then, in a symbolic gesture, a multitude of people gathered around the Liberty Tree—a gigantic oak that grew just beyond Christopher Gadsden's property. The tree had been imbued with deep signifi- cance ever since the autumn of 1766, when patriot partisans had assembled to listen to a forceful Gadsden rail against the Stamp Act. Now, almost ten years later, Major Barnard Elliott captivated the crowd as he proclaimed the new nation's separation from the mother country.[6]

Despite all of the huzzahs and cheers, not everyone was elated. In what may be Henry Laurens's most famous letter, the merchant-planter told his son John that the announcement of the Declaration of Independence made him shed tears of sorrow. Even at this relatively late stage in the Anglo-American crisis, the Whig leader continued to yearn for reconciliation with Britain. "At this moment,"

Laurens lamented, "my heart is full of the lively sensations of a dutiful Son, thrust by the hand of violence out of a Father's House into the wide World."[7]

As far as Laurens was concerned, it was the British who had forced patriots such as himself into severing ties with the Crown. Along with many others, he believed they had done this most recently in three distinct ways. First, they had attempted to incite black slaves against their Whig masters. Second, they had actively instigated the July attacks by the Cherokee. And finally, they had stirred up a "dangerous Insurrection" among "common" backcountry Tories. With respect to the first charge, Laurens placed the blame for the slave trade on Whitehall itself. Distancing himself from the business that had made him one of the wealthiest men in America, the Whig leader declared, "I abhor slavery." According to Laurens, England had been involved in a "complicated wicked-ness." Not only had the nation profited immensely from the Atlantic slave trade, but it was now using enslaved blacks to help suppress the rebellion of their white masters. "These Negroes were first enslaved by the English," Laurens insisted, and now the British government chose to "employ their Men of War to steal those Negroes from the Americans to whom they had sold them." The merchant-planter claimed that the whole notion of the British granting freedom to slaves was a farce. Citing no evidence, he asserted that the Crown had merely pretended "to set the poor wretches free" but instead had them "basely" trepanned and sold "into ten fold worse Slavery in the West Indies." With no small measure of irony, the merchant claimed that these unfortunate slaves, having been duped by the British government, would "become the property of English Men again & of some who sit in Parliament." Laurens concluded: "O England, how changed! how fallen!"

As for the second charge, the patriot leader claimed that the Cherokee had acted duplicitously and had gotten involved in a conflict that they had promised to avoid. According to Laurens, the tribe had "amused" the South Carolinians "by the most flattering Talks, full of assurances of friendship & promises" to follow patriot advice, "which had always been that they should observe a strict neutrality." Instead of remaining passive, the "Savage Indians" had aligned themselves with the Crown "& other Ministerial Agents," and "suddenly, with-out any pretence to Provocation those treacherous Devils in various parties headed by White Men & pushed on by those who are in employment for this cruel purpose, made an Inroad upon our settlements burned several Houses & Murdered about sixty Persons chiefly Women & Children." Referring to Andrew Williamson's retaliatory campaign, Laurens hoped that success against the Cherokee would ensure that "the Creeks & other Indians may continue to be *simple Spectators of our contest with British ships & soldiers* [emphasis mine]."

If Williamson should fail, the Whig leader feared, white Carolinians "would be attacked on all sides & greatly distressed."

From the contents of the Laurens letter, it is clear that the white back-country colonists remained deeply divided. Despite the objections made by John Stuart and Alexander Cameron, a number of loyalists had participated in (and may have instigated) the Cherokee attacks. The notion that the British agents had involved Indians in the Anglo-American conflict prompted a number of Tories to renounce their ties to the Crown. Most notable among them was Colonel Robert Cunningham, whose brother Patrick had stolen the patriot shipment of gunpowder to the Cherokee in early November 1775. According to Laurens, Cunningham "would not at first believe that the British Administration were so wicked as to Instigate the Savages to War against us. As soon therefore as he was convinced of the truth his Conscience freed him from old obligations & he most heartily desired to take the Oath of fidelity to the United Colonies." Although the Whig leader claimed that a number of Tories had joined Cunningham in renouncing their allegiance to Britain, he was forced to concede that not all of the loyalists on the frontier were eager to join the ranks of the patriot party. A number of "Common fellows," who had been captured by South Carolina provincial authorities, had broken their paroles (as Georgia Governor James Wright had done on February 11, 1776) and were "now among the Indians."

Epilogue

For white contemporaries both in and out of South Carolina, the Thomas Jeremiah affair seems to have been a major item of news.[1] Evidence suggests that there were heated polemics for and against Jeremiah's innocence on both sides of the Atlantic.[2] Royal Governor Thomas Hutchinson of Massachusetts, for instance, was well aware of Jeremiah's trials and of the Negro Act itself and described them as overt examples of patriot tyranny.[3] First Lord of Admiralty John Montague, fourth Earl of Sandwich, gave a speech in the British Parliament specifically mentioning Jeremiah, condemning the guilty verdict and subsequent execution by Whigs as acts of "cruelty and baseness."[4] In contrast, white patriots in South Carolina, such as Henry Laurens, saw the case of Jeremiah as a prime example of what could—and should—happen to a black upstart who had overstepped his bounds, exceeded his station, and conspired against provincial authority. In an effort to justify the execution, Laurens wrote that Jeremiah "was a forward fellow, puffed up by prosperity, ruined by Luxury & debauchery & grown to amazing pitch of vanity & ambition." There was no doubt, as far as he was concerned, that "Jerry" was "withal a very Silly Coxcomb," guilty of "a design & attempt to encourage our Negroes to Rebellion & joining the King's Troops if any had been Sent here."[5]

Given the unsettled times, Whigs in South Carolina were also intensely anxious, however, about the various ways in which the affair would be received by contemporaries elsewhere, so much so that on Sunday, August 20, 1775, the day after Campbell first wrote to Dartmouth about the affair, Henry Laurens sent to his son John, then in London, a detailed account of the trial, in order to "contradict false reports" and lies, "which may be, among others, propagated to the prejudice of the poor Carolinians." Suspecting that the affair would some-how be used to blacken the patriot cause, Laurens wrote: "the trial was con-ducted not only with great deliberation but with an uncommon degree of delay—it was above three Weeks on the Carpet the Governor did not act offi-cially, in this case, 'tis not his Province to sign the Death Warrant, although he has the Power of Pardoning—there is a mystery in this business which I can-not yet unravel—because I will not indulge uncharitable suspicions—but I will be upon my guard."[6]

Two days later, Peter Timothy wrote to William Henry Drayton (then in the backcountry): "The fishing Season is over here—The Hurricane Season being come in, we have thought it necessary that all the Tories boats should be laid up—Jerry was hanged last Friday—more force was exerted for his being saved than there would be for you or [me]."[7]

In early October 1775, John Laurens would report back to his father that the "story of the Negro man Jerry" was indeed a frequent topic of discussion, claim-ing that the widely known English version of the affair would have a highly detrimental effect on attitudes toward the "character of our countrymen for justice and humanity."[8] The prevailing loyalist perspective to which young Laurens alluded undoubtedly derived from the observations of Lord Campbell, who had sent word to England on August 19 and again on August 31 that Jeremiah's trial was a travesty of justice—the judicial murder of an innocent man, who, as an industrious pillar of the seaport community, had become the victim of "numberless arts" and "notorious falsehoods propagated" by provin-cial elites to whip up the frenzy of the mob.[9]

In order to distance themselves from the charge of "instigating insurrec-tion," loyalists such as Milligen and Campbell would argue that the evidence given by blacks against Jeremiah was false and only given "to save themselves from a whipping." In their own backhanded way, Tory officials defended the accused blacks by asserting their ignorance:

> the constant exercising of the Militia, and other martial appearances,
> joined to their imprudent conversations [among Whigs] at their
> tables before their domestics, could not escape the notice of those
> unhappy wretches, and naturally led them to converse among
> themselves on the reasons for it. One of these conversations, was, it
> is said, overheard, and several of those poor ignorant creatures taken
> up, who terrified at the recollection of former cruelties were easily
> induced to accuse themselves, and others to escape punishment.[10]

In his letter to Lord Dartmouth, the royal governor argued that Jeremiah's keen sensibility, prodigious income, and possession of slaves were concrete proof that the man could not have been an insurrectionary: "It was needless to urge the improbability of a fellow in affluent circumstances, who was universally acknowledged to be sensible and sagacious, possessed of Slaves of his own, entering into so wild a scheme as instigate an insurrection without support, without encouragement (for happily not a shadow of evidence appeared that any white man was concerned)."[11]

Perhaps Campbell was correct. Maybe Jeremiah did have too much of a stake in the existing slave system to be an insurrectionary. On the other hand, the boatman must have been acutely aware of the limitations and boundaries placed on him inherent in the existing power structure. As a wealthy and well-connected black man who hovered for years around the insular circle of the white community, Jerry may have had a greater stake in inciting a slave revolt than anyone else. The full nature of Thomas Jeremiah's insurrectionary status remains hard to determine but begs a number of questions: Was this black harbor pilot in fact an innocent victim—a Christian who the white rebels put to death in order to prevent their own insubordination from being punished by the Crown? Did Jeremiah really intend to foment a counterrevolutionary racial uprising against Whig authority? Was this merely yet another example of that great colonial American paradox—of liberties granted to some and freedoms denied to others? Or is the story more complicated?

Should the name Thomas Jeremiah deserve to be mentioned in that pantheon of African American freedom fighters along with Gabriel Prosser, Denmark Vesey, and Nat Turner? Or should posterity view Jerry as a counterpoint to Crispus Attucks—a martyr who has eluded American memory if only because of his apparent willingness to support the side that ultimately lost? How will subsequent ages look back on the curious ordeal of Thomas Jeremiah? Will this "disagreeable subject" continue to be brushed under the rug and ignored, or will the tale and its context become ingrained into the fabric of that grand tapestry which binds America's narrative history together?

Having pondered the above queries for close to a decade, I am aware that we must keep in mind that the individual actors described in this study lived in an age that we can never fully grasp. Try as we might to write objectively drawing on bits of primary sources, snippets of information, and judicious use of pertinent quotes, historians can never fully do justice to the stories and subjects they think and write about. The sheer nature of the discipline, not to mention the range and complexity of human emotion and experience simply preclude it. What may appear odd, aberrant, or unsavory to this generation was often taken as a given during the late eighteenth century. The men who took the colony of South Carolina into independence from Great Britain experienced a myriad of constitutional, racial, economic, and political challenges that we can only vaguely begin to sketch out, let alone fully understand. That does not by any means excuse the some of the more horrific acts of cruelty that mar these pages. Atrocities, as the latter part of the war would demonstrate, would be carried out by all sides as the war languished on.[12] It is difficult to say what decisions we moderns would have made had we lived in a period of such incredible turmoil and duress.

It is now nearly ten years since I first began this project. As I put the final touches on this story, even today, I don't believe anyone living can state with absolute certainty whether Thomas Jeremiah plotted in the summer of 1775 to turn his world upside down and fan the flames of a British instigated insurrection in South Carolina. But it would be unwise to discount that possibility entirely. Perhaps our protagonist did hope to exploit the rift between the colonists and the Crown in order to liberate his brothers and sisters ensnared in hereditary bondage. As far as this author is concerned, such questions can, and will, be dealt with only by the highest authority in the hereafter. The Almighty God has reserved judgment for himself. According to his appointed time, his right hand will mete out perfect justice.

Appendix A

Documents Relating to the Trials and Execution of Thomas Jeremiah

A. Governor Lord William Campbell to Earl of Dartmouth, August 19, 1775 [excerpt]

Source: CO 5/396/20X4–207d, NA; CO 5/410/200–207, NAUK

We are now in such a situation I cannot attempt to send duplicates of my last letters, as I must be under the necessity of letting this Mail take its chance in a defenseless Packet Boat, for I cannot in our present State send the poor solitary, worm eaten Sloop we have got here, out of the Harbour, as I may now expect the next packet every day, & I am still in hopes of hearing from General Gage, and the Admiral soon. Your Lordship will I am afraid imagine I dwell too much, & too warmly on the wretched state we are left in here, by my zeal for the King's Service my thorough conviction of the ill consequences that has attended the total neglect of this Province, as well as Georgia, & N. Carolina, will not suffer me to remain silent. Since my arrival here, I have seen Georgia a Province at present, of the last consequence to the W. India Islands, warp'd from its duty by a very insignificant internal faction, aided by the people in this Province. The friends of Government here have been so sunk, so abandon'd to despair, for some time, that it is hardly possible to make them believe the British Nation is determined to assert their just rights over the Colonies, & it is to very little purpose I mention the great force to the Northward, when it is not in my power to produce a single line from either of the Commanders in that part of America, to enable me to contradict the numberless falsehoods which are everyday propagated, & which does more mischief than I can express. This is a very disagreeable subject for me to dwell on, but my Duty requires I should represent the true state of the Province, and of my unfortunate Vicinage of N. Carolina, & Georgia, which is equally neglected, equally abandon'd. Your Lordship will I am sure excuse my warmth when I acquaint you, that yesterday under the color of Law, they hanged & burned, an unfortunate wretch, a Free Negroe of considerable property, one of the most valuable & useful men in his way in the Province, on suspicion of instigating an Insurrection, for which I am convinced there was not the least ground. I could not save him My Lord! the very reflection Harrows my Soul! I have only the comfort to think I left no means untried to preserve him. They have now dipt their hands in Blood, God Almighty knows where it will end, but I am determined to remain till the last extremity in hopes to promote the King's Service, 'tho my familys being here adds not a little to my distress. Another act of Barbarity, tho happily not of so tragical a Nature was committed a few days ago, on a poor man the Gunner of Fort Johnson, who for expressing his loyalty was tarr'd, & feather'd 10 or 12 times, in different parts of the Town, & otherwise treated with great cruelty, stopping him at the doors of those Crown Officers who were most obnoxious; & the Mob so grossly insulted Mr. Milligen in particular who is Surgeon to the Forts, & Garrisons in this Province, that he was under a necessity of taking refuge on board the King's Ship till the Packet Boat sails. I intend committing this Packet to the care of Mr. Milligen who I hope will have the honor of delivering it to Your Lordship. I beg leave to introduce him as a most honorable and worthy man, who has lived many years in this Province beloved, and respected by all ranks till his Zeal for the King's service in these happy times, made him obnoxious to the Mob. This Gentleman is perfectly acquainted with the state of the Province, & I can assure your Lordship you may put your entire confidence in his Honor and Veracity. I enclose with this a Letter I rec[eive]d from Colonel Fletchal with my answer: sorry I am to find myself unable to protect, or assist the King's Loyal Subjects here, it is a cruel mortification. I also send my answer to an Address from a society of Quakers, in the back part of the Country; they consist of about 800 family's, & are warmly attached to Government. Your Lordship will likewise receive a Copy of an Oath tender'd to all those who refused to sign the Association, my own private Secretary not excepted, & a message I sent to the Assembly some days ago, with their answer, all which will plainly convince Your Lordship on what ticklish ground we stand here. The Armed Vessel that was fitted out from this Port has seized a quantity of powder, part of it the property of his Majesty on board a Ship lying off Augustine Bar in E. Florida, & carried it to Beaufort in this Province. Last Sunday 30 of the Militia of this Town were sent to convey it here, & I am told that by one means or other, they have amass'd great quantities of warlike stores, ammunition particularly, which they can easily do, as there is no force by Sea, or Land to prevent them, & they allow Rice to be exported on no other terms, but paying in Arms, & Ammunition. The new raised Troops which are quarter'd in the Barracks may be near 800 consisting if Vagabonds & Thieves of all Countries, & the Charles Town Militia may be pretty near the same number. The Regiment of Horse was to be raised in the back Country; but I am told the levies there have been much check'd by Fletchal, Robinson, & one Cunningham, mention'd by Coll. Fletchal in his letter, who is a very active man, & remarkably spirited. Mr. Milligen will give your Lordship a very particular account of these matters that have fallen within his knowledge, as he is sensible and intelligent. As the fate of the Crown Officers is not determined by the Comm[itte]e, if Mr. Innes is forced from me, which I will not endeavor by all means to prevent, he has offer'd at any risk to endeavor an escape into the back Country, join Col[onel] Fletchal & endeavor to maintain his ground at Fort Charlotte, in concert with Mr. Cameron the Dep[ut]y Superintendent, but I will not now think of that Scheme.

I have the Honor to be with the most perfect Regard,

My Lord
Your Lordship's most Obliged
& most Obed[ien]t H[um]ble Serv[an]t
William Campbell

N.B.: I shall encourage the King's faithful Subjects as much as in my power I can do no more. Some expense maybe incurr'd by my Orders to Col. Fletchal, I have no power to do it, but I cannot hesitate at such a juncture.

B. Governor Lord William Campbell to Earl of Dartmouth, August 31, 1775

Source: CO 5/396/225RH start to 230LH end, NAUK

My Lord,

In my letter No. 5. I just mention'd the dreadful Trajedy acted here on Friday the 18th of this month. I must now be more particular in the account of this matter, and of the unhappy man who was the sufferer, as it will lead me to an investigation of some part of the accursed politicks of this Country.

I need not acquaint your Lordship that number less arts have been used, and that the most notorious falsehoods propagated, to work up the people in every part of America to that pitch of madness and fury, to which they are arrived. The Leaders of the Faction in this Province have not come short of their Brethren to the Northward in this most diabolical system, and I think have improved upon them in some respects by the matchless cruelty they have exercised in the prosecution of their infamous plan. In the first place they have long taken uncommon pains to impress the minds of the People with the worst opinion of His Majesty's Ministers. They represented them as capable of adopting the most ruinous measures, and that torrent of abuse which was poured out at home in flagitious publications, without any effect, was carefully retailed here, and poison'd the minds of great numbers, as no antidotes could be administered from the Press, none of the printers daring to insert anything in their Papers that was not perfectly agreeable to the Faction. The people thus prepared, during the settling of the Provincial Congress, as very little before my arrival here, a letter is produced from a Mr. Lee in London to a leading Man in this place in which he boldly asserts the Ministry had in agitation not only to bring down the Indians on the Inhabitants of this Province, but also to instigate, and encourage an insurrection amongst the Slaves. It was also reported, and universally believed, that to effect this plan 14[,]000 Stand of Arms were actually on board the Scorpion, the Sloop of War I came out in. Words, I am told, cannot express the flame this occasion'd amongst all ranks and degrees, the cruelty and savage barbarity of the scheme was the conversation of all Companies, and no one dared venture to contradict intelligence conveyed from such respectable authority. But it was necessary to go further, they must endeavor to establish the fact to answer the purposes they proposed by this most infernal falsehood. They had about this time heard that Mr. Stuart, the King's Superintendant for the Southern District, had received letters from General Gage, and the[y] scrupled not to say they contained directions to put the Indians in motion. Mr. Stuart was then in the Country in a very bad state of health, but as his warm attachment to Government was well known, the report was easily believed, and death and destruction to him and his family was denounced. Upon this Mr. Stuart tho' in a very weak state determined to go to Georgia, and there remain till he heard what could be alleged against him. On being informed that this letter from General Gage and his correspondence in consequence of it with Mr. Cameron his Deputy in this Province, was the only charge, he sent for one or two of the violent party in Savannah, produced his letter book, and showed them what he had wrote to Mr. Cameron, and the Deputy's answer. The first acquainted Mr. Cameron that Mr. Stuart was informed by General Gage that attempts had been made to the Northward to seduce the six Nations from their Allegiance, that like means might be used with the Indians to the Southward, therefore desiring his utmost vigilance to prevent their succeeding his Department. Mr. Cameron in answer not only assures Mr. Stuart of the good disposition of the Indians to Government, but was it necessary, that a large body might be drawn together for its service. This account of Mr. Stuart's was transmitted to the Committee here, but so far from answering the end proposed by the communication, it only added fuel to the flame. Mr. Stuart did not consider he had to deal with People who did not wish to be convinced of his innocence, or that of the Ministry, on the contrary it was absolutely necessary for the carrying on of their designs, that they should be believed guilty, and this last expression of Mr. Cameron's furnish'd them with a plausible pretext to accuse Mr. Stuart of want of candour, in not disclosing the whole of the letter, or why should Mr. Cameron exceed his duty in saying the Indians were ready to take an active part in the quarrel. Their threats against Mr. Stuart were again renewed, and as he had reason to apprehend a design was formed to seize his person he withdrew to St. Augustine, which retreat was held as a confirmation of his guilt, and it was pretended put the matter out of all doubt.

But as incursions from the Indians tho' well calculated to alarm and terrify was a danger at some distance, and no hostility, nor appearance of any happening, it was necessary to have recourse to the instigated insurrection amongst their slaves, effectually to gain the point proposed, and they could not be long at a loss for pretexts to establish this. The constant exercising of the Militia, and other martial appearances, joined to their imprudent conversations at their tables before their domestics, could not escape the notice of those unhappy wretches, and naturally led them to converse among themselves on the reasons for it. One of these conversations, was, it is said, overheard, and several of those poor ignorant creatures taken up, who terrified at the recollection of former cruelties were easily induced to accuse themselves, and others to escape punishment. Among the rest one Thos. Jeremiah a free black (commonly called Jerry) was taken into custody on the accusation of one of those wretches. This unfortunate man my Lord, had by his industry acquired a property upwards of 1000 pounds sterling, was in a very thriving situation, had several slaves of his own, who he employed in fishing, and was one of the best pilots in the harbour. He often piloted in Men of War, and it was strongly suspected (which I believed was his only crime) that he would have no objection to have been employed again in the same service. It was needless to urge the improbability of a fellow in affluent circumstances, who was universally acknowledged to be remarkably sensible and sagacious, possessed of slaves of his own, entering into so wild a scheme as to instigate an insurrection, without support, without encouragement (for happily not a shadow of evidence appeared tha[t] any white man was concerned) it was needless to urge this, or any other argument in his favour, to trial he was brought a few days after my arrival, before two justices and five freeholders according to the Negro Act, and after sitting a week, and taking uncommon pains to get evidence, no proof could be produced to convict him, or give sufficient grounds to believe any attempt of the kind they pretended to fear, was ever intended, and the matter for that time ended, with ordering slight corporal punishments to be inflicted on two or three slaves for imprudent language, but Jerry was order'd to be remanded to prison and his tryal resumed two months afterwards, by which time they hoped to procure more evidence. It is with horror my Lord that I relate the remainder of this story; on Friday the 11th of this month, this unhappy man, was brought to trial, if such a process deserved that name and was sentenced to be hanged and afterwards, burned. A wretched slave who was one of the evidences against him received sentence of death at the same time both to be executed the 18th following. I waited for two or three days expecting a petition in favor of the prisoner (for in Negro cases no report is made to the Governor no warrant for execution is necessary but that of his Judges, which is often immediate) but none appearing I sent one of the Justices before whom he was tried to attend me, with the proceedings against this poor man, and the whole of the evidence. I assure you my Lord my blood ran cold when I read on what ground they had doomed a fellow creature to death; I easily saw that without a petition from his judges I should not be able to save him. I therefore expressed to the Justice in the strongest terms my sense of the weakness of the evidence, and entreated that for his own sake, and that of his fellows, he would get a Petition signed by them. At the same time I resolved to lay the affair before the Judges, and the Attorney General, therefore order'd the Justices to attend, and give every information necessary to enable those Gentlemen to make a report to me. Whilst this was transacting, my attempting to interfere in the matter raised such a Clamor amongst the People, as is incredible, and they openly declared that if I granted the man a pardon they would hang him at my door. I received too a letter from a man of the first Property in the Province, who had always express'd great friendship, representing in the strongest terms the dreadful consequences that would attend my pardoning him, concluding with this remarkable expression, that it would raise a flame all the water in Cooper River would not extinguish. In the meantime the Chief Judge and the Attorney General called & informed me they had met the other Judges, considered the evidence, and would be ready to report their opinion that evening if I desired it, but that however favorable it might be to the unhappy prisoner, they were well assured his death was determined on, and with particular circumstances of insult to me should I interpose, whither in this situation it would be proper for me to insist on it. I leave your Lordship to conceive of the poignancy of my agony and distress on this occasion. I was almost distracted, and wished to have been able to fly to the remotest corner of the Earth, from a set of Barbarians who are worse than the most cruel Savages any History has described. Still more to heighten this horrid scene, having heard a report that the man had confessed his guilt to the Revd. Mr. Smith one of the Ministers of this town, I sent for that Gentleman and enquired about it. He candidly told me that he attended the Black as much from a desire to ascertain the reality of an instigated insurrection as from the motives of humanity; That he used every argument every art to draw him to confession, endeavoring to make him contradict himself in the many conversations he had with him but in vain. His behavior was modest, his conversation sensible to a degree that astonished him, and at the same time he was perfectly resigned to his unhappy, undeserved fate. He declared that he wished not for life, he was in a happy frame of mind, and prepared for death. Mr. Smith concluded this affecting story with acquainting me, that the wretch one of the evidences against Jerry, and condemn'd with him, retracted what he said against him, and voluntarily declared his perfect innocence. Altho' I had little hopes of saving the man's life, I determined on one effort more. I desired Mr. Smith to attend the Committee then sitting. I flattered myself that the testimony of a Clergyman one of their own party in high estimation with them and violent in their Cause might have some influence when he laid these Circumstances before them. The recantation of the wretch who had been a principal evidence against Jerry and condemned to death with him I sent to Laurens the Chairman of their Committee, and another copy to the Justices before whom the man was tried, with a short notice to each, wrote in such terms as I hoped might rouse their consciences. One of the Justices did attempt to get a Petition signed, but in vain, the other, I mean Laurens, would not interfere, but his answer, and some subsequent correspondence between him and Capt. Innes I mean to preserve, altho' I will not now trouble your Lordship with it—To conclude this heart-rendering story the man was murder'd. I can call it nothing else, he asserted his innocence to the last, behaved with the greatest intrepidity as well as decency, and told his implacable, and ungrateful Persecutors, God's judgement [sic] would one day overtake them for shedding his innocent blood. I call them ungrateful because this unhappy man's Publick services were universally acknowledged, particularly in Cases of fire, where by his skill and intrepidity he had been often remarkably useful.

Such is the spirit my Lord of the party that now governs this Province, such is the foundation on which they have the matchless assurance to publish to the world that His Majesty's Ministers have instigated insurrections amongst their slaves, and directed the Indians to fall upon the Inhabitants. By these falsehoods they prevailed on a majority of the Provincial Congress to agree to levy Troops, and fortify Charlestown and by these arts the Committee of Safety have got the Government into their hands which they exercise in the most arbitrary, cruel and wanton manner. Happy it was for the friends of Government in this Country that the wretched creatures who were doomed to death could not be prevailed upon to accuse any white person, tho' repeatedly told it was the only chance they had for life, and often desired not to be afraid to mention names let their Rank or station be what it would. Tho' this evidence could not have been legally used against a white person, I am convinced if they had been accused they must have fallen a sacrifice to the fury of the Mob.

I will now conclude this disagreeable subject with acquainting your Lordship that I thought it is my duty to desire the judges to deliver their report altho' the man had been destroyed. Three with the Attorney General were of one opinion, the other two differ'd from their brethren and gave theirs separately. I have the honor to enclose them all. Your Lordship will easily conceive that things are hastening fast to that extremity which will in all probability oblige me to withdraw from Charles Town, to avoid fresh indignities, and what will make this retreat the more mortifying, I shall leave several thousand faithful subjects in the back Country who are ready to take arms in the defense of the Constitution, had they the least support, but as they have neither proper Arms, nor ammunition, it would be the greatest cruelty as the highest madness, to expose them to the fury of the Rebels. Two of the principal incendiaries Wm. Henry Drayton and one Tennant a clergyman were sent sometime ago to poison the minds of the poor ignorant People in the back part of the Province, but succeeded so badly, that they have been under a necessity of drawing together the whole strength they could muster in the middle of settlements and marching to 96 District, to effect by force, what they could not accomplish by threats, bribes or persuasion. In this situation I see no prospect of succor, no chance of relief, it is now near nine weeks since Captain Tollemache sailed for Boston in the Scorpion and I have not had a single line from General Gage, or the Admiral. I did not expect the General could at present spare Troops, but I flattered myself a ship or two might have been sent, and that this important Province would not have been left to the care of one poor solitary worm eaten Sloop. The Vessels the Rebels have lately fitted out have already robbed different ships at sea of 20 Tons of Gunpowder, & every day Vessels are pouring in Arms & Ammunition from the French and Dutch Islands.

I have the Honor to be with the greatest respect,

My Lord
Your Lordship's most obed[ien]t
& most obliged servant
William Campbell

N.B.: I am to acknowledge the receipt of your Lordship's letter with the melancholy news of the death of the Queen of Denmark. I also received several Acts of Parliament to restrain the Trade of this Province, and other parts of America, which I have published, but as there is no means of enforcing them, they are merely waste paper.

(Endorsed)
15th November

C. Report of Thomas Knox Gordon, Edward Savage, William Gregory, and James Simpson to Lord William Campbell [first part of an enclosure Lord Campbell sent to Earl of Dartmouth, August 31, 1775]

Source: CO 5/396/231RH start to 232 LH end, NAUK

To His Excellency Lord William Campbell, Captain General, Governor & Commander in Chief, in and over His Majesty's Province of South Carolina. The Report of the Judges and Attorney General on the case of Jerry, a free Negro, now under sentence of death, for an attempt to raise an Insurrection.

May it please your Excellency,
    Mr. Coram one of the Justices of the Peace, and Mr. Cannon one of the Freeholders, before whom Jerry was tried, having waited upon us, and delivered to us Notes of the Evidence given upon the Trial, and having informed us, that upon that Evidence, they were fully satisfyed[sic] in their Consciences of his guilt, and that his crime was within the meaning of an Act of Assembly passed in the 13th year of His late Majesty King George the 2nd commonly called the Negroe Act; they had therefore adjudged him to be hanged, and then burned to ashes, on Friday the 18th instance. And the said Mr. Coram and Mr. Cannon having withdrawn, We, in obedience to your Excellency's commands, took the said evidence and Act of Assembly into consideration and then adjourned our Meeting until Evening, that each of us (in the interim) might have an opportunity to consider the matter *Seriatim and Seperatim.*
    We further report to your Excellency, that in the evening We all met, when We, whose names are hereunto described, agreed in the following opinion.

That the said Act of Assembly, being an Act of a very penal nature, must receive a strict and literal construction.

That the 17th section of the Said Act, is the only part thereof, that makes the Crime of *attempting* to raise an Insurrection, Capital. The Words are "And every *Slave* who shall raise or *attempt* to raise an Insurrection in this Province, shall upon conviction suffer Death."

That the said Jerry being a *free Negroe* and *not a slave* is clearly not within the words of the said 17th section.

That the makers of the Law, cou'd never have had it in contemplation to include *Free Negroes* in the said recited words of the 17th section, because in many parts of the Act, there is a plain and palpable distinction made between *Slaves* and *Free Negroes*, And because in the very preceding clause the 16th *Free Negroes* were in the contemplation of the Legislature, and are thereby subjected to the pains of death, equally as *Slaves*, for certain crimes therein mentioned, and had it been the intention of the Legislature, to have included *them* in the subsequent section, they never cou'd have so immediately forgot them.

That *Free Negroes* not being within the aforesaid words of the 17th section of the said Act of Assembly, are only punishable for an attempt to raise an Insurrection, in a like manner as white men.

That a bare attempt to raise an Insurrection evidenced *only by words without any overt Act in consequence of them*, (which from a copy of the Evidence, hereunto subjointed, appears to be the present case) is not a levying of War within the meaning of the Act of Parliament passed in the 25th year of King Edw[ar]d the 3[r]d and consequently does not amount to Treason.

We are therefore upon the whole, most clearly of the opinion, That the Justices and Freeholders in the present case, have mistaken the Law, and that the sentence of death by them passed, upon the s[ai]d Jerry is illegal.

As one of the Justices differed in opinion from us, and another declined giving any opinion at all, We must beg leave to refer your Excellency to those gentlemen for their particular reasons.

All which is most humbly submitted to your Excellency by us.

Thos. Knox Gordon
Edward Savage
Wm. Gregory
JaS Simpson

Charlestown
August 17th 1775

D. Report made by Charles Mathew Coslett to Lord William Campbell [second part of an enclosure Lord Campbell sent to Earl of Dartmouth, August 31, 1775]

Source: CO 5/396/233 RH start to 234 RH end, NAUK

In obedience to your Excellencie's Commands Mr. Coram one of the Justices of the Peace who tried Jeremy a free Negroe did lay before the Judges and His Majestie's Attorney General the Evidence give on that trial, tho' very incorrectly he declared, however, that the Witnesses were examined at different times and always confirmed what they had said on their first examination—As I recollect [we] were of the opinion, that we could not make any report viva voce Evidence which we ourselves had not heard and that it was always the Judge who heard and saw the Witness examined who reported to his Majesty.

The other point my Lord, was, whether being a free Negroe the judgement passed upon him was warranted by the Negro Law. I have had the misfortune to differ from my brethren and the Attorney General upon this point, it however is my duty to give my opinion however ill it may be supported. I ground my opinion entirely upon the Negro Act of the 13th of Geo 2nd. The 14th section of that Act enacts that the evidence of any free Indian or Slave with Oath shall be allowed and admitted in all cases against any free Negroes, &c and all Crimes and Offences committed by Free Negroes &c shall be proceeded in, heard, tried and adjudged by the Justices and Freeholders appointed by this Act for the trial of slaves, in like manner as is hereby directed for the trial of Crimes committed by Slaves any Law &c to the Contrary. The construction I put upon this clause is, that the Justices and Freeholders have a power to try and convict all free Negroes for any crime which a slave under this Act can be tried or convicted for except in 29th Sec: where free Negroes are fined only for harbouring slaves.

The 17th Sec: only uses the word "slave" who shall raise or attempt to raise an Insurrection, on conviction shall suffer death—yet if it is not to be construed that the free Negroes are liable to the same punishment for this same offense, they will not be punishable at all under this Law, or any other that I know of— besides, the policy and peculiar circumstances of this Province would never permit the Legislature to make any difference in the punishment of a slave and a free Negroe in an offense of so enormous a nature, at least as equally danger-ous as the other. This is a penal law it is true and therefore according to the usual rule it ought to be taken strictly, but in the 53[r]d Sec: it is enacted that all Clauses therein contained shall be construed most largely for the promoting and carrying into Execution this Act.

Besides, I could not help reflecting, that there was a vast multitude of slaves and free Negroes Mullatoes &c in the Province, and that it might be of the most fatal consequence to the lives and properties of the white Inhabitants, if these fellows once got into their heads that free Negroes &c were not punishable under this Act for such an enormous crime.

Charles Mathews Coslett

E. Report of John Fewtrell to Lord William Campbell [third part of an enclosure Lord Campbell sent to Earl of Dartmouth, August 31, 1775]

Source: CO 5/396/235 RH, NAUK

May it please your Excellency,

Agreeably to your Excell[en]cy's Command, of giving my opinion or answer in Writing, I humbly think the Legislature of this Province has invested the execution of the Negro Laws of this Province in Criminal Matters Capital or not Capital in the Justices and Freeholders The Act of Assembly 13 Geo: 2 1740. says they shall proceed to examine Witnesses and other evidence & *finally* hear & determine the matter brought before them. Another Section gives them the power in Cases Capital to mitigate the Sentence, except for the homicide of a white person, to corporal punishment in such discretion as they see fit Act of Assembly of 24. Geo: 2. 1751. says the Justices & Freeholders or a Majority of them may mitigate the Punishment inflicted. Such full powers therefore being placed in the Justices & Freeholders in Criminal Matters I apprehend takes away all jurisdiction from the Judges & that they cannot anyways interfere. I have the Honor to be—Your Excell[en]cy's &c

August 19th 1775
John Fewtrell

F. Report of Whig JP John Coram to Lord William Campbell [fourth part of an enclosure Lord Campbell sent to Earl of Dartmouth, August 31, 1775]

Source: CO 5/396/237 RH, NAUK

South Carolina
Charles Town District.

Before Me John Coram one of his Majesty's Justices of the Peace for the said District, Personally came and appeared Jemmy a Negro Man Slave, the Property of Mr. Peter Croft, who upon his solemn declaration saith, that about ten weeks since being in Charles Town at Mr. Preolias Wharf, one Thomas Jeremiah, a Free Negro who declared he had something to give Dewar a runaway slave belonging to Mr Tweed, and wished to see him, and asked Jemmy to take a few Guns to said Dewar, to be placed in Negroes hands to fight against the Inhabitants of this Province, and that he Jeremiah was to have Chief Command of the Said Negroes; that Jeremiah said he believed he had the Powder enough already, but that he wanted more Arms which he would try to get as many as he could.

Declared before me this 16 June 1775
John Coram

Sambo says that about 2 or 3 months ago being at Simmon's Wharf, Jerry says to him Sambo do you hear anything of the War that is coming, Sambo answered no, Jerry replys yes there is a great War coming soon—Sambo replies, what shall we poor Negroes do in Schooner—Jerry says set the Schooner on fire, jump on shore and join the soldiers—that the war was come to help the Poor Negroes

G. Report by George Milligen, September 15, 1775 [excerpt]

Source: CO 5/396/208–216d, NAUK

[The Provincial] Congress consisted of about 170 members chosen by the several parishes and other divisions of the province, and among them were moderate men, friends to His Majesty's government and the legal constitution; but the republican party, ever violent, secret and active, conscious of their rebellion practices and dreading the resentment of an insulted King, contrived this Association which would make all that subscribed it guilty themselves, hoping that amongst a multitude of sinners they, even they, might escape punishment. The very artful expression of "instigated insurrections" in the Association paper had all the wished for effect on the fears of the people who were made to believe that His Majesty's ministers and other servants instigated their slaves to rebel against their masters and cut their throats, and this was credited by the ignorant and unwary, strong as proofs of Scripture writ; and to keep up their fears and distraction of mind, reports were daily circulated that the Negroes of this plantation had refused to work, that in another they had obtained arms and were gone into the woods, that others had actually murdered their masters and families etc., but all without foundation. Letters were likewise said to be received from England and New York to support this assertion. By this jesuitical management and by the several threats of utter ruin to many individuals should they refuse, thus the Association was generally subscribed, though I know many whose hearts revolted while they put their hands to it, and I have heard them declare that they submitted to this illegal power as they would to a highwayman who held a pistol to their breasts; some few notwithstanding the terror over their heads, when they signed it, added saving their allegiance to His Majesty.

This bugbear of instigated insurrections gained another great point for the disaffected faction. They wanted an armed force to be entirely at their disposal to protect themselves and to intimidate and distress His Majesty's loyal subjects. They obtained their desire: the Congress voted money to raise two regiments of foot and a regiment of light horse, a committee was formed to take upon them the management of this army from whom the officers receive their commissions, orders etc.

The reports from the country of insurrections among the Negroes proving false and many people beginning to doubt the truth of instigations being used, therefore to carry on the tragedy several Negroes were taken up on suspicion and committed to the workhouse where there is a prison for them. About the end of June they were examined by the General Committee and all dismissed excepting two, one of them a freeman named Jerry, a very good fisherman and pilot for the bar. He was accused of sending firearms to Negroes in the country and advising them to go in to His Majesty's troops when any should arrive, for they were then all to be made free; but at this time they had not even in their own jaundiced opinions proof sufficient to condemn him for this great crime. He was therefore remanded to the workhouse till further proof could be got against him. On the 11 of August he was again brought to his trial, and as there was either further proof produced, or it was pretended so, against him, he was found guilty and condemned to be hanged and the dead body burnt, which sentence was executed on the 18th. Thus this poor fellow fell a sacrifice to the groundless fears of some and the wicked policy of others, for from the best information I could get his real crime was being a good pilot and his inclination to be of use to his Majesty's ships. All pilots were forbid at their peril to go on board or in any manner assist the King's ships or transports to come into the harbour. Besides, the man's trial was illegal. He was tried by the Negro Act, a provincial Act for the trial of slaves, the court consisted of two Justices of the Peace and five freeholders, and the witnesses against him could not give evidence on oaths, for they were slaves and not Christians—whereas this man was free and a Christian and possessed of property to the amount of six or seven hundred pounds sterling, therefore he ought to have been tried by the King's court and a jury. His excellency Lord William Campbell did everything in his power to save the poor man's life, but that monster the mob which now governs Charleston threatened to erect a gallows by his lordships door and oblige him to hang the man himself. Jerry met death like a man and a Christian, avowing his innocence to the last moment of his life, and I am well informed that the witnesses against him declared him innocent, that the evidence they had given against him was not true and given only to save themselves from a whipping, the only punishment they were told would be inflicted on Jerry. Surely there is no murder so cruel and dangerous as that committed under the appearance of law and justice.

H. Henry Laurens to John Laurens, Charles Town, June 18, 1775 [excerpt]

Source: Laurens, *Papers* 10: 184–185

Trials of Several Negroes Suspected & charged of plotting an Insurrection have been conducted this Week I mean the past Week, Jerry the pilot is among the most Criminal—two or three White people are Committed to prison on Strong Negro Evidence—& just as we were adjourning this Morning a Message was delivered from parson [Oliver] Hart that a Woman belonging to him & another to Josh[u]a Ward Esqr. could make very ample discoveries—these were immediately ordered into Custody for examination to Morrow.

I. Henry Laurens to John Laurens, Charles Town, June 23, 1775 [excerpt]

Source: Laurens, *Papers* 10: 191–192

Reports from the Committee appointed to conduct trials of Negroes Suspected of designs to Rebel—also from the Magistrates & upon the whole there appears very little foundation for Parson Tennants great fear & our amazing bustle—however one or two Negroes are to be Severely flogged & banished—I ask for what? if they deserve any punishment nothing less than Death Should be the Sentence, & at this critical time no pardon or mitigation should be granted—the old answer, why they don't appear to have been so guilty as to deserve death but must receive Some punishment for example

Sake—Strange doctrine indeed!—One of the acting Magistrates who related the process to me, Seemed heartily tired & ashamed, Said he could get no freeholders to act—no Sign of danger in this, in a Town where the Inhabitants are as suddenly blown up by apprehensions as Gun powder is by Fire—The White Men Suspected will be Set at large, nothing is brought in Evidence against them yet tis Said the populace are determined to drive them out of the Country—Jerry is Still to take his trial but he is not in close confinement—this was relaxed as the people's fears abated—mean time the Companies of Militia are kept on Duty Night & Day—& murmurs begin to Spread.

J. Henry Laurens to John Laurens, Charles Town, August 20, 1775

Source: Laurens, *Papers* 10: 320–322

Three days ago the Negro Man was executed; uncommon pains had been taken to Save him, the fellow had Money & and many friends among people of his own Colour, Some among the White—I Say uncommon pains, tis remarkable that both Clergymen of our Church visited him frequently & became Solicitous for him—Your uncle well knows that that Sort of Duty had been generally left to the Dissenting Ministers when White Men have been under Sentence of Death.

The Law by which he was tried was called into question, the Judges & Attorney General were called upon for their opinions, & for a while those Sages were pleased to aver that a Free Negro was not amenable to that Act, & one of them threw the Magna Charta in the faces of the people—but loose opinions would not pass & the Gentlemen dared not venture to Subscribe to a declaration which must have called Something more valuable than their Law knowledge into question.

after that Bar was removed, one of the witnesses named Jemmey, it Seemed retracted from his Evidence & declared Jerry was Innocent, this declaration was made in a variety of Answers by Jemmy to the Rev[eren]d Mr. Smith's questions—which are introduced by Mr. Smith on a piece of Paper in these words, "After Some conversation with Jemmy, I put the following Questions."—Jemmy's Recantation was immediately sent to the Governor—& immediately by His Lordship to me Sitting in the Chair in General Committee—evidently intended for the Committee although His Excellency avoided the Recognition of Such an Assembly—the Committee on their part refused to take the Letter under their Consideration—good manners obliged me to write Such an answer; but it was done in haste & very late at night therefore I may be excused for not expressing my thoughts so clearly as I might have done at a little more leisure a Short correspondence followed which gave me Some pain, Capt. Innes I believe to be a Man of honour & a good Soldier but his passions & prejudices are bad qualities in a Secretary to a Gentleman of Lord Williams abilities—you will See the correspondence in papers inclosed with this.—the retraction by Jemmy could have no weight with Men who would give themselves time to consider that his first Evidence was corroborated by two other Witnesses, that a Sambo who was the main Witness would not retract—& that Jerry when he was first confronted by Jemmy, positively[sic] denied that he knew his person—that he knew the Man—although upon enquiry it clearly appeared that they were old acquaintance & nearly allied by Jerry's connection as a husband to the other Man's Sister—these & many other particulars were unknown to me when the Governor first wrote—I am now fully satisfied that Jerry was guilty of a design & attempt to encourage our Negroes to Rebellion & joining the King's troops if any had been Sent here—the uncommon pains taken to Save his Life had filled the minds of many people with great Jealousies against certain Crown Officers acting under direction—but I declare upon my honour that I entertain no Such thoughts of any of them in particular—& I altogether acquit the Governor. My regard for him induced me to alarm him by writing plainly as I did in my first answer, I believe it had the desired effect—I am glad of it—for although I know none of the out of the Door Secrets of the people, & carefully avoid Such knowledge, yet I had heard enough to fill me with horror from a prospect of what might be done by Men enraged as Men would have been had a pardon been Issued—Jerry was a forward fellow, puffed up by prosperity, ruined by Luxury & debauchery & grown to amazing pitch of vanity & ambition—withal a very Silly Coxcomb—Such Characters are found in all Countries, & Men may be ruined by prosperity when perhaps their whole estate real & personal would not yield an hundred Guineas—Riches are great or Small comparatively—as a Negro Fisher Man Jerry was comparatively as Rich as a Vannuk, in the Circle of Stock holders.—I have not Said so much on this head merely to furnish you with a narrative of Jerry's latter history as to enable you in case of need to contradict false reports which may be, among others, propagated to the prejudice of the poor Carolinians whose impolicy &, in many instances mad conduct, will appear glaring enough without the aid of one Lie.

K. Enclosure that Henry Laurens sent to John Laurens, August 20, 1775

Source: Laurens, *Papers* 10: 328–335

Charles Town 17 August Past 7. O'Clock
Sir
I beg leave to inclose a paper for your perusal which has affected me more than words can surely express Surely Sir I may appeal to your feelings for me as the Representative of Majesty in this unhappy Province, Think Sir of the weight of Blood, I am told I cannot attempt to save this Man without bringing greater Guilt on this Country than I can bear to even think of

I am Sir
Your Humble S[ervan]t to Command
William Campbell

I have sent the Original to the Justices who condemned this Man
Send me back this Copy

To Henry Laurens Esq.
[Copy of Answer to the above]
My Lord.
Your Lordships Letter of 7. O Clock this Evening did not reach me till 9—It was brought to me in General Committee & being informed by the Messenger that it was intended so—I offered it immediately as a matter proposed to the Committee—The Letter and the paper which had come inclosed in it were therefore read. But when the Committee heard the Contents they utterly refused to take them under Consideration.

For my own part my Lord as I have not heard the Evidence fully against Jerry I will not take upon me to declare him innocent or Guilty, but with submission to your Lordship I will presume to say that if the retraction of Evidence by one who had been an accomplice & after he had secured his own pardon and Reward, was to be admitted at the Old Bailey many Rogues would escape Punishment and many of his Majestys Proclamations prove worse than Nugatory, but such a retraction I also presume would not even be listen'd to in a case where there had been another firm Evidence.

I understand the unhappy Man in Question was found Guilty after a fair Legal trial, that the Justices and freeholders were unanimous in their opinion of his Guilt—In the Calamitous Situation of this Colony under the threats of Insurrections, strong proofs of which the people are possessed of, no wonder they are alarmed at the Sound of Pardon to a Man circumstanced in all respects as Jerry is,—especially after the recent Instance of one of their Negro Pilots being illegally carried away by the Commander of one of His Majestys Sloops of War.

I pray God to direct your Lordship—And I assure your
Lordship—that I am with the utmost respect
Your Lordships
Ob[edien]t. & most hum[ble]. S[ervan]t.
HL
Ansonburgh. Thursday 1/2 p. 10 O Clock. P.M
17th August 1775.

[*not a word in answer to this—I know the history but as it was communicated to me in confidence I dare not inflame the people by divulging it to them—but I thought it necessary to let the Governor know—that I had some feeling for the Majesty of the People—as well as for the "Representative of Majesty."]

Charles Town 18th August 1775.
[(Copy)]
Sir
I have it in Command from his Excellency to inform you that the Voluntary Confession of the Wretch Jemmy was made to Mr. Smith before His Lordship knew such a person was even under Confinement—

No application was made to the Governor in his behalf till past 12. Yesterday. his Excellency signed the Pardon at 6 O Clock and by desire of Mr Smith, Jemmy is now ignorant of it, unless Mr Coram to whom Mr. Nesbitt was obliged to apply for such information as was necessary to enable him to draw the Pardon has acquainted him with it—

In your hurry last night you omitted inclosing Mr. Smiths Conversation with the wretched Creature His Excellency requests it may be sent [to the] Bearer—

I am Sir
Your most Obed[ien]t & most H[um]b[l]e Servant—
Alex: Innes

Henry Laurens Esq.
[Copy of the Answer to the above]
Sir
Inclosed is the paper which his Excellency desired to be returned I beg his Lordships pardon for omitting to inclose it last night—

I should be uncandid if, in answer to that part of your Note of this morning intimating that no application in behalf of Jerry has been made to the Governor till past 12 Yesterday, I did not inform you that it was about 12 the preceeding [sic] day when the Justice voluntarily acquainted the people that his Lordship had recommended to him to procure or promote a petition in behalf of the Criminal,* and that in speaking of the Evidence which had been given against him his Excellency had said, ["]the People should consider the Consequence of executing him upon such Evidence in case the times should alter["]—a remark which greatly affected the minds of those to whom it was repeated—with regard to Jemmy I know not his person but he is certainly a liar of the most abominable order of Liars, therefore I am, as I presume every man—who knows no more of particulars than I do, must be, at a loss what kind or degree of Credit to give his testimony.

I am Sir [&c]

[HL]

Friday Morning 18th August 1775

1/2 P. 7. O Clock

[*this fact stands uncontroverted—]

[Copy of Mr. Innes's reply to the foregoing]

Charles Town 18 August 1775

Sir,

If you will be so kind as to look at my Note again you will find no reason to Complain of my want of Candour. You will find you have mistaken Jemmy for Jerry. I repeat that no application was made for Jemmy till 12 Yesterday when Mr. Brewton was in the House with his Lordship and I also repeat that till that time his Excellency did not know Jemmy was under Confinement, how cruel then that Suggestion in Mr. Laurens Letter of last Night, that either pardon or reward was offered to procure his recantation. Mr. Smith can satisfy Mr. Laurens in that point if a doubt remains in his breast. The Persons of both the wretches are totally unknown to me & I most cordially agree with you that Jemmy is the most abominable of Liars, I have the Authority of his Excellency to acquaint you he never made use of that expression that "the People should consider what might be the consequence of executing him upon such evidence in case the times should change." his Excellency shudder'd at the very thoughts of an innocent Mans suffering an Ignominious death but will venture to Assert had he been convinced of his Guilt his Lordship would have been the last Man that would have attempted to save him from the Punishment due to a Crime of so Black a dye.

However unhappy his Lordship has been in his endeavors to save this unfortunate person, Hell itself cannot (with even the Color of probability) suggest one motive that could have actuated the Governor on this occasion but what proceeded from Humanity Justice and Mercy. Adieu Sir I beg pardon for detaining you so long the horrid Scene will soon be closed and this Matter decided by that eternal God to whom all hearts are open & before whom the most Secret thoughts cannot be hid.

I am Sir
Your most Ob[e]d[ien]t. & most H[um]ble Servt.
Alexr Innes

[HL's answer to Mr. Innes's second Letter of the 18 August & conclusion of the correspondence]

Sir

Upon Reviewing your Letter of this morning I perceive that I had mistaken the name of Jemmy for Jerry and I now understand that no application was made in favor of the former till Yesterday Noon but I solemnly declare it was not my intention nor was it in my heart to complain of a want of Candour on your part by that misnomer and I am assured upon recurring to my answer this fact will be established—Upon reflection you will be also satisfied that I could not mean an unkind Suggestion when I signified my opinion of the efficacy of retracted Evidence after a fair trial and Conviction of a Criminal at a Court of Oyer and Terminer in Great Britain in Cases where by His Majestys Proclamations not only Pardon but Rewards are offered to accomplices for discovering their Confederates which often happens and often to a Proverb ["]the greatest rogue turns Kings Evidence["] nor did I by any means intend to Infer from thence that Pardon and Reward had been offered to Jemmy by the Governor or by his authority directly or indirectly

I am sorry the Magistrate has been so criminal as to misinform the people in that important declaration which his Excellency says is not warranted by his expressions—he must have taken pains to be wicked in this point by averring a falsehood in writing one day and deliberately Confirming it upon the day following—*

My dear Sir I do not believe nor will I be persuaded by the insinuations of any Man to believe that his Excellency was actuated in his endeavors to save the Life of Jerry by any other motive but such as proceeded from humanity and his Lordships Apprehensions of Justice and Mercy—but at the same time I must declare that I also now believe Jerry was Guilty and I am fully persuaded the

Governor and you are so open to Conviction that I should have no difficulty in bringing you both to be of my opinion on this he[a]d.

I was till this morning unacquainted with particular circumstances because I had avoided the knowledge of the whole of this horrible Insurrection Report, as much as possible, and I was in hopes of having steered clear of an affair which in the sequel has given me some uneasiness. but I learn that the Scene is closed! Justice is satisfied! I beg our correspondence on this disagreeable Subject may here end and that you will believe me to be with great regard

Sir

Your Obed[ien]t. Serv[an]t.

[HL]

Ansonburgh 18th August 1775.

[*The Justice persisted in the declaration to Lord William's Face, His Lordship said he had mistaken him some how or other—but Mr. Coram is clear & possitive [sic] & was very prudently cautious.]

[Copy of a very extraordinary Letter from the "Representative of Majesty."—attempting to prove a Negative—charging two Justices & three Freeholders with the shedding of Innocent blood—because after a fair & patient hearing, they were unanimously of opinion that Jerry was Guilty—the trial was conducted not only with great deliberation but with an uncommon degree of delay—it was above three weeks on the Carpet the Governor did not act officially, in this case, 'tis not his Province to sign the Death Warrant, although he has the Power of Pardoning—there is a mystery in this business which I cannot yet unravel.—because I will not indulge uncharitable suspicions—but I will be upon my guard]

Charles Town 17th August past 7 oClock

Sir

Without attempting to comment upon the contents of this paper, I only Send it for your perusal. In Case of Blood I wave Ceremony, I would even give up Dignity to Save the Life of an Innocent Man.—Consider it Seriously Sir, lay it before your Brother Justice, & the Freeholders, between God & your own Consciences be it, I take every Holy Power to witness I am innocent of this Mans death, upon your Heads be it, for without your interposition I find I cannot Save him.

I am Sir

Your Humble Serv[an]t

William Campbell

John Coram Esquire

N.B. I have a copy of Mr. Smith's Declaration but I have Sent you the Original which I desire you will carefully return.

L. John Laurens to Henry Laurens, October 4, 1775

Source: Laurens, *Papers* 10: 450–451

London, October 4, 1775

I have before me, My Dear Father's kind letters of the 18th and 20th of July, with a copy of 30th August, the original of which I have not yet received—the deplorable state of Carolina grieves me very much, your unremitting Labours in its service I am afraid are not so efficacious as if they were seconded by men of like Wisdom and Firmness with yourself—the Defection of such a considerable number of your own People, the Instability of your newly raised Troops, would make you fall an easy prey, if the Ministers should send Regulars among you in these Circumstances—luckily for the Provinces I do not believe it to be their present Intention, but forbearance in this respect cannot be answered for long, especially where there is such a temptation for it. Certain it is, that vigorous preparations are making, against the Continent in general, and it becomes each Province to be upon its Guard. I am sorry to think that our People should descend to tar and feather a Gunner of Ft. Johnson and suffer a Fletchal to live within their Territories—however I hope the first was merely the Fury of an enraged Riot, and that by steadiness and better conduct than we have hitherto pursued, we shall triumph over all the efforts of secret Treachery or open Violence. Our Countrymen seem wrong headed upon many occasions, and not sufficiently in earnest when exertion is really required. This disbanding is a terrible affair and I am afraid owing to mismanagement of the officers. The affair of the negro man Jerry has been quite differently represented here. I shall set it in a proper light whenever it occurs here in conversation, for according to the prevailing story the character of our countrymen for justice and humanity would suffer very much. The paragraph you desire to be published will appear in to morrow's Morning Chronicle, it could not be admitted in the evening paper. The description which you give of yourself My dearest Friend and Father rends my heart. Your want of Society and load of Public Business, are circumstances too cruel not to demand pity even from a stranger. Oh that I could relieve you by any means. I wish to be with you sometimes but when I reflect upon the conduct of my countrymen, I dread that men who are in earnest will fall a sacrifice to vain boasters, and wish you to be in England and out of a country where all your Patriotism I am afraid will be countenanced by rash and wrong headed men.

I have such a cold that I can scarce hold up my head. I must therefore beg my Dear Papa's excuse till the next opportunity which will be in a few days and commend him to God's protection. Remaining his most dutiful

and affectionate
JOHN LAURENS.

P S Parliamentary Registers No 11, 12, 13 & Remembrance No 4 go with this.

M. Diary Entry of Thomas Hutchinson, October 5, 1775

Source: Hutchinson, *Diary* 1: 543

Sir Egerton Leigh says that at South Carolina the Negroes are very insolent: that they [the whites] have a Company of Indians in Charleston, as a guard against the Negroes: that they have an Act called the Negro Act, prescribing a particular mode of trial of Negroes: that under this Act they tried a free Negro, a Pilot, for saying that—If the King should send troops, he would join them— found him guilty of exciting the Negroes to an insurrection, and sentenced him to die: that upon an apprehension that Lord Wm Campbell, the Governor, would respite him, a message was sent him that if he offered to stay the execution, they would erect a gallows before his door, and make him the executioner of the Negro: and so he suffered the poor fellow to be hanged. Surely such tyranny cannot last.

N. Extract of a letter to a gentleman in Philadelphia, Charles Town, August 20, 1775

Source: Force, *American Archives* 3: 180

Everything here is suspended but warlike preparations. It is said there are scarce two hundred men in town not enrolled. The country is unanimous. Our two regiments of foot are everyday training, and almost complete. About a week ago a small sloop from this town boarded a snow from *England*, in *Augustine* Bay, and carried off between twelve and fourteen thousand pounds of powder, mostly belonging to the King. She had been sent privately with thirty resolute men well armed by our committee, in order to intercept the vessel on the coast, but was disappointed, being rather too late, for there were fourty thousand pounds landed, with four brass field-pieces, the day before our troop boarded her. There were twelve soldiers sent from *Augustine* to assist and defend the snow, to whom our people gave ten guineas for helping them out with the powder, and being so modest as to not rennt. A man-of-war was in sight, but fortunately aground the few hours our people stayed. We spiked up the snow's guns, and then went off triumphant, although attacked by three boats full of armed men. One got within one hundred and fifty yards, it being quite calm, but that moment a fresh gale spacing up. Our people brought their boats safely to Beaufort, a town on the coast, about seventy miles S.W. of this place. It was reported they were pursued by the armed vessels from *Augustine*, to which place, on hearing of this, our Council of Safety dispatched fifteen Artillery-men and 15 Grenadiers, by water, and a compiling of Provincials to Beaufort, to assist the county people in defense of the acquisition. We are putting the town in a posture of defense, and all are determined to oppose whatever troops may come here. Yesterday a negro was hanged and burned for intended sedition, and burning the town, & c.

O. An Act for the Better Ordering and Governing Negroes and Other Slaves in this Province—1740—No. 670 [excerpts]

Source: Cooper and McCord, *Statutes at Large* 7: 397–417

[Preamble]
Whereas in his Majesty's plantations in America, slavery has been induced and allowed, and the people commonly called Negroes, Indians, mulattoes and mustizoes, have been deemed absolute slaves, and the subjects of property in the hands of particular persons, the extent of whose power over such slaves ought to be settled and limited by positive laws, so that the slave may be kept in due subjection and obedience, and the owners and other persons having the care and government of slaves may be restrained from exercising too great rigour and cruelty over them, and that the public peace and order of the Province may be preserved: We pray your most sacred Majesty that it may be enacted.

[Sections of the act cited by Gordon, Savage, Gregory, Simpson, and Coslett]

XIV. And *whereas*, slaves may be harbored and encouraged to commit offences, and concealed and received by free Negroes, and such free Negroes may escape the punishment due to their crimes, for want of sufficient and legal evidence against them; *Be it therefore further enacted* by the authority aforesaid, That the evidence of any free Indian or slave without oath, shall in a like manner be allowed and admitted in all cases against any free Negroes, Indians (free Indians in amity with this government, only excepted,) mulattoe or mustizoe; and all crimes and offences committed by free Negroes, Indians, (except as before excepted,) mulattoes or mustizoes, shall be proceeded in, heard, tried, adjudged and determined by the justices and freeholders appointed by this Act for the trial of slaves, in like manner, order and form, as is hereby directed and appointed for the proceedings and trial of crimes and offenses committed by slaves; any law, statute, usage or custom to the contrary notwithstanding.

XVI. And *whereas*, some crimes and offenses of an enormous nature and of the most pernicious consequence, may be committed by slaves, as well as other persons, which being peculiar to the condition and situation of this Province, could not fall within the provision of the laws of England; *Be it therefore enacted* by the authority aforesaid, That the several crimes and offences herein after particularly enumerated, are hereby declared to be felony, without the benefit of clergy, that is to say:—if any slave, free negro, mulatto, Indian or mustizoe, shall willfully and maliciously burn or destroy any stack of rice, corn or other grain, of the product, growth or manufacture of this Province, or shall willfully and maliciously set fire to, burn or destroy any tar kiln, barrels of pitch, tar, turpentine or rosin, or any other goods or commodities of the growth, produce or manufacture of this Province, or shall feloniously steal, take or carry away any slave, being the property of another, with intent to carry such slave out of this Province, or shall willfully or maliciously poison or administer poison to any person, free man, woman, servant or slave, every such slave, free negro, mulattoe, Indian, (except as before excepted,) and mustizoe, shall suffer death as a felon.

XVII. *And be it further enacted* by the authority aforesaid, That any slave who shall be guilty of homicide of any sort, upon any white person, except by misadventure, or in defense of his master or other person under whose care and government such slave shall be, shall, upon conviction thereof as aforesaid, suffer death; and every slave who shall raise or attempt to raise an insurrection in this Province, shall endeavor to delude or entice any slave to run away and leave this Province, every such slave and slaves, and his and their accomplices, aiders and abettors, shall, upon conviction as aforesaid suffer death; *Provided always*, that it shall and may be lawful to and for the justices who shall pronounce sentence against such slaves, by and with the advice and consent of the freeholders as aforesaid, if several slaves shall receive sentence at one time, to mitigate and alter the sentence of any slave other than such as shall be convicted of the homicide of a white person, who they shall think may deserve mercy, and may inflict such corporal punishment, (other than death,) on any such slave, as they in their discretion shall think fit; any thing herein contained to the contrary thereof notwithstanding; *Provided always*, that one or more of the said slaves who shall be convicted of the crimes or offences aforesaid, where several are concerned, shall be executed for example, to deter others from offending in the like kind.

XXIX. *And be it further enacted* by the authority aforesaid, That if any free Negro, mulatto, or mustizo, or any slave, shall harbor, conceal or entertain any slave that shall run away or shall be charged or accused with any criminal matter, every free negro, mulatto and mustizo, and every slave, who shall harbour, conceal or entertain any such slave, being duly convicted thereof, according to the directions of this Act, if a slave, shall suffer such corporal punishment, not extending to life or limb, as the justice or justices who shall try such slave shall, in his or their discretion, think fit; and if a free negro, mulatto or mustizo, shall forfeit the sum of ten pounds, current money, for the first day, and twenty schillings for every day after, to the use of the owner or owners of such slave so to be harboured, concealed or entertained, in like manner as debts are directed to be recovered by the Act for trial of small and mean causes; and that in case such forfeitures cannot be levied, or such free Negroes, mulattoes or mustizoes shall not pay the same, together with the charges attending the prosecution, such free negro, mulatto or mustizo shall be ordered by the said justice to be sold at public outcry, and the money arising by such sale shall, in the first place, be paid and applied for and towards the forfeiture due, made payable to the owner or owners, and the charges attending the prosecution and sale, and the overplus, (if any,) shall be paid by the said justice into the hands of the public treasurer, to be afterwards paid and applied in such manner as by the General Assembly of the Province shall be directed and appointed.

Appendix B

Documents Relating to the Slave Shadwell and the Free Black Scipio Handley

A. Council of Safety to Captain Edward Thornbrough, October 28, 1775 [excerpt]

Source: Laurens, *Papers* 10: 504–505

Sir.

We have received information that a Negro Man named Shadwell, a Mariner by profession, & the property of John Allen Walters Esqr. is employed on board his Majestys Sloop Tamar, under your command.

As the said Negro, is a runaway & harbouring him is highly penal, the carrying such a one off the Colony, [is a] Felony, by the laws of this Country, Circumstances of which you may not be apprised; we think it necessary to give you this intimation, in order that the Negro may be delivered to his lawful owner.

We would not be misunderstood as insinuating that you, Sir, give any Encouragement for Slaves to leave their Masters, we reasonably conclude that this Negro if he is on board the Tamar has imposed himself upon you as a Freeman: & Therefore we doubt not if our information is true, but that you will cause him to be delivered up. to Mr. J[ohn] C[alvert]. the bearer of this Letter

By Order of the Council of Safety,
Henry Laurens, President

200 able bodied Seamen upon their arrival Wages to commence a £3 Mo.5

Mr. Calvert being called informed the Board that Captain Thornbrough appeared angry at the contents of the letter, & declared his astonishment & concern that any Gentleman could Suspect that any runaway Negro could be on board his Sloop, & assured him that no such or any Negro but one whom he shewed him & who belonged to the Schooner late Messrs. Stone & Duvales was on board. Capt[ain]. Thorn. retained him until he returned from on board the Cherokee where he went to show the letter to the Governor, when he discharged him telling him that when he should have fully considered the letter he would send an answer.

B. Memorial of Scipio Handley

Source: AO 12/47/117; AO 12/109/160, NAUK

To The Commissioners appointed by Act of Parliament for enquiring into the losses and Services of the American Loyalists
The Memorial of Scipio Handley of Charles Town South Carolina a Black Humbly Sheweth
That your Memorialist at the time Lord William Campbell was obliged to leave Charles Town on Account of the Descentions which happened there in or about the year 1775, he your Memorialist being a free Man and followed Fishing he took the opportunity of Carrying Letters to his Lordships from Town and having Performed in such like manner several times your Memorialist was at last discovered and fired on by the Rebels and your Memorialist endeavoring to make his Escape he was run on Shore and one of the Boats men dangerously wounded.

That your Memorialist being taken Prisoner and heavily Ironed was put in close confinement and your Memorialist hearing that he was to be put to Death for acting against the Congress, your Memorialist by the hand of a Friend Received a File, with which he acquitted himself of his Irons and broak out of Gaol, and being a two story from the ground leaped down. By which means your Memorialist was so unfortunate as to get a Rupture.

That your memorialist making his way Escape left the Province and left what little Property he had behind him and is now in this city without money or Friends.

Your Memorialist therefore prays that his lease may be taken into your consideration in order that your Mem. may be enabled to receive such Aid or relief as his Losses and services maybe found to deserve.

Scipio Handley

Estimate of Losses of Scipio Handley
when taken by the Americans in the year 1775 on account of his Loyalty Viz ±

To one Fishing Boat—value——2,, 2,,—
Cash had with him when taken——3,,11,,—
Goods to the amount of ——1,, 4,,—
Money sent by Handley to from a Gentleman in Charles Town to a Gent on
board
My Lords Ship——5,, 16,,—
Household Furniture, three Beds etc. etc. 33,, 33,,
Cash in my House——etc. etc. 28,,—,,
Two Trunks, Cloathes Linen etc.——15,,—,,
Ten head of Hogs——8,,—,,—

Sterling—£. 97,, 9,,—

Esc—d
Evidence on the foregoing Memorial of
Scipio Handley a Black

The Claimant, Sworn.
Says he has been Christened about 12 Months ago in England, was born in
Charles Town South Carolina was free born, when the troubles broke out carried on business in fishing and buying and selling fruit about the Town, lived
in Charles Town but never carried Arms or took any oath to the Rebels as he
was carrying things from Town to Lord William Campbell and put in Gaol in
Irons. they took his Boat which was his own with all that was on board. he was
confined 6 weeks when he made his escape and went away to St. Augustine
and from thence to Barbadoes, when Georgia was taken he went to Savannah
with the troops but never returned to Charles Town.

Property—Says he lost the several Articles mentioned in his memorial the
Furniture was his own. it was left in the House when he was taken besides the
cash trunks and linen he had 7 hogs besides. Says Colonel Furtune drew up his
Memorial and he has set down everything lower than he ought he received £5
from the Treasury in full.

Eleanor Lister formerly resident at Charles Town, Sworn.
Knew the Claimant at Charles Town he went a Fishing they said he was a free
man at Charles Town his mother was a free Women she used to bake Ginger
bread and Cakes and such things, he was a Fisherman Knows he went to carry

things to L. W. Campbell and was catche'd and put in Gaol, and took himself away, and it was buzzed about that he was a Loyalist

Knows there was furniture in his Mothers House but whether it was his or his Mothers she can't tell, the Mother hired a Negro of her and paid her honestly, the furniture was good enough for Negroes, does not know whether there was any Mahogany Furniture

Esc—d

C. Claims and Memorials Petition of Scipio Handley of South Carolina

Source: AO 13/119/431, NAUK

To the Honourable Lords Commissioners of his Majesty's Treasury
The humble Petition of Scipio Handley
Sheweth
That the said Scipio Handley after leaving Chas.town in South Carolina in the year One Thousand seven hundred & seventy five on account of Lord William Campbell as was already mentioned in a former Petition to your Honors, was obliged to go to Barbadoes in the West Indies

and stayed there until he heard that Georgia in Savannah was taken by the British troops and then the said Scipio Handley left Barbadoes and went to Georgia in a ship called Eagle commanded by Captn. Tuner;

and there remained until the Rebels & French troops came and laid siege to the Town of Georgia,

and as it was very bare of troops all that was in it were Employed both White & Black, in order to Endeavour to keep them off, as if they had succeeded in their attempt they would have had no mercy on many,

your Petitioner could Expect none, as they had often threatned his life if Ever he should be caught for quitting Charlestown in One Thousand Seven hundred & Seventy five when they were contriving to put him to death.

Your petitioner during the time of the Siege of Georgia was Employed at the *Armoury Shop*, Running grape shot and Carrying them out to the Redoubts and Batteries.

The Siege Continued for near six weeks, Your Petitioner in performing the dutys of his Station unluckily received a Musket Ball in his right leg, which proved to be a very dangerous wound, as the surgeons thought they would be obliged to Cut it off

but after a long & Tedious while it got healed tho far from being entirely well as it fails him & the pain of it at times so very great that he is Obliged to keep his Bed for two or three days and therefore rendered entirely unfit for service.

This Accident happened about 4 oClock on a Saturday morning in the year of our Lord One Thousand Seven hundred & Eighty.

Your Petitioner humbly implores your Honours will take the Case of a poor infirmed stranger into Consideration & grant him such assistance as your honours shall Judge proper and in so doing your humble Petitioner will Ever Consider himself in duty bound to Pray for Your Honours Health Happiness & Prosperity.

Scipio Handley
London January 13th 1784
No. 3 W.P.

Notes

NOTES TO INTRODUCTION

1. Henry Laurens to John Laurens, December 12, 1774, in Laurens, *Papers* 10: 1–5; For a vivid description of the sumptuous former slave trader's Ansonborough mansion in Charles Town, Rattray Green, see Carp, *Rebels Rising*, 147–151, 155, 156, 163, *Wells's Register*, 94.

2. Coker, *Charleston's Maritime Heritage*, 35–37; Bonds, "Opening the Bar," 230–231.

3. Coker, *Charleston's Maritime Heritage*, 35–37; Wood, *Black Majority*, 204–205; Cooper and McCord, *Statutes at Large* 12: 419–420; 7: 368, 382, 409–410; *South Carolina Gazette*, April 30, 1771; Wood, "'It was a Negro,'" 164–168, 174.

4. Philip D. Morgan, *American National Biographical Dictionary*, 12: 1. Morgan proffers that Jeremiah was born into slavery but does not substantiate this claim. It is conceivable that he was born free or biracial, however, none of the documents seem to indicate this.

5. Lord William Campbell to Earl of Dartmouth, August 31, 1775, CO 5/396, folios 225RH start to 230LH end, NAUK. With the Great Fire of 1740 fresh in their minds, eighteenth-century Charlestonians venerated firefighters as guardians of the public weal and of private property. After 1740, Charles Town residents rapidly made important advances in protecting their city from conflagration. In fact, Charles Town was one of the first colonial cities to take steps towards a paid fire department. Although not as well paid for their services as whites, black firefighters, according to Carl Bridenbaugh, did receive compensation. For "turning out," he says, "Negroes received but ten schillings." But for operating the one of the city's five fire engines, African-American firefighters in Charles Town received twenty schillings per hour. Unlike white firefighters, however, blacks who refused to answer the cry of fire and the call of duty received thirty-nine lashes with a whip. See Bridenbaugh, *Cities in Revolt*, 105. For a recent treatment of urban firefighters, see Carp, "Fire of Liberty," 781–818.

6. Lord William Campbell to Earl of Dartmouth, August 31, 1775, CO 5/396, folios 225RH start to 230LH end, NAUK.

7. Robert M. Weir points out that as a young man Thomas Jeremiah also made the news due to some apparent blunders on his part. "In 1755, the *South Carolina Gazette* alluded to a nearly fatal accident that was attributed to the "Carelessness of a Negro Pilot (Jerry)." Quoted in Weir, *Colonial South Carolina*, 200–201.

8. Lord William Campbell to Earl of Dartmouth, August 31, 1775, CO 5/396, folios 225RH start to 230LH end, NAUK.

9. Report by George Milligen, September 15, 1775, CO 5/396/208–216d, NAUK.

10. Philip D. Morgan, *American National Biographical Dictionary*, 12: 1. For information relating to the wealth of Thomas Jeremiah, see Campbell to Dartmouth, August 19, 1775, CO 5/396/204–207d, NAUK; Campbell to Dartmouth, August 31, 1775, CO 5/396 folios 225RH start to 230LH end, NAUK; Report by George Milligen, September 15, 1775, CO 5/396/208–216d, NAUK; Henry Laurens to John Laurens, August 20, 1775, in Laurens, *Papers* 10: 322. For data on the wealth of South Carolina whites, see Ramsay, *History of South Carolina* 1: 123; Taylor, "Wholesale Commodity Prices"; Weir, *Colonial South Carolina*, 141; Coclanis, *Shadow of a Dream*, 7; McCusker and Menard, *Economy of British America*, 58–59, 88; Jones, *Wealth of a Nation*.

11. Lord William Campbell to Earl of Dartmouth, August 31, 1775, CO 5/396, folios 225RH start to 230LH end, NAUK.

12. In reference to Jerry, Laurens wrote his son John that "the fellow had Money & many friends among people of his own Colour, Some among the White." Henry Laurens to John Laurens, August 20, 1775, in Laurens, *Papers* 10: 320.

13. Jeremiah's riches could have certainly helped finance the material for a servile insurrection, but his wealth alone was not the primary reason he was singled out and put to death by Whig authorities. According to John Drayton, "the charge on which he was executed, was a conspiracy to excite an insurrection of the slaves, and to set fire to Charlestown. It was also said the principal charge was, that Jerry said 'If the British ships come here, he would pilot them over the Charlestown Bar.' Jerry was a Pilot." See Drayton, *Memoirs* 2: 24. It is worth noting here that three other Low Country residents, each affiliated with port security, were targeted and brutalized by patriots during the summer of 1775. None was as wealthy as Jerry, but they all could have aided, in one way or another, a British naval invasion of the lower South. The three men victimized were George Walker, the gunner of the strategic Fort Johnson on James Island in Charles Town Harbor; Laughlin Martin, whom Laurens described as "an under Wharfinger & of Some Credit in Town;" and John Hopkins, a river pilot who worked the waters in and around the mouth of the Savannah. All of them were white and all of them were tarred, feathered, and publicly humiliated. (For more on Martin and Walker, see chapters 2 and 3.) On July 25, 1775, the unfortunate Hopkins was dunked in hot tar and slathered in bird feathers. He was even threatened with hanging unless he publicly condemned the King and made a toast to the rebel cause. The hapless pilot was subsequently found guilty of treason by the state of Georgia in 1778. See Crary, *The Price of Loyalty*, 62–64; Candler, *Revolutionary Records*, 1: 330. Sampson, a black pilot whom we will encounter later on, actually committed the crime that South Carolina patriots tried to prevent by hanging and incinerating Jeremiah for piloting British ships

across the Charles Town Bar during the Battle of Fort Sullivan in 1776. As the war dragged on, the radical patriot Peter Timothy demanded that hand over French allies Sampson their captive, so that he could be "made an Example of Terror," suggesting that it would be "highly exemplary to hang [him] up at a Yard Arm." The more sedate John Rutledge conceded that the boatman had indeed been "very useful" to the enemy as well as "hurtful" to the state of South Carolina. The governor entreated Benjamin Lincoln to release the pilot in to "Custody, [so] that he may receive the Punishment due to his Crimes." For a discussion of this exchange, see Piecuch, *Three Peoples*, 169. As these instances illustrate, an impending Royal Navy invasion, particularly one intended to draw on the black majority (or other intestine enemies) for support, accounts for such seemingly anomalous examples of patriot cruelty.

14. See Miscellaneous Records Book OO (1767–1771), 624, SCDAH.

15. The notion that the North was the focal point of the Revolution has long been a part of popular consciousness and historical imagination. In the year of the bicentennial, Nash wrote: "The northern cities were the first areas of revolutionary ferment, the communication centers where newspapers and pamphlets spread the revolutionary message, and the arenas of change in British North America where most of the trends over taking Colonial American society were first and most intensely felt" (Nash, "Social Change," 6–7). While there are a few exceptions, the narratives that continue to follow this model are too numerous to mention. The "shift to the South" is generally attributed to the British defeat at Saratoga on October 17, 1777. Admittedly, this was a critical turning point in the War for American Independence. In addition to proving to the French that the Americans were "worthy" of assistance, the loss at Saratoga precipitated a change in the Crown's military strategy. Throughout the early stages of the Revolutionary War, royal officials wrote home about the staunch loyalism of Carolina's backcountry residents and urged Whitehall to draw on them for support. Convinced by the optimism of these communiqués and ignoring the advice of General William Howe, colonial secretary Lord George Germain urged Britannia's forces to turn their attention to the South. The reports of besieged royal officials and of embittered loyalist exiles turned out to be exaggerated, however, and the attempt to capitalize on the perceived loyalty of the backcountry ended in disaster. Despite the fall of Savannah (December 29, 1778) and of Charles Town (May 12, 1780), the refocus on the South and the Crown's dependence on backcountry loyalists would herald defeat for Cornwallis and the British forces at Yorktown (October 19, 1781). But what if Whitehall, instead of drawing from a small pool of disaffected loyalists, played on the worst fears of Southern colonists by basing its war effort on the support of African-American slaves and/or Native Americans? The history of South Carolina, not to mention the War for Independence, might well have had a different outcome. As I argue here, such possibilities seemed entirely plausible during the period between the summer of '74 and the summer of '76. It was the fear of such possibilities that ultimately helped push South Carolinians to pen their first state constitution, on March 26, 1776. Although this conservative constitution was meant to be temporary and geared toward reconciliation, after the Battle of Fort Moultrie on June 28, 1776, the colony's independence was a foregone conclusion. See Higginbotham, "The War for Independence," 309; Olwell, "'Domestick Enemies.'"

16. *The Patriot*, film directed by Roland Emmerich, 2000, Columbia Pictures.

17. Southerners have long charged that academics have privileged the Northeast over the South with respect to writing on the American Revolution. Just more than twenty years ago, Jack Greene gave voice to that sentiment in his controversial study *Pursuits of Happiness*. Greene, who sought to mainstream the South from the confines of parochialism, asserted that far more attention had indeed been directed to the North and New England than to the geographical region that would become distinctly Southern after the war's end. Recently, the eminent late historian R. Don Higginbotham weighed in on the South's role in the American Revolution. According to Higginbotham, it was, in fact, "the South, not fiery New England, [that] initiated the concrete steps leading to imperial separation," pointing to the example of North Carolina. Although he made that concession, Higginbotham questioned the extent to which "large slave populations and resentful Indian tribes in the southern colonies" drove "political leaders to favor independence." While Higginbotham admitted that that sort of dynamic was at work in Virginia, as Holton so deftly demonstrated, he asserted that the validity of such arguments did not hold up in other contexts (or other colonies). The historian boldly declared: "Patriots in all the southern colonies expressed these apprehensions, but only in Virginia were numerous bondmen actually encouraged to flee to the royal standard prior to July 1776." He went on to state emphatically: "More convincing evidence is required before we can accept the view that slavery was paramount or even a somewhat lesser motive for independence." Arguing that constitutional explanations trump race, class, and sectional conflicts as explanations for the final break with Britain, Higginbotham stated: "The revolutionary stalwarts engaged in great risks in participating in a war against the world's foremost superpower and in being unaware how much of the white, slave, and Indian elements might support the imperial side." He expressed concern that an "excessive emphasis on the racial motive could lead to the erroneous notion that the southern parts of America would not have joined their northern neighbors had the southern peoples been as predominantly white as were those in the middle and New England provinces." As valid as the latter concern is, this study will attempt to show that race and slavery were indeed factors in the South's move toward independence. While Southern demography may have never trumped constitutional concerns, that does not mean that the factor should be discounted out of hand. Nor does it mean that Southerners were "unaware" of the perils of revolting against Britain. In a land where the majority populace was black and enslaved, where mercenary Indians lurked on the frontier, and where poor backcountry residents envisioned (in some cases) a different sort of politics from that of their wealthy Low Country counterparts, such demographic concerns most certainly colored and, in some cases, shaped the decision making of all parties. That the conflict in the lower South took on a different character from the North and that constitutional causes fail to explain all facets of the quarrel demonstrate how much we still have to learn. See Greene, *Pursuits of Happiness*, 4; Holton, *Forced Founders*; Olwell, "'Domestick Enemies'"; Higginbotham, "Some Reflections," 659–662.

18. Frey, *Water from the Rock*; Schama, *Rough Crossings*; Piecuch, *Three Peoples*; Holton, *Forced Founders*; Pybus, *Epic Journeys*; Bolster, *Black Jacks*.

19. Jones, *Wealth of a Nation;* McCusker and Menard, *Economy of British America;* Ball, *Slaves in the Family;* Wallace, *Life of Henry Laurens;* McDonough, *Christopher Gadsden and Henry Laurens;* Laurens, *Papers.*

20. According to Rosemary Niner Estes, Gadsden may have been the titular leader of the Sons of Liberty, but Daniel Cannon was the true driving force behind the mechanic class. Estes asserts that the wealthy carpenter/sawmill owner let others assume the limelight; yet "in the long term his leadership was repeatedly affirmed." See Estes, *Charles Town's Sons of Liberty: A closer look,* 180–183, 252–277; Walsh, *Charleston's Sons of Liberty;* Poston, *Buildings of Charleston,* 480, 620.

21. While Jeremiah was locked in the workhouse, on July 30, 1775, Henry Laurens wrote to his son John, then in England, and told him to print the following statement in a London newspaper:

> Ministerial emissaries have been exceedingly diligent in that quarter (Western and Northern Frontiers of the Province) and some adjacent counties within the line of North Carolina, a happy discovery of which was alluded to, when I said in a letter "Christianity and Methodism must differ very widely"—No stone has been left unturned by Administration, and by their creatures, to disunite us poor distressed Americans. Insurrections of our Negroes, attended by the most horrible butcheries of innocent women and children. Inroads by Indians always accompanied by inhuman massacre. Civil discord between fellow citizens and neighbor farmers, productive of fraud, perjury and assassination, are all comprehended within their plans, and attempts have been made to carry them all into execution. I do not desire you to take my word for proof of this assertion; I can prove the facts by producing letters from a Secretary of State, a Governor of one of the Colonies and a Superintendant [sic] of Indian Affairs.—Are these dark hellish plots for subjugating the colonies consistent with Lord Dartmouth's religious tenets? with his majesty's declaration of "Readiness to gratify the wishes, and remove the apprehensions, of his subjects in America?" I will not comment, every human breast must be filled with horror at the bare recital; indignation against our common enemies— enemies to the King and to the welfare of the British realm, will be excited by a proof of these facts—Lord Dartmouth dare not deny his part—Governor Martin his—nor J[ohn] S[tuart] the part he has taken—Many rash, many impolitic steps, it is true, have been adopted by the Americans,—but when I reflect that aggression lies not on their side—when I consider these devilish machinations of a rash, wrong-headed ministry, I see an apology for everything we have done, and cannot forbear repeating, what had been a thousand times repeated—"Oppression will make a wise man mad."

On October 4, John Laurens wrote back to his father that he had done as he was instructed. The next day, the merchant-planter's anonymous statement appeared as an "Extract of a Letter from South Carolina" in the *Morning Chronicle and London Advertiser.* In the same letter, John wrote to his father: "The affair of the negro man

Jerry has been quite differently represented here. I shall set it in a proper light whenever it occurs here in conversation, for according to the prevailing story the character of our countrymen for justice and humanity would suffer very much." The quote from the newspaper (extract above) is the original from *Morning Chronicle and London Advertiser*, October 5, 1775. The concluding remark "Oppression will make a wise man mad" is a paraphrase from *KJV*, Ecc 7:7; For the edited version, see Henry Laurens to John Laurens, July 30, 1775, in Laurens, *Papers* 10: 258–259; John Laurens to Henry Laurens, October 4, 1775, in Laurens, *Papers* 10: 450–451. For other Whig lamentations related to the Brits' alleged use of Indians and slaves, see Thomas Lynch to Ralph Izard, November 19, 1775, in Izard, *Correspondence* 1: 154; "Extract of a Letter from Chariestown, South-Carolina, to a Gentleman in Philadelphia," February 7, 1776 in Force, *American Archives* 4: 949.

22. Henry Laurens to John Laurens, August 20, 1775, in Laurens, *Papers* 10: 320; Campbell to Dartmouth, August 31, 1775, CO 5/396, folios 225RH start to 230LH end, NAUK; Report by George Milligen, September 15, 1775, CO 5/396/208–216d, NAUK; Hood, *The Governor's Palace*, 307–313.

23. On the eve of the Revolutionary War, the entire eastern seaboard felt the increasing strain of the "three way tug-of-war" among patriots, loyalists, and African-Americans. However, it was in the colony of South Carolina, with its unique black majority, that these tensions became most acute. The racial demography of that province in the eighteenth century, and of the Low Country in particular, fostered hostility on the part of enslaved blacks and a palpable air of suspicion among the white minority. According to a recent estimate, for the entire colony (below the Cherokee territory) in 1775, there were roughly 500 Native Americans, 71,600 whites, and 107,300 African-Americans (almost all of whom were enslaved). Conditions for overt confrontation between white and black had been building for generations, occasionally erupting into open violence, as in the Stono Rebellion of 1739. Heightened social and political tensions during the decade that followed the Stamp Act controversy of 1765 increased the prospects for further conflagration by the spring of 1775. Wood, "'Dream Deferred,'" 172; Frey, *Water from the Rock*, 56; Wood, "Changing Population," 38. In 1775, Dr. George Johnston, then surgeon to His Majesty's forces, arrived at a similar number when he surmised that "the number of white inhabitants had increased to 70,000" and that "the number of negroes had like wise increased to 100,000." According to the physician, the value of "Negroes" had also "increased from £10 to £15 per head." See Milling, *Colonial South Carolina*, 109. For an alternative estimate, see Coclanis, *Shadow of a Dream*, 63–68. According to Coclanis, the total population of South Carolina in 1770 was approximately 124,244 (49,066 whites and 75,178 blacks). The author estimates that African-Americans made up 60.51 percent of the total population.

24. Cooper, *Statutes at Large* 7: 97–101; Jones, *Wealth of a Nation*; McCusker and Menard, *Economy of British America*; Carp, *Rebels Rising*, 225.

25. For the period between 1768 and 1772, Nash estimates the annual averages for Charles Town, South Carolina, as follows: rice, 284,000 pounds sterling; indigo, 119,000 pounds sterling; deerskins, 15,000 pounds sterling; grains and provisions, 12,000 pounds sterling; naval stores, 5,000 pounds sterling; total, 435,000 pounds

sterling. The data for rice and indigo pertain to South Carolina as a whole; yet, as Nash points out, most of those exports were indeed shipped from Charles Town. See Nash, "Urbanization in the Colonial South," 7, quoted in Van Ruymbeke, "Huguenots of Proprietary South Carolina," 42.

26. McCusker and Menard, *Economy of British America*, 85.

27. For an account of the Low Country's economic rise and fall, see Coclanis, *Shadow of a Dream*.

28. Nash, *Urban Crucible*, 1–2; Carp, *Rebels Rising*, 1.

29. This parallel between New York and Charleston Harbor is largely derived from an enjoyable conversation I had on December 19, 2008, with an actual Charleston Harbor pilot, the current commissioner of the Pilotage, Robert Bennett.

30. Quoted in Jenrette, *Adventures with Old Houses*, 62.

31. Laurie and Chamberlain, *South Carolina Aquarium Guide*, 151–161; Wood, "'It Was a Negro,'" 164–168, 174; Wood, *Black Majority*, 196–205; Morgan, "Black Life"; Morgan, *Slave Counterpoint*.

32. Around the eve of the "Second War for Independence," Charles Dickens, using a rhetorical device, claimed he was given a tour of Charles Town and its harbor by a guide he called "Venatico": "Venatico, as I will call him, begins to talk about the fishing vessels that lie in flocks and spots out yonder to the west, fishing for a fish with a wonderful Indian name which I can neither spell nor pronounce, and which is only found in the sea round Charleston. The crews are all hired negroes, he says, and are all profitable to their temporary masters. Venatico, bids me also to remark that, like Venice, at first view Charleston city seems growing out of the waves." Interestingly, Dickens noted in reference to the Exchange Building that "the poorest Negro is proud to show the old Custom House where the Britishers imprisoned the patriots." See Dickens, *All the Year Round*, 462–463.

33. Glen, quoted in Sellers, *Charleston Business*, 5; Fraser, *Charleston!* 127.

34. Quincy, quoted in Howe, "Journal of Josiah Quincy, Junior." 441.

35. Gayle, "Nature and Volume of Exports;" 25–33. The main ship anchorage in Charles Town Harbor between Shute's Folly and Sullivan's Island was, and still is, known as Rebellion Road. Although many are inclined to believe that the roadstead's name had something to do with the War for Independence or with the American Civil War, this is a misconception. According to P. C. Coker III, Charleston's foremost maritime authority, the anchorage, "received its name by an act of the Colonial Assembly in 1696, which declared that any vessel that anchored in that location was considered in 'rebellion' against the Crown. At the time the roadstead was out of the range of the city's guns. Consequently any vessel anchoring there was outside of the enforcement of the law and thus considered in 'rebellion.'" See Coker, *Charleston's Maritime Heritage*, 31; conversation with Charleston pilot Richard Bennett.

36. Barry, "Almanac of 1776," 149. One of the vivid descriptions of the harbor in motion comes yet again from Dickens: "How deftly the little fishing-boats scad in, with a sweep and swirl, taking down and huddling up their blowzy brown sails, as they float calmly into the inner harbour, where idle craft rock and flap in the tepid green water!" Dickens, *All the Year Round*, 462. For the diversity of craft in the harbor, see Coker, *Charleston's Maritime Heritage*, 1.

37. Fraser, *Patriots, Pistols and Petticoats*, 2–8; Sellers, *Charleston Business*, 19; George C. Rogers Jr. estimated that the November 18, 1740, fire destroyed 300 homes. According to Rogers, the swath of territory stretching from the corner of Broad and Church Street to Granville's Bastion was reduced to ashes. The entire west side of Church Street from Broad to Tradd was incinerated. As the six-hour conflagration ran its course, some of the most important houses and stores in the city were lost. To compensate the 171 residents who suffered damages, Parliament awarded the hefty sum of 20,000 pounds sterling. Fears of devastating fires in Charles Town were greatly warranted and never completely went away. They would crop up again in the Jeremiah episode and come to fruition in 1778, 1796, and again during the nineteenth century. See Rogers, *Charleston in the Age*, 28; McCrady, *History of South Carolina under the Royal Government*, 239–240.

38. In 1774, Cannon became one of the city's five of firemasters. As a firemaster, he may have witnessed Jerry's firefighting skills in action or worked with him in a supervisory capacity. What role this possible connection between the two men may have played in Cannon's eventual decision to find the defendant guilty is unclear. The four other firemasters were Gabriel Manigault, Thomas Smith, David Deas and John Edwards. See *S.C. Gazette*, June 3, 13, 27; July 25; Oct 3, 1774; Estes, *Charles Town's Sons of Liberty: A closer look*, 99; Cooper, *Statutes at Large* 2: 42.

39. In 1773, members of the all-white grand jury fretted over the fact that "large quantities of naval stores and other combustible matters lie on the wharves to which the Sparks of Fire might be easily communicated." Journals of the Court of General Sessions, SCDAH, February 16, 1773, quoted in Zornow, "Troublesome Community," 28 n. 33.

40. Allegedly, patriots devised a scheme to obtain gunpowder by trading it in exchange for rice. In mid-August 1775, Campbell claimed "they [the Whigs] allow Rice to be exported on no other terms, but paying in Arms, & Ammunition." See Lord William Campbell to Earl of Dartmouth, August 19, 1775, CO 5/396/204–207d, NA; CO 5/410/200–207, NAUK; Lipscomb, *South Carolina Revolutionary War Battles*, 3.

41. Plan of the City and Neck of Charleston, S.C. Reduced from Authentic Documents & Engraved by W. Keenan. Pub. Septr. 1844, David Rumsey Collection.

42. Report of John Coram, CO 5/396/237 RH, NAUK.

43. Berlin, *Many Thousands Gone*, 148–149; Bullard, *Cumberland Island*, 74.

44. Cooper, *Statutes at Large* 4: 81.

45. Over time, the daring of these buzzards increased, so much so that by 1774, the scavengers allegedly followed customers down the street looking for scraps and handouts. Apparently, the birds were an accepted part of city life because they played an important role in cleaning up waste. See Sellers, *Charleston Business*, 21; Cashin, *William Bartram*, 8.

46. Cooper, *Statutes at Large* 9: 705, 706.

47. Ibid.; Zornow, "Troublesome Community," 6–38. Garden's quote is from Smith, *Selection*, 349. See Morgan, *Slave Counterpoint*, 240.

48. Report of John Coram, CO 5/396/237 RH, NAUK; Heitzler and Kirchner, *Goose Creek*, 245. Prioleau's Wharf is where Jeremiah allegedly tried to enlist recruits

for a slave rebellion. It is also where George Washington landed when he visited Charleston in 1791. Washington took the ferry to the location from Haddrell's Point across the Cooper. See Matthews, *Forgotten Founder*, 74.

49. Rediker, *Between the Devil*, 53–56; Rogers, *Charleston in the Age*, 5–8.

50. Sellers, *Charleston Business*, 35.

51. As Fraser noted, "The love of dancing and music among the female elites of Charles Town and the lowcountry was unparalleled in colonial America. Many of the wives of the new rich sought musical instruction for themselves and for their daughters, and by the early 1770s more than twenty-three music, singing, and dancing masters offered lessons in Charles Town." Instruction in the harpsichord for Low Country women was particularly popular. Ann Windsor, the first female music teacher in the city, placed an advertisement in the *South Carolina Gazette* announcing her services as a teacher of "young ladies upon the Harpsichord." Lady William Campbell, the governor's wife, of the Izard clan, had an "Elegant Harpsichord, double Rows of Keys, Fineerd & Ca" worth 84 pounds sterling in her drawing room. See T 1/541, NAUK. See Fraser, *Charleston!* 131; Pearson, "'Planters Full of Money,'" 303–325.

52. In February 1861, Dickens noted that "the heat is African, the laborers are also ... Here, up and down the embrasured terraces, at right angles to each other, the fair yellow mulattoes and shiny black negress nurses wander, with their faces turned to the sea, wooing the fluttering breeze that fans black cheeks and white cheeks with Divine Impartiality." See Dickens, *All the Year Round*, 462; Cashin, *William Bartram*, 8.

53. For a vivid contemporary account of Southern flora, see Bartram, *Travels*. See also Laurie and Chamberlain, *South Carolina Aquarium Guide*.

54. In Charles Town, residents of African descent continued to outnumber their European counterparts well into the eighteenth century. In 1984, Philip D. Morgan calculated that 5,833 enslaved blacks, 24 free blacks, and approximately 5,000 whites resided in the town during the 1770s. While we can only speculate at the exact number of Charles Town residents on the eve of the Revolution, recent estimates point toward the number 12,000 and confirm a slight black majority. A Jamaican merchant visiting the South Carolina metropolis in 1773, surprised by the city's demography, noted: "There are swarms of Negroes about the Town and many Mulattoes." Quoted in Fraser, *Patriots*, 10. For demographic estimates, see Morgan, "Black Life," 188; Carp, *Rebels Rising*, 225.

55. Fraser, *Charleston!* 98–110, 112.

56. For an excellent discussion of these cotillions, see Fraser, *Charleston!* 130. For the impact of African or Gullah modes of speech on the white elite, see Rogers, *Charleston in the Age*, 79; Baranowski, *Phonological Variation*, 73–79.

57. In the Low Country, where the black majority was most substantial, enslaved blacks outnumbered free whites during the mid-1770s at a rate of four to one (roughly 80,000 African-Americans to 20,000 whites). Within individual parishes along the coastal waterway, the population disparity was often much more noticeable. In 1762, for example, St. John's Berkeley parish was inhabited by more than 1,000 adult male slaves and only 76 adult white males. Olwell, *Masters, Slaves and Subjects*, 32; Olwell,

"'Domestick Enemies,'" 22. The statistics for St. John's Berkeley parish are from Knepper, "Political Structure," 36.

58. Wood, *Black Majority*, 308–326.

59. Zornow, "Troublesome Community," 62–82.

60. Throughout the history of colonial South Carolina, the policy of European colonists was to create and sustain unnatural hostilities between blacks and Indians in order to ensure white survival. In 1758 Governor Glen told his successor William Henry Lyttleton, "it has always [sic] been the policy of this gover[nmen]t to creat [sic] an aversion in them [Indians] to Negroes." Seventeen years later in 1775, Lyttleton, by then an English MP, would advocate exploiting southern demography as a matter of British military policy. See Willis, "Divide and Rule," 165. As Nash asserted in 1974:

> Indian uprisings that punctuated the colonial period and a succession of slave uprisings and insurrectionary plots that were nipped in the bud kept South Carolinians sickeningly aware that only through the greatest vigilance and through policies designed to keep their enemies divided could they hope to remain in control of the situation. That white Carolinians were able to retain a hold on the situation testifies to their ability to play one Indian tribe against another and to their partial success at keeping Indians and Negro slaves divided.

See Nash, *Red, White, and Black*, 286–290; Wood, *Black Majority*, 116–117.

61. Gadsden, *Writings*, 93.

62. Gipson, *British Empire*, 72; William Lyttleton's Speech, October 26, 1775, in Simmons and Thomas, *Proceedings and Debates* 6: 96; Johnson, *Taxation No Tyranny*; "Viator," *Thoughts of a Traveller*.

63. Lyttleton's chain analogy may have been a creative reworking of the well-known "Join, or Die" woodcut by Benjamin Franklin (1754), depicting the American colonies as a serpent divided into eight distinct segments. William Lyttleton's Speech, October 26, 1775, in Simmons and Thomas, *Proceedings and Debates* 6: 96; George Johnstone's Speech, in Simmons and Thomas, *Proceedings and Debates* 6: 105; Frey, *Water from the Rock*, 67; Ralph Izard to "A friend in Bath," October 27, 1775, in Izard, *Correspondence*1: 135; Piecuch, *Three Peoples*, 40, 345 n. 28–31.

64. John, *Spreading the News*, 17–18.

65. According to Ray Raphael, many blacks "appear to have been aware of the important decision in the Sommersett case back in Great Britain: in 1772 Lord Mansfield, Chief Justice of the King's Bench, determined that James Sommersett, who had been purchased in Virginia, taken to England, and then escaped, could not be forcibly returned to his master. African slaves took this case to heart: if they could somehow reach the shores of England, they too would be set free." On June 30, 1774, for example, a notice appeared in the *Virginia Gazette* speculating that a runaway named Bacchus would attempt "to board a vessel for Great Britain...from the knowledge he has of Somerset's Case." See Raphael, *People's History*, 247; Mullin, *Flight and Rebellion*, 131. For a fuller discussion of the case of

Sommersett v. Stuart, see Blumrosen and Blumrosen, *Slave Nation;* Schama, *Rough Crossings.*

66. Schama, *Rough Crossings;* Pybus, *Epic Journeys;* Ryan, "'Under the Color of Law.'"

67. Johnson, *Taxation No Tyranny;* Holton, *Forced Founders;* McDonnell, *Politics of War;* Nash, *Unknown American Revolution;* Washington to Lee, December 26, 1775, in Washington, *Papers* 2: 611.

68. Quoted in Nash, *Unknown American Revolution*, 166; *Pennsylvania Evening Post*, December 14, 1775; Carp, *Rebels Rising*, 143–172.

69. According to a letter written on July 21, 1775, by the Southern royal superintendent for Indian affairs, John Stuart:

> a report was propagated everywhere throughout the province that I had sent to call down the Cherokee and Catawba Indians which so irritated the people as to render my friends apprehensive that my person was in danger. At the same time it was given out that the Negroes were immediately to be set free by government and that arms were to be given them to fall upon their masters. As nothing can be more alarming to the Carolinians than the idea of an attack from Indians and Negroes, the leaders of the disaffected party easily carried into execution their plan of arming the people and giving such a turn to their disposition as might favour their views, which were to receive the sanction of a Provincial Congress to meet the first of June.

See letter from Stuart to Dartmouth, July 21, 1775, CO 5/76/150, NAUK.

70. See chapters 6 and 7 below.

71. McCrady, *The History of South Carolina under the Royal Government*, 239–240.

72. The issue of what to call this man has proven to be a thorny one for historians. In addition to "Thomas Jeremiah," he has been referred to as "Jeremiah Thomas," "Jerimiah," and simply "Jeremiah" with no first name. This may be a result of the fact that the man's contemporaries often didn't know his proper name, either. On July 17, 1771, the judge presiding over Thomas Jeremiah's assault charge was apparently confused about the boatman's moniker. Finding him innocent, the judge declared that the court precincts "do Pardon, Remit and Release the said Thomas Jerry or by whatever name he is called." See Maier, "Charleston Mob"; Nash, *Unknown American Revolution;* Pybus, *Epic Journeys.* For Jeremiah's 1771 pardon, see Miscellaneous Records Book OO (1767–1771), 624, SCDAH. Two very good recent books have described aspects of the Jerry affair. However, both make the claim that Jeremiah's prominence is what did him in. According to Jim Piecuch, "Jeremiah, a free black whose skills as a harbor pilot had enabled him to amass considerable wealth, apparently angered the Whigs simply because he was a successful black man in a slave society." Benjamin L. Carp asserts, "Jeremiah's white neighbors feared his prominence." See Piecuch, *Three Peoples*, 79; Carp, *Rebels Rising*, 167.

73. Carp, *Rebels Rising*, 167.

74. In his book about the 1780 British invasion of Carolina capital, author Carl Borick devoted his entire fifth chapter to the strategic import of the Charles Town Bar. See Borick, *A Gallant Defense*, 71–85; Lipscomb, *Carolina Lowcountry*, 26–27; Piecuch, *Three Peoples*, 169; Schama, *Rough Crossings*, 106;

NOTES TO CHAPTER I

1. Weir, *Colonial South Carolina*, 314.
2. Fraser, *Charleston!* 138.
3. Drayton, *Memoirs*1: 126–127.
4. Fraser, *Charleston!* 138.
5. Drayton, *Memoirs* 1: 131–132; Fraser, *Charleston!* 138; Weir, *Colonial South Carolina*, 315.
6. Drayton, *Memoirs* 1: 133.
7. Fraser, *Charleston!* 138–139; Weir, *Colonial South Carolina*, 315; Drayton, *Memoirs* 1: 131–135. Maitland may have angered the people for other reasons. He was apparently hiding a thirteen-year-old black boy named Isaac Vauton in steerage. Vauton, who was four feet ten inches tall, claimed that he was born free in Rhode Island and that he was employed as a waiting boy by a Dr. Sweed. Unconvinced by the boy's story and suspecting that he was a runaway, Charles Town authorities remanded Vauton to the magistrate, Fenwick Bull, Esq. See *South Carolina Gazette and Country Journal (SCGCJ)*, August 2, 1774.
8. See note 35 in the introduction.
9. On Thursday, August 5, Richard Maitland cleared Charles Town Harbor for London in the *Magna Charta*. *SCGCJ*, August 9, 1774.
10. Drayton, *Memoirs* 1: 135–136.
11. John Julius Pringle (from Charles Town) to William Tilghman (at Philadelphia), July 30, 1774, Preston Davie Collection (3406) folder 47, UNCSHC. John Julius Pringle (July 22, 1753–March 16, 1843) should not be confused with Sir John Pringle, an older Scottish contemporary who went on to become "the father of military medicine" and physician to George III. An ardent patriot, John Julius Pringle would become a successful judge and a wealthy rice planter with extensive landholdings on the Ashley River. In early 1776, he would take over the lavish residence at 70 Tradd Street built by his father, a Scottish merchant by the name of Robert Pringle. John Julius Pringle was the attorney general of South Carolina for sixteen years and declined an offer made by Thomas Jefferson in 1805 to become attorney general for the entire United States. His tenth son, William Bull Pringle, would marry Mary Motte Alston. When her father, Colonel Alston, died in 1839, the Pringle couple became extraordinarily wealthy. That wealth was augmented greatly by the 1843 death of William's father, John Julius Pringle. Besides the slaves, the extensive plantation holdings, and the money, the couple took possession of the former home of the deceased slave trader Miles Brewton at 27 King Street. The residence is widely considered to be one of the finest examples of Georgian Palladian architecture in America. The black iron gate at the entrance to the home

was fitted with a spiked cheval-de-frise in response to the discovery of the Denmark Vesey Plot in 1822. For an excellent account of the life and times of the Pringle-Alston clan, see Côté, *Mary's World*. For biographical information on John Julius Pringle, see "Entries in the Bible." For the apparently unrelated Sir John Pringle, see "Sir John Pringle."

12. John Bullman, "a stout good looking man, only much pitted with smallpox," came to South Carolina on December 19, 1770. Hired as the assistant rector of St. Michael's, the preacher made a substantial living "of upwards of £200 sterl.g p. Ann." In addition to his employment at St. Michael's, he ran a "very good" school for boys, which paid him handsomely. See John Pringle (from Charles Town) to William Tilghman (at Philadelphia), September 15, 1774, Preston Davie Collection (3406), folder 47, UNCSHC. See Williams, *Early Ministers*, 29–30.

13. Drayton, *Memoirs* 1: 142.

14. Pringle to Tilghman, September 15, 1774; Drayton, *Memoirs* 1: 142.

15. Drayton, *Memoirs* 1: 143.

16. Ibid.

17. Pringle to Tilghman, September 15, 1774; Drayton, *Memoirs* 1: 142–143; Fraser, *Patriots*, 139.

18. Fraser, *Patriots*, 63.

19. Drayton, *Memoirs* 1: 144.

20. Wood, "'Liberty Is Sweet,'" 156–159.

21. Maier, *From Resistance to Revolution*, 133.

22. *SCGCJ*, August 16, 1774.

23. *SCGCJ*, September 6, 1774.

24. Ibid.

25. Drayton, *Memoirs* 1: 144.

26. *SCGCJ*, October 18, 1774.

27. Drayton, *Memoirs* 1: 144.

28. Holton, *Forced Founders*, 121–124; Cole, *Wholesale Commodity Prices*, 61–68; Ammerman, *In the Common Cause*, 82–83; Fraser, *Patriots*, 63–64; Weir, *Colonial South Carolina*, 316.

29. Ammerman, *In the Common Cause*, 82–83.

30. Holton, *Forced Founders*, 121–124; Fraser, *Patriots*, 63–64; Weir, *Colonial South Carolina*, 316.

31. A report from Georgia in the *South Carolina Gazette and Country Journal* dated October 11 mentioned slaves seeking refuge with the Creek Indians:

By accounts from Georgia, we are informed that the last Message sent to the Creeks by the Superintendent [John Stuart], brought these Indians to Reason; they have put two more of the Murderers to Death, named Sihoya and Nottawega, the other two, Houmahata and Sousea, escaped after being fired at: All Run-away Negroes, and Stolen Horses and Cattle are to be returned; in short, they promise every Thing we can require or wish for, and express an earnest Desire to make up the differences.

A dispatch dated November 1 in the same newspaper also mentioned a conflict between Georgians and the Creeks in which black slaves played a prominent role:

> By last Accounts from Savannah, in Georgia, we informed, "That on the 20th ult. the Governor [James Wright] and Superintendent [John Stuart] met the Creek Indians about Ten o'Clock in the Morning, and finished ultimately with them at Four in the Afternoon, having concluded a Treaty, the stipulations of which are, 1. A Ratification of all former Treaties and Agreements. 2. That the two Murderers, Houmahta and Sosea, shall be put to Death whenever and wherever found. 3. All Negroes harbored in Creek Country shall be delivered up. 4. All Horses and Cattle stolen from the white people during the late Disturbances, shall be restored. 5. Henceforward, the Indians are not to make any Settlements on the Okonee and Ockmulguee Rivers. 6. The Indians are to direct their People not to hunt on this side of the Okonee River. 7. The Satisfaction given and to be given is to be accepted and admitted as full Satisfaction for the Murders committed in the Provinces of Georgia and West-Florida. And, 8. That in Confidence of the Indians performing their Engagements, the Trade is to be immediately opened."

See *SCGCJ*, October 11, 25 (supp.), 1774.

32. Court of General Sessions, 1769–1776, Grand Jury Presentments, SCDAH; Morgan, "Black Life," 187–232.

33. *SCGCJ*, October 25, 1774. The *Maria* arrived in Charles Town Harbor on October 17, 1774, after a seventy-three-day voyage from Isles de Los (Iles de Los). The vessel, owned by the firm of Powell, Hopton, and Company, carried a human cargo of thirty-six Sierra Leonean slaves. The slaves were quarantined for ten days at the pesthouse on Sullivan's Island, before being sold at auction on October 27. See Donnan, *Documents* 4: 467. Word of the insurrection reached Boston in November; *Massachusetts Gazette and News Letter*, December 1, 1774.

34. *SCGCJ*, October 25, 1774.

35. See Court of General Sessions, 1769–1776, Grand Jury Presentments, SCDAH. In the document, there is some controversy about Margate's origins. He may have actually been an American slave who escaped to England and attempted to cover up his identity by claiming an African birth. See Adam Zele, "Becoming Sensible."

36. James Habersham to Robert Keen, *CGHS* 6: 243–244.

37. Given his presence in England in the circle of the Countess of Huntingdon, Margate would certainly have been familiar with the ruling. See Blumrosen and Blumrosen, *Slave Nation*, 1–14.

38. Edwards to the Countess of Huntingdon, January 16, 1775, A3/6/10, Countess of Huntingdon's American Papers, Westminster College; Zele, "Becoming Sensible"; Morgan, *Slave Counterpoint*, 650 n. 161.

39. Morgan, "Black Life," 208–209.

40. James Habersham to Robert Keen, *CGHS* 6: 243–244. See Edwards to the Countess of Huntingdon, January 16, 1775, A3/6/10; Edwards to the Countess of Huntingdon, January 11, 1775, A3/6/9; Piercey to the Countess of Huntingdon, November 28, 1774, A4/1/9, all in Countess of Huntingdon's American Papers, Westminster College. Quoted in Morgan, "Black Life," 208–209. See also Wood, "'Liberty Is Sweet,'" 166.

41. *SCGCJ*, November 8, 1774, carried the following announcement:

On Tuesday last the Ship Britannia, Samuel Ball, Master, arrived here from London, with whom came Passengers Thomas Atwood, Esq; appointed Chief Justice of the Behania Islands, William Gregory, Esq; appointed one of the Assistant Judges and Justices of this Province, in the Room of John Murray, Esq; deceased, James Cusack, Esq; and Mr. Wrong, Mrs. Mac Dounough and her Family, Mrs. and Miss Andrews, Mrs. Hoster, Mr. William Holliday, Mr. Zephaniah Kinsey, Mr. Gray, Mr. Peele, and several others.

See also Fraser, *Patriots*, 57.

42. Weir, *Colonial South Carolina*, 316; Fraser, *Charleston!* 139–140; *Drayton, Memoirs* 1: 154–155.

43. The news arrived on Tuesday, November 15, when the *Fair American* made its way into Charles Town Harbor. The following information was published a week after the vessel's arrival: "That on the First of October, an express arrived there from Sir William Meredith, Bart. one of the Members for that Town, then at London, with Advice that his Majesty had been pleased to dissolve his Parliament, and to order new Writs to be issued for electing another Immediately." See *SCGCJ*, November 22, 1774; Drayton, *Memoirs* 1: 165.

44. Fraser, *Charleston!* 140.

45. Ibid.

46. Drayton, *Memoirs* 1: 167–168.

47. Ibid., 169.

48. Ibid.

49. Ibid., 170.

50. According to Coker, "The American Revolution shattered the indigo industry, as southern plantations were thrust into open-market conditions." See Coker, *Charleston's Maritime Heritage*, 44. Commenting on Gadsden's speech, Laurens noted that the radical leader "attempted to exonerate himself & made such a defence of his own conduct as fell little Short of an impeachment of that of his Colleagues who are much displeased with him, he confessed that he acted against his judgement & as there was but one other Side which he could take his Interest he made upon the whole but an uncouth figure." Henry Laurens to John Laurens, Charles Town, January 18, 1775, in Laurens, *Papers* 10: 28.

51. Drayton, *Memoirs* 1: 172.

52. Ibid., 172–173.

53. Ibid., 173.

54. At the time this compromise was agreed upon, rice was valued at 55 shillings per barrel. The price of indigo was 30 shillings per pound. The price of hemp was 8 pounds sterling per hundred pounds. Corn was valued at 12 shillings and 6 penniesper bushel. The price of high-quality flour was 4 pounds 10 shillings per hundred pounds. The price of standard-quality flour was valued at 4 pounds sterling for the same amount. Pork was valued at 13 pounds sterling per barrel. The cost of butter was 3 shillings per pound. Lumber, measured in inch pine boards per 1,000 feet, went for 20 pounds sterling in Charles Town, 15 pounds in Beaufort, and 15 pounds in George Town. Ibid., 167–169, 172–176.

55. William Bradford to James Madison, January 4, 1775, in Madison, *Papers* 1: 132; Edmund Burke, *Speeches* 1: 299; Alden, "John Stuart Accuses," 318.

56. A report in *SCGCJ* on March 28, 1775, noted that on March 24, "the Ship Charming Sally, Capt. Fortune, sailed on her return for Bristol, having on board five balls of sailduck, the only part of her inward cargo that had not been thrown into Hog Island Creek, which was imported into this Province contrary to the Non-Importation Agreement entered into by the Inhabitants."

57. Wealthy merchant and slave trader John Neufville, who opposed nonimportation when it was discussed publicly in July 1774, was the consignee of the cargoes aboard the *Charming Sally* as well as the *Katherine*. A report in *SCGCJ* on November 29, 1774, indicated that the ship *Two Brothers* from Gambia was also slated to land in Charles Town Harbor. However, the vessel had evidently become "so shattered" after a rough gale of wind that it was obliged to change course and "put into Cockspur Harbor" at the mouth of the Savannah River. The newspaper noted that "Pilot boats are sent to bring the Negroes round, and if they arrive in Time, they will be advertised and sold here." See Donnan, *Documents* 4: 470–471; *South Carolina Gazette (SCG)*, February 13, 20, 27, 1775.

58. In Article 2 of the Continental Association, patriots promised to "neither import, nor purchase, any slave imported after the first day of December next [1774]; after which time we will wholly discontinue the slave trade; and will neither be concerned in it ourselves, nor will we hire our vessels, nor sell our commodities or manufactures, to those who are concerned in it. See Drayton, *Memoirs* 1: 190.

59. *SCGCJ*, March 21, 1775, noted that "On Tuesday last the Snow Proteus, John Paplay, Master, arrived here from London, with whom came Passengers, Mr. Robert Smyth, with his son, and Master Ward, Son of John Ward, Esq.

60. Fraser, *Charleston!* 140; Drayton, *Memoirs* 1: 182–187.

61. Drayton, *Memoirs* 1: 182–187.

62. Ibid.

63. Ibid.

64. Ibid., 184.

65. Ibid., 184–186.

66. See *SCGCJ*, March 21, 1775; *SCG*, March 27, 1775; Fraser, *Charleston!* 140; Drayton, *Memoirs* 1: 182–183.

67. Drayton, *Memoirs* 1: 186–187.

68. See John Laurens to Henry Laurens, London, February 18, 1775, in Laurens, *Papers* 10: 75–76.

69. Fraser, *Charleston!* 141.

70. See *South Carolina General Gazette (SCGG)*, March 27, 1775.

71. The *Katherine* departed on Friday, March 24. See Donnan, *Documents* 4: 470–471.

NOTES TO CHAPTER 2

1. Drayton, *Memoirs* 1: 216.

2. *SCGG*, May 5, 1775; Haw, *John & Edward Rutledge*, 71.

3. Holton, *Forced Founders*, 143–144.

4. Lipscomb, *South Carolina Revolutionary War Battles*, 3.

5. *SCGG*, April 28, 1775.

6. Lipscomb, *South Carolina Revolutionary War Battles*, 3.

7. "By a private letter of authority from London, we have intelligence, that it is in the contemplation of [the British] Administration to encourage our slaves to act against us! We have thought it prudent, without loss of time, to provide against such machinations: enclosed we transmit to you extracts of our Resolves upon this alarming subject." Quoted in Frey, *Water from the Rock*, 56.

8. See *SCG*, May 12, 1775; letter from the General Committee to Delegates for South Carolina at Philadelphia, May 8, 1775, in Laurens, *Papers* 10: 114 n. 2, 4.

9. The first session took place between January 11 and 17. The opening of the second session took place on Thursday, June 1, 1775. See Alden, "John Stuart Accuses" 318.

10. Although somewhat dated, the best description of the royal government is still McCrady, *History of South Carolina under the Royal Government*.

11. A copy of the Association was sent by Henry Laurens to his son on May 15, 1775:

The actual Commencement of Hostilities against this Continent—the threats of arbitrary impositions from abroad & the dread of instigated Insurrections at home—are causes sufficient to drive an oppressed people to the use of Arms: We therefore the subscribers, Inhabitants of this unhappy Colony, holding ourselves bound by that most sacred of obligations, the duty of good Citizens towards an injured Country, & thoroughly convinced that under our present distressed circumstances we shall be justified before God & Man in resisting force by force; do unite ourselves under every tie of Religion & of honour & associate as a band in her defence[sic] against every Foe. & we do solemnly promise that whenever her Continental or Provincial Councils shall decree it necessary we will go forth & be ready to sacrifice our Lives & fortunes in attempting to secure her Freedom & Safety.

Henry Laurens to John Laurens, May 15, 1775, in Laurens, *Papers* 10: 118–119.

12. Captain Inness, a Scotsman, arrived in Charles Town on April 19, 1775. He would serve Governor Campbell as a personal secretary and send home secret reports on political developments to the Earl of Dartmouth. See Innes to Dartmouth, June 10, 1775, reprinted in Bargar, "Charles Town Loyalism," 125–136.

13. Fraser, *Charleston!* 143.

14. Quoted in Linebaugh and Rediker, *The Many-Headed Hydra*, 232.

15. Henry Laurens to John Laurens, June 8, 1775, in Laurens, *Papers* 10: 172–179.

16. According to the editors of Laurens, *Papers*, on September 1, 1775, a list of those "inimical to the Liberties of America" appeared in *SCGG* and included twenty-two names. All but one of them, for whom there is no obvious connection, were members of the royal administration in South Carolina. The list included William Wragg (former councilor); Thomas Knox Gordon (chief justice, Court of Common Pleas); Edward Savage, John Fewtrell, Charles Mathew Coslett, and William Gregory (justices, Court of Common Pleas); James Trail (clerk, Court of Common Pleas); James Simpson (attorney general); Richard Lambton (deputy attorney general); Thomas Skottowe (register of the Court of Ordinary and secretary of the province); Alexander Innes (secretary to the governor); Colonel Probart Howarth and Captain White Outerbridge (officers at Fort Johnson); Robert Dalway Holliday (collector); George Roupell (searcher and commissioner of forfeiture); Robert McCulloch (deputy collector); John Morris (comptroller of customs); John Morgridge, Mark Walkman, and William Rhodes (waiters); George Milligen (chief surgeon to His Majesty's forces in South Carolina); and John Cart (for whom there was no obvious connection). See Laurens, *Papers* 10: 323 n. 7; *Wells's Register*, 89–94.

17. Henry Laurens to John Laurens, Charles Town, June 8, 1775, in Laurens, *Papers* 10: 172.

18. According to the editors of Laurens, *Papers*, "The Athanasian Creed, named for fourth century Alexandrian bishop [St. Athanasius] affirms Christian beliefs in the Trinity and the Incarnation. HL's objection arose from the fact that it is prefaced and concluded with the assertion that salvation is impossible without strict adherence to these doctrines. Printed immediately before the litany in the Book of Common Prayer, the Church of England adopted the creed in 1662 to replace the Apostles' Creed." Laurens, *Papers* 10: 176 n. 25. For the patriot leader's thoughts on the matter, see Henry Laurens to John Laurens, June 8, 1775, in Laurens, *Papers* 10: 176–177. For a further discussion of the Athanasian Creed, see also Cross, *Oxford Dictionary*,100–101.

19. On June 7, Laurens wrote:

We were fortunate enough to overrule the Mad schemes of a few of our Zealots, which if they had been carried into execution would have cost this Province half a Million of our Currency, & this would have been the smallest part of the Evil, we should have ruined Charles Town & the adjacent Country, run Counter to the advice (since received) of the Continental Congress, drawn the heaviest degree of Great Britain's resentment against us & have remained objects of the derision of all the World—yet one or two of that Hellfire party cannot cordially forgive me for the success of my opposition to their wild projects—every body else are satisfied & every day gives them cause to be even more so.

See Henry Laurens to James Laurens, June 7, 1775, in Laurens, *Papers* 10: 163.

20. Clearly, the patriot leader knew his history. His allusion was to an incident that occurred during the Spanish occupation of the Low Countries in the 1580s. In order to ward off an impending Habsburg attack, the Dutch sank vessels into the Scheldt River and ruined the previously thriving port of Antwerp. As a result, the city's trade suffered for years. The Antwerp harbor (unbeknownst to Laurens) would not reopen until 1792 when France reopened the Scheldt River. Henry Laurens to John Laurens, May 30, 1775, in Laurens, *Papers* 10: 159–160 n. 9. See also Kossman, *Low Countries*, 14–15, 21.

21. Henry Laurens to John Laurens, June 8, 1775, in Laurens, *Papers* 10: 165.

22. According to the editors of *The Papers of Henry Laurens*, "The ship *Maria Wilhelmina*, captained by William Williams, arrived April 4 from New York. She had begun loading for Gosport by April 18, was cleared for sailing by June 2, but remained windbound for several weeks. The vessel finally sailed after July 28." See Laurens, *Papers* 10: 165 n. 3; *SCGG*, April 7, 18; June 2, 9, 16, 30; July 28, 1775. Several days after the vessel departed, radical member of the Council of Safety Arthur Middleton wrote to fellow "firebrand" William Henry Drayton:

We shall be driven to a Sea war at last; I hope our dear little *Maria Wilhelmina* will be replaced and Admiral Tennant fight over his ideal battles in reality, for behold a resolution of the Continental Congress much to our purpose. "That it be recommended to each Colony to appoint a Committee of Safety to superintend & direct all matters necessary for the security & defense of their respective Colonies in the recess of their Assemblies & Conventions—and that each Colony at their *own expense* make such provision by *armed Vessels or otherwise* as their respective Assemblies, Conventions or Committees of Safety shall judge expedient & suitable to their circumstances & situations for protection of their *harbours & navigation on their Seacosts* against all *unlawful Invasions, Attacks & depredations from Cutters and Ships of War.*"

See Barnwell, "Correspondence, " 124–125. See Sellers, *Charleston Business*, 64.

23. The man-of-war *Tamar*, captained by the elderly Edward Thornbrough, remained in Carolina from May 5, 1772, until March 30, 1776, when the she finally departed for Nova Scotia. See May, "His Majesty's Ship's," 169; Henry Laurens to John Laurens, June 8, 1775, in Laurens, *Papers* 10: 165, 165 n. 4.

24. Henry Laurens to John Laurens, June 8, 1775, in Laurens, *Papers* 10: 165–166.

25. Innes to Dartmouth, June 10, 1775, reprinted in Bargar, "Charles Town Loyalism," 133.

26. See Douglass, *Peerage of Scotland* 1: 118; Cheves, "Izard of South Carolina," 234–235; May, "His Majesty's Ships," 168; Lipscomb, *South Carolina Revolutionary War Battles*, 10–11; See Hood, *Governor's Palace*, 307–313; Innes to Dartmouth, June 10, 1775, reprinted in Bargar, "Charles Town Loyalism," 133; Henry Laurens to John Laurens, June 8, 1775, in Laurens, *Papers* 10: 164–165.

27. Henry Laurens to John Laurens, June 8, 1775, in Laurens, *Papers* 10: 164–165.

28. Ibid., 165.

29. The debate over the blockade would continue throughout the summer and into the fall. On July 30, for example, Laurens wrote to his son:

Yesterday we concluded upon, no plan, to do what I esteem in our circumstances worse than nothing, to "Fortify Charles Town or to put it in Some posture of defense," this I say will be worse than doing nothing, for diverse reasons which are obvious & for one which is invincible but I am not at liberty to divulge it—the Council of Safety have been constantly persecuted into a Consent, by a few persons who have been constantly pushing for ruinous measures which they call vigorous—a little time will Shew their error, but the Consequences may be fatal to Charles Town.

See Henry Laurens to John Laurens, July 30, 1775, in Laurens, *Papers* 10: 256.

30. Wood, "'Dream Deferred,'" 175–176.

31. Innes to Dartmouth, June 10, 1775, reprinted in Bargar, "Charles Town Loyalism," 133.

32. Alden, "John Stuart Accuses," 320.

33. Josiah Smith Jr. to James Poyas, May 18, 1775, Josiah Smith Letterbook,UNCSHC. Quoted in Crow, "Slave Rebelliousness," 84–85; Wood, "'Dream Deferred,' 175–176; and Olwell, *Masters, Slaves and Subjects*, 230.

34. Drayton, *Memoirs* 2: 179–180. Quoted in Olwell, *Masters, Slaves and Subjects*, 230.

35. Josiah Smith to George Appleby, June 16, 1775, Josiah Smith Letterbook UNCSHC, UNCSHC. According to Milligen:

This bugbear of instigated insurrections gained another great point for the disaffected faction. They wanted an armed force to be entirely at their disposal to protect themselves and to intimidate and distress his Majesty's loyal subjects. They obtained their desire: the Congress voted money to raise two regiments of foot and a regiment of light horse, a committee formed to take upon them the management of this army from whom the officers receive their commissions, orders, etc.

See also Report by George Milligen, September 15, 1775, CO 5/396/208–216d, NAUK; Davies, *Documents* 10: 109–114.

36. *SCGCJ*, June 13, 1775. According to a report filed in 1776 by the British Administration, "Colonel of the Malitia Mr Pinckney ordered the Inhabitants to do

Patrole Duty and to Mount Guard every night, which duty had till then been done by a Town Guard," on the basis of "Certain Information which they pretended to have received that an insurrection was meditated." See Alden, "John Stuart Accuses," 320; quoted in Wood, "Taking Care," 282.

37. Henry Laurens to John Laurens, May 15, 1775, in Laurens, *Papers* 10: 119. In that letter, Laurens noted that "upwards of one hundred Men besides the common Town Watch mount guard every Night & Committees of observation, of Intelligence & of safety find employment every Day."

38. Force, *American Archives* 2: 1130.

39. By his own account, Campbell was agitated and embarrassed by the reception. He wrote to Dartmouth, "My Lord, I have the honour to acquaint your lordship that I arrived here late in the evening of the 17 ult. in His Majesty's ship *Scorpion*, landed the next day and took possession of the government in the usual manner." See See Campbell to Dartmouth, July 2, 1775, CO 5/396/151, NAUK; Davies, *Documents* 10: 32–35.

40. Rogers, *Charleston in the Age*, xiii. According to Laurens:

His Lordship was received by the Grenadier Company at his Landing escorted by them in front of the common Militia, the Artillery & Light Infantry Companies.... His Lordship was not Honoured by a long train of attendants—two of the Council, two or three Judges, the Secretary & Some Officers of the Scorpion with barely one or two more made up his Retinue— the Lieut. Governor [William Bull] declined coming to Town, complaints of Slight & ill usage & tis Said intends to resign his Commission—Lord William went through the necessary Acts of taking the Oaths, reading his Commission & etc. at the Council Chamber & Granville's Bastion & then proceeded to Mr. Brewton's where he is to reside until his House is made ready for him—tomorrow I Shall pay my respects half an hour can be redeemed from Congress.

See Henry Laurens to John Laurens, June 18, 1775, in Laurens, *Papers* 10: 183–184.

41. Drayton, *Memoirs* 1: 257–258. According to Campbell, "Three Councillors could barely be found to admit me into my office: Mr. Gordon, the chief justice; Mr. Irving, the receiver general; and Mr. Gregory one of the Judges." See Campbell to Dartmouth, July 2, 1775, CO 5/396/151, NAUK; Davies, *Documents* 10: 32–35. This tiny retinue of loyalists, along with Secretary Alexander Innes and Dr. George Milligen, were virtually the governor's only allies in Low Country South Carolina. Gordon, Gregory, Fewtrell, and Coslett would later report to Campbell during his efforts to pardon Thomas Jeremiah.

42. Campbell wrote:

I have not seen or heard from the lieut.-governor: ever since my arrival he has remained at his country house [Ashley Hall] about 12 miles from town without favoring me with the smallest attention or giving the least assistance to government. I should have been extremely sorry had I been conscious to myself of personally deserving from Mr. Bull so pointed and contemptuous a neglect, but in the present case I have only to lament that a gentleman who for so many years has filled an important station with credit to himself and advantage to his country should treat the commission of his Sovereign with such studied disrespect.... Such my lord is the present distracted state of this province, such the very difficult and embarrassed state in which I find myself, abandoned by the lieut-governor, without a Council, without support of any kind.

See Campbell to Dartmouth, July 2, 1775, CO 5/396/151, NAUK; Davies, *Documents* 10: 32–35.

43. Drayton, *Memoirs* 1: 257–258.

44. Henry Laurens to John Laurens, August 20, 1775, in Laurens, *Papers* 10: 328.

45. Campbell to Dartmouth, July 2, 1775, CO 5/396/151, NAUK; Davies, *Documents* 10: 32–35.

46. Drayton, *Memoirs* 1: 266–269; Governor Lord William Campbell to Earl of Dartmouth, August 31, 1775, CO 5/396/225RH start to 230LH end, NAUK; Davies, *Documents* 10: 93–98.

47. Fraser, *Charleston!* 141.

48. Campbell to Dartmouth, Charles Town, August 31, 1775, CO 5/396/225RH start to 230LH end, NAUK; Davies, *Documents* 10: 93–98.

49. See Palmer, *Biographical Sketches*, 327. According to Gordon, "the Malcontents being very anxious to have some plausible pretence for arming with great industry propagated a Report that the Negroes were meditating an Insurrection." See Loyalist Claims Memorial, AO 12/51/289, NAUK; Quoted in Wood, "'Liberty Is Sweet,'" 162. According to a report filed by the British administration in 1776, "The pretended Discovery of an intention to Instigate Insurrections of the Negroes and Bring Down the Indians was the pretense for tendering an Instrument of Association to every person in the Province." See Alden, "John Stuart Accuses," 318–319.

50. Report by George Milligen, September 15, 1775, CO 5/396/208–216d, NAUK; Davies, *Documents* 10: 109–114. In his letter to Dartmouth, Campbell argued that he was the victim of "numberless arts" and "notorious falsehoods propagated," and that the patriots were deliberately churning out misinformation to "work up the people in every part of America" into a "pitch of madness and fury." See Campbell to Dartmouth, Charles Town, August 31, 1775,CO 5/396/225RH start to 230LH end, NAUK. Dr. George Milligen first went to America as surgeon's mate in Oglethorpe's Georgia Regiment and settled at Charleston a year later. By 1775, he held a royal commission as chief surgeon to His Majesty's forces in South Carolina. When summoned before the General Committee, he explained that his royal commission precluded his signing of the Association. A highly visible loyalist, in August, he was threatened by the mob and given notice to appear again before the Committee. In light of these circumstances, Campbell advised him to take refuge aboard the *Tamar*. On August 22, 1775, Milligen sailed for England aboard the *Eagle*. Prior to filing his claim

as a loyalist, he added "Johnston" to his surname. See Henry Laurens to John Laurens, Charles Town, August 20, 1775, in Laurens, *Papers* 10: 324 n. 8.

51. Report by George Milligen, September 15, 1775, CO 5/396/208–216d, NAUK; Davies, *Documents* 10: 109–114.Such reports were prevalent in other colonies. Toward the end of the summer, for example, a patriot preacher in Maryland would write to London, "The governor of Virginia, the captains of the men of war, and mariners have been tampering with our Negroes; and have nightly meetings with them; all for the glorious purpose of enticing them to cut their masters' throats while they are asleep. Gracious God! that men noble by birth and fortune should descend to such ignoble base servility." See "Extracts of a Letter from a Clergyman in Maryland to his Friend in England," August 2, 1775, in Force, *American Archives* 3: 10; Hoffman, "'Disaffected,'" 281; Wood, "'Taking Care,'" 279.

52. According to an official report made by the British administration in 1776, "The newspapers were full of Publications calculated to excite the fears of the People— Massacres and Instigated Insurrections were in the mouth of every Child." See Alden, "John Stuart Accuses," 318–319; quoted in Wood, "'Taking Care,'" 281.

53. Report by George Milligen, September 15, 1775, CO 5/396/208–216d, NAUK; Davies, *Documents* 10: 109–114.

54. *SCG*, May 29, 1775; quoted in Olwell, *Masters and Slaves*, 229; Wood "'Liberty Is Sweet,'" 166.

55. Drayton, *Memoirs* 2: 300–301.

56. According to Laurens, Martin was an "under Wharfinger" of "Some Credit in Town." See Henry Laurens to John Laurens, June 8, 1775, in Laurens, *Papers* 10: 167.

57. Drayton, *Memoirs* 2: 300–301.

58. Henry Laurens to John Laurens, Charles Town, June 8, 1775, in Laurens, *Papers* 10: 167.

59. Ibid., 167–168.

60. Innes to Dartmouth, June 10, 1775, reprinted in Bargar, "Charles Town Loyalism," 133.

61. Walsh, *Charleston's Sons of Liberty*, 71.

62. On June 13, the apology appeared in the *SCGCJ*, and on the same day, Captain John Lasley set sail for Bristol on the *Liberty* with James Dealy onboard. See Henry Laurens to John Laurens, June 8, 1775, in Laurens, *Papers* 10: 168 n. 11.

63. Joseph Manigault to Gabriel Manigault, Charles Town, June 4, 1775, Manigault Family Papers, USCSCL.

64. The merchant planter remarked that the "Poor creatures" were "sensibly effected & with many thanks promised to follow my advice and to accept the offer of my protection." See Henry Laurens to James Laurens, June 7, 1775, in Laurens, *Papers* 10: 162–163.

65. This dispatch from New Bern was dated May 19. According to historian Samuel A. Ashe, several days later, an emissary arrived in the North Carolina capital from New York "and informed Governor Martin that General Gage was about to send him the arms and munitions desired, and there was reason to suppose that the shipment had been discovered. A report also had been propagated that the governor had formed a design of arming the Negroes and proclaiming freedom to those who

should resort to the king's standard, and the public mind was much inflamed against him." See Ashe, *History* 1: 435–436.

66. *SCG*, July 8, 1775.

67. Campbell to Dartmouth, Charles Town, August 31, 1775, CO 5/396/225RH start to 230LH end, NAUK; Davies, *Documents* 10: 93–98.

68. Davies, *Documents* 10: 72. Ibid.

69. Ibid.

70. Ibid.

71. Henry Laurens to John Laurens, June 18, 1775, in Laurens, *Papers* 10: 184–185.

72. Report by George Milligen, September 15, 1775, CO 5/396/208–216d, NAUK; Davies, *Documents* 10: 109–114.

73. Henry Laurens to John Laurens, June 23, 1775, in Laurens, *Papers* 10: 191–192.

74. Hemphill and Wates, *Extracts*, 66.

75. Henry Laurens to John Laurens, June 23, 1775, in Laurens, *Papers* 10: 191.

76. Campbell to Dartmouth, Charles Town, August 31, 1775, CO 5/396/225RH start to 230LH end, NAUK; Davies, *Documents* 10: 93–98.

77. Henry Laurens to John Laurens, June 23, 1775, in Laurens, *Papers* 10: 191.

78. Campbell to Dartmouth, Charles Town, August 31, 1775, CO 5/396/225RH start to 230LH end, NAUK; Davies, *Documents* 10: 93–98.

79. Report by George Milligen, September 15, 1775, CO 5/396/208–216d, NAUK; Davies, *Documents* 10: 109–114. The other black who remained under suspicion was Jemmy, who was later sentenced to death along with Jeremiah but was pardoned on Thursday, August 17, the day before the scheduled execution.

NOTES TO CHAPTER 3

1. Henry Laurens to John Laurens, June 23, 1775, in Laurens, *Papers* 10: 191–192.

2. Manigault, "Papers," 2; quoted in Wood, "Taking Care," 283.

3. Letter from Woodmanstone, England, September 5, 1775, in Manigault Family Papers, USCSCL.

4. This statement was striken from the actual letter. In its place (and in order to avoid accusations of antipathy toward the Scots) was put a milder statement about the community's wish that Burnet had "never come to this Province." See Thomas Hutchinson to the Council of Safety, July 5, 1775, in Laurens, *Papers* 10: 206 n.2.

5. Ibid., 207–208.

6. Ibid., 206–208.

7. Ibid., 207.

8. Council of Safety to the St. Bartholomew Committee, July 18, 1775, in Laurens, *Papers* 10: 231.

9. Ibid., 231–232.

10. Henry Laurens to John Laurens, August 20, 1775, in Laurens, *Papers* 10: 329 n. 14, 330.

11. On June 26, Colonel William Henry Moultrie and Lieutenant Colonel Isaac Huger applied to the Council of Safety for advice concerning the "enlistment of men, who are said to have deserted from sea service." Despite Laurens's objections and the warning by Captain Tollemache that if he lost any men, he would do everything in his power to "distress the trade" of the province, the Council antagonized the naval officer by replying: "We did not know that we had enlisted any of your men; but if any have them enlisted, we dare not give them up." See *Collections of the South Carolina Historical Society* 2: 30. See letter from Henry Laurens to John Laurens, July 14, 1775, in Laurens, *Papers* 10: 220 n. 7.

12. See chapters 4, 5, and 6.

13. Governor Lord William Campbell to Earl of Dartmouth, July 19 & 20, 1775, CO 5/395/168, NAUK; Davies, *Documents* 10: 49–53.

14. See chapters 5 and 6. The pilot Lord Campbell referred to may have been a runaway slave named Shadwell or a free black mariner named Scipio Handley.

15. Henry Laurens to John Laurens, Charles Town, August 20, 1775, in Laurens, *Papers* 10: 321.

16. Report by George Milligen, September 15, 1775, CO 5/396/208–216d, NAUK; Davies, *Documents* 10: 109–114. Just as Jeremiah was targeted as a strategic liability for being a black harbor pilot, Walker was singled out for his position as the Tory "gunner" of Fort Johnson. Perched high above the southern entrance to the harbor, Fort Johnson was a strategic outpost of immense importance. Both patriots and loyalists were well aware that whoever held the fortress held Charles Town. As the issue of defense became increasingly critical, the Tory soldiers guarding the outpost quickly became a potential target.

17. Former councilor William Wragg (1714–1777), a devoted loyalist, was exiled to his plantation. See Barnwell, "Correspondence," 126.

18. According to McCrady, Fenwicke Bull was a recent immigrant from England and "not one of the either Bull or Fenwicke families of the province." See McCrady, *History of South Carolina in the Revolution*, 58.

19. Barnwell, "Correspondence," 129. Wells edited the *South Carolina and American General Gazette*, the rival publication to Timothy's *South Carolina Gazette*. See McCrady, *History of South Carolina in the Revolution*, 58–59.

20. Report by George Milligen, September 15, 1775, CO 5/396/208–216d, NAUK; Davies, *Documents* 10: 109–114; Governor Campbell to the Earl of Dartmouth, September 19, 1775, CO 5/396/241, NAUK; Davies, *Documents* 10: 116–118.

21. Campbell to Dartmouth, August 31, 1775, CO 5/396/225RH start to 230LH end, NAUK; Davies, *Documents* 10: 93–98.

22. Henry Laurens to John Laurens, August 20, 1775, in Laurens, *Papers* 10: 331.

23. Ibid., 331–334.

24. The gentleman alluded to might have been Miles Brewton, a wealthy Charles Town resident and member of the Commons House, or it might have even been

Henry Laurens. The most likely candidate, however, would have been the wealthy loyalist William Wragg. I am grateful to an anonymous Oxford University Press reviewer for the last suggestion.

25. Campbell to Dartmouth, August 31, 1775, CO 5/396/225RH start to 230LH end, NAUK; Davies, *Documents* 10: 93–98.

26. Ibid.

27. See Henry Laurens to John Laurens, Charles Town, August 20, 1775, in Laurens, *Papers* 10: 320.

28. Campbell to Dartmouth,, August 31, 1775, CO 5/396/225RH start to 230LH end, NAUK; Davies, *Documents* 10: 93–98.

29. Ibid.

30. Milligen claimed that a "house carpenter," Daniel Cannon, and the clerk of St. Philip's Church, Edward Weyman, "about the latter end of June," summoned him and ordered him to subscribe to the Patriot Association. When Milligen refused, Cannon told the surgeon he "must expect to be treated agreeable to the rules of sound policy." See Report by George Milligen, September 15, 1775, CO 5/396/208–216d, NAUK; Davies, *Documents* 10: 109–114.

31. Campbell to Dartmouth, Charles Town, August 31, 1775, CO 5/396/225RH start to 230LH end, NAUK; Davies, *Documents* 10: 93–98.

32. Report by Gordon, Savage, Simpson and Gregory, CO 5/396/231RH start to 232 LH end, NAUK.

33. Ibid.

34. Ibid.; Report by George Milligen, September 15, 1775, CO 5/396/208–216d, NAUK, Davies, *Documents* 10: 109–114.

35. Report by Coslett, CO 5/396/233 RH start to 234 RH end, NAUK.

36. Campbell to Dartmouth, August 31, 1775, CO 5/410/207–224, NA; *DAR*, 10: 72.

37. Ibid.

38. Ibid.

39. Fewtrell submitted his report in writing to Lord Campbell on Saturday, August 19, the day after Jeremiah's execution. See Report by Fewtrell, CO 5/396/235 RH, NAUK.

40. This may have been a mistake. Fewtrell probably meant the Council of Safety (the executive) and not "the legislature of the province," which was actually the Provincial Congress. Ibid.

41. Ibid.

42. Campbell to Dartmouth, Charles Town, August 31, 1775, CO 5/396/225RH start to 230LH end, NAUK; Davies, *Documents* 10: 93–98.

43. Henry Laurens to John Laurens, Charles Town, August 20, 1775, in Laurens, *Papers* 10: 320.

44. Ibid., 330. According to a letter written by Alexander Innes, which Laurens sent to his son, the Reverend Smith applied for a pardon for Jemmy earlier that day at noon, but Campbell did not sign it until six P.M.

45. Campbell to Dartmouth, August 31, 1775, CO 5/396/225RH start to 230LH end, NAUK; Davies, *Documents* 10: 93–98.; Henry Laurens to John Laurens, August 20, 1775, in Laurens, *Papers* 10: 321, 328, 334–335.

46. Campbell to Dartmouth, August 31, 1775, CO 5/396/225RH start to 230LH end, NAUK; Davies, *Documents* 10: 93–98.

47. This letter was later given to Laurens, who referred to it as a "very extraordinary Letter from the 'Representative of Majesty.' Attempting to prove a Negative—charging two Justices & three Freeholders with the shedding of Innocent blood—because after a fair & patient hearing, they were unanimously of opinion that Jerry was Guilty." See Henry Laurens to John Laurens, August 20, 1775, in Laurens, *Papers* 10: 334.

48. This line in particular irritated Laurens a great deal, and he would later mockingly refer to Campbell by that epithet.

49. Henry Laurens to John Laurens, August 20, 1775, in Laurens, *Papers* 10: 321.

50. Ibid. Laurens was not alone in his distaste for the secretary; other patriot leaders, especially William Henry Drayton, expressed some disdain for him. Drayton wrote in July: "I have not been able, or rather it has not lain in way till the other day, to exchange even a word with Captain Innis. People in general seem averse to him. His carriage seems haughty, and from some late proceedings he seems perfectly disposed to be *viceroy over him* [meaning Campbell]." See letter from William H. Drayton to William Drayton, Charles Town, July 4, 1775, Davies, *Documents* 10: 37.

51. Henry Laurens to John Laurens, August 20, 1775, in Laurens, *Papers* 10: 329.

52. Ibid.

53. Campbell was directly involved with three other black harbor pilots: a slave named Shadwell, a free black named Scipio Handley, and a boatman named Sampson.

54. Henry Laurens to John Laurens, August 20, 1775, in Laurens, *Papers* 10: 330.

55. Probably William Nesbitt.

56. Laurens's response to Innes's letter was sent out at 7:30 A.M. Considering that Innes's initial letter was also written that day, the secretary must have penned it in the wee hours.

57. Henry Laurens to John Laurens, August 20, 1775, in Laurens, *Papers* 10: 331.

58. Ibid., 331–334.

59. Report by George Milligen, September 15, 1775, CO 5/396/208–216d, NAUK; Davies, *Documents* 10: 109–114; Campbell to Dartmouth, August 31, 1775, CO 5/396/225RH start to 230LH end, NAUK; Davies, *Documents* 10: 93–98. As Peter H. Wood noted, "Among white residents of Charleston, neither his accusers nor his defenders could fully comprehend the meaning of his life and death. But fellow blacks, both enslaved and free, must have sensed his real and symbolic importance in a powerful way." See Wood, "Taking Care," 286–287.

60. Campbell to Dartmouth, August 31, 1775, CO 5/396/225RH start to 230LH end, NAUK; Davies, *Documents* 10: 93–98.

61. Report by George Milligen, September 15, 1775, CO 5/396/208–216d, NAUK; Davies, *Documents* 10:109–114.

62. No specific time is given, but the letter was sent by Laurens on the afternoon of the 18th from the Charles Town district of Ansonborough. See Henry Laurens to John Laurens, August 20, 1775, in Laurens, *Papers* 10: 333–334.

63. Ibid., 333.

64. Ibid., 334.

65. Ibid., 333–334.

66. Extract of a letter to a gentleman in Philadelphia, August 20, 1775, in Force, *American Archives* 3: 180. Force dated the document August 20, but because the "gentleman" wrote "yesterday" in regard to Jeremiah's execution, the letter must have been written on the 19th.

67. Lord William Campbell to Earl of Dartmouth, August 19, 1775, CO 5/396/204–207d, NAUK; CO 5/410/200–207, NAUK.

68. Williams, *Hurricane of Independence*, 1–19.

NOTES TO CHAPTER 4

1. Lipscomb, *South Carolina Revolutionary War Battles*, 11.

2. Ibid.

3. Ibid.

4. John Ball to Isaac Ball, Charles Town, September 19, 1775, Ball Family Papers, 1631–1891, SCHS; Drayton, *Memoirs* 2: 31.

5. Drayton, *Memoirs* 2: 31–34.

6. Drayton, *Memoirs*, 2: 30–35; Council of Safety to William Henry Drayton, Charles Town, September 15, 1775, in Laurens, *Papers* 10: 386–387; Charles Drayton to William Henry Drayton, Charles Town, September 16, 1775, in Gibbes, *Documentary History* 1: 183–184; John Ball to Isaac Ball, Charles Town, September 19, 1775, Ball Family Papers, 1631–1891, SCHS.

7. Charles Drayton echoed these sentiments when he noted that "his trepanned lordship" advised "the back country people not to take up arms, unless they think they are full strong enough—if they think they are, they may—and that they will be soon be relieved by troops expected to be here soon." See Charles Drayton to William Henry Drayton, Charles Town, September 16, 1775, in Gibbes, *Documentary History* 1: 183.

8. John Ball to Isaac Ball, Charles Town, September 19, 1775, Ball Family Papers, 1631–1891, SCHS. Shortly after the incident, Henry Laurens remarked in a letter to William Henry Drayton that the governor's "pretended friendship" was designed to work to the patriots' "destruction." See Council of Safety to William Henry Drayton, Charles Town, September 15, 1775, in Laurens, *Papers* 10: 386.

9. John Ball to Isaac Ball, Charles Town, September 19, 1775, Ball Family Papers, 1631–1891, SCHS; Drayton, *Memoirs* 2: 34–35.

10. Council of Safety to South Carolina Delegates in Congress, Charles Town, September 18, 1775, in Laurens, *Papers* 10: 399.

11. Drayton, *Memoirs* 2: 35.

12. Ibid. 36.

13. Charles Drayton to William Henry Drayton, Charles Town, September 16, 1775, in Gibbes, *Documentary History* 1: 183; Council of Safety to South Carolina Delegates in Congress, Charles Town, September 18, 1775, in Laurens, *Papers* 10: 399;

Council of Safety to William Henry Drayton, Charles Town, September 15, 1775, in Laurens, *Papers* 10: 387–388; Drayton, *Memoirs* 2: 35–36.

14. Fortunately for both sides that evening, Moultrie and his men had been detained when their vessels got stuck in the mud. According to John Drayton, this was an act of divine Providence: "It hence appeared, the detention in landing had been a fortunate interference of Providence to prevent bloodshed. For, had they landed in the night as was intended, the fort would probably have been stormed, while Innis and his seamen were busied in their ruinous work: and the press of troops would have been so great into the fort, and the surprize so unlooked for, as scarcely to have ended in any thing else, than the loss of some lives—and in the actual commencement of hostilities in this part of America." Drayton, *Memoirs* 2: 38.

15. According to Edward McCrady, "A creek then ran up what is now Water Street and then passed the rear end of the lot of the Governor's residence, from which communication by small boats was easily maintained with the vessels of war in the harbor." See McCrady, *History of South Carolina in the Revolution*, 64; Rogers, *Charleston in the Age*, 44; Poston, *The Buildings of Charleston*, 149.

16. See Holton, *Forced Founders*, 133; Ready, *Tar Heel State*, 109.

17. Drayton, *Memoirs* 2: 40.

18. His Majesty's armed ship *Cherokee*, captained by John Ferguson, arrived at Charles Town on September 7, 1775. The *Swallow* packet, under William Copeland, arrived at Charles Town from Falmouth on September 13. See Laurens, *Papers* 10: 388 n. 7, n. 8.

19. Drayton, *Memoirs* 2: 51–52; Council of Safety to William Henry Drayton, Charles Town, September 15, 1775, in Laurens, *Papers* 10: 388.

20. According to John Drayton, the crescent became part of the flag "on account of the first and second regiments' detachments then at the fort; who wore a silver crescent on the front of their caps—and their uniform was blue." See Drayton, *Memoirs* 2: 52–53.

21. Ibid., 51.

22. Alexander Garden to Henry Laurens, Charles Town, September 17, 1775, in Laurens, *Papers* 10: 395.

23. Drayton, *Memoirs* 2: 53.

24. See Laurens, *Papers* 10: 405 n. 1.

25. Council of Safety to Edward Thornbrough, Charles Town, September 19, 1775, in Laurens, *Papers* 10: 405–406.

26. Ibid.

27. Edward Thornbrough to Henry Laurens, Rebellion Road, September 19, 1775, in Laurens, *Papers* 10: 406.

28. Ibid.

29. Isaac Motte to Henry Laurens, Fort Johnson, September 19, 1775, half past 3 o'clock, in Laurens, *Papers* 10: 407.

30. Ibid.

31. Ibid.

32. Ibid.

33. Elias (Elisha) Painter, the boatswain of the *Swallow*, was eventually taken into service aboard the *Cherokee*. Painter deserted his post and was subsequently aided by the South Carolina Council of Safety in getting to Georgia, where he hoped to obtain passage to his native England. See *Collections of the South Carolina Historical Society* 3: 42.

34. See *SCGG*, April 28, 1775.

35. Isaac Motte to Henry Laurens, Fort Johnson, September 19, 1775, half past 3 o'clock, in Laurens, *Papers* 10: 409.

36. Ibid.

37. Isaac Motte to Henry Laurens, Fort Johnson, September 19, 1775, 10 o'clock at night, in Laurens, *Papers* 10: 408–409.

38. Council of Safety to William Henry Drayton, Charles Town, September 20, 1775, in Laurens, *Papers* 10: 412.

39. Drayton, *Memoirs* 2: 54.

40. Henry Laurens to James Laurens, Charles Town, September 22, 1775, in Laurens, *Papers* 10: 414.

41. Around the time that the Committee began to revive the proposal, Laurens wrote to his son:

> Our people after talking of various offensive & defensive Plans without bringing anything to maturity except trifles in the first Class from whence they can never reap either honor or profit, are now upon the exploded scheme of stopping up the Channels called Lawford's & the Ship in order to keep out Ships of War, a scheme which I formerly opposed with great success & which I shall still contend against although I have little ground to hope for success, because they have revived a motion in Committee which was reprobated in a Congress—this former may consist of 30 or 40—the latter contained near 200 Members.—the measure in my Idea proposes too much or too little—if they stop the Bar effectually this Town & the most valuable part of the Country will be ruined—if they fail we shall incur a vast fruitless expence & be exposed to ridicule & censure through future ages—& in neither case can we ward off the vengeance of Great Britain if she is foolishly determined to hurt herself by punishing us for such foolish conduct.

See Henry Laurens to John Laurens, Charles Town, September 23, 1775, in Laurens, *Papers* 10: 422–423.

42. Drayton, *Memoirs* 2: 55.

43. Ibid., 54–55.

44. Henry Laurens to John Laurens, Charles Town, September 26, 1775, in Laurens, *Papers* 10: 426–427.

45. Drayton, *Memoirs* 2: 55.

46. The men were George Gabriel Powell, Edward Blake, John Izard, Daniel Cannon, Roger Smith, Michael Kalteisen, and John Edwards. Committee Appointed to

Obstruct the Passages over the Bar of Charleston to the Council of Safety, Charleston, October 5, 1775, in Gibbes, *Documentary History* 1: 199.

47. Drayton, *Memoirs* 2: 55–56.

48. General Committee to Lord William Campbell, State House, September 29, 1775, in Laurens, *Papers* 10: 434–435.

49. Ibid. A similar letter was sent to the governor's wife, Lady Campbell, notifying her of the Council's wish that her husband return to Charles Town. See Henry Laurens to Lady William Campbell, Ansonborough, September 29, 1775, in Laurens, *Papers* 10: 435–436.

50. Lord William Campbell to Henry Laurens, Tamar, September 30, 1775, in Laurens, *Papers* 10: 442–443.

51. See Thomas Ferguson to Christopher Gadsden, Charles Town, October 3, 1775, in Gibbes, *Documentary History* 1: 198–199.

52. The radicals accused the moderates of using questionable tactics to obtain the signatures. According to Thomas Ferguson, "Very unfair means were used to get the people to sign. A great many came and desired their names to be struck off." See Thomas Ferguson to Christopher Gadsden, Charles Town, October 5, 1775, in Gibbes, *Documentary History* 1: 200–201; Drayton, *Memoirs* 2: 56.

53. Drayton, *Memoirs* 2: 56.

54. Thomas Ferguson to Christopher Gadsden, Charles Town, October 3, 1775, in Gibbes, *Documentary History* 1: 198.

55. This individual may have been Gabriel Manigault. Drayton, *Memoirs* 2: 56.

56. This was actually yet another attempt to revive an old plan. In the mid-1750s, engineer William De Brahm sent detailed plans to Royal Governor Glen for a fortified Canal measuring 11,600 feet to connect the Ashley and Cooper Rivers, so that Charles Town Neck would become an island, "protected against an Insurrection of the Negroes or an Indian War." See De Vorsey, *De Brahm's Report*, 91.

57. Drayton, *Memoirs* 2: 56–57.

58. Ibid.

59. Committee Appointed to Obstruct the Passages over the Bar of Charleston to the Council of Safety, Charleston, October 5, 1775, in Gibbes, *Documentary History* 1: 199.

60. Thomas Ferguson to Christopher Gadsden, Charles Town, October 5, 1775, in Gibbes, *Documentary History* 1: 200–201.

61. Ibid.

62. Drayton, *Memoirs* 2: 58.

63. Hemphill and Wates, *Extracts*, 94–96.

64. Drayton, *Memoirs* 2: 58, 100–103.

65. Report of the Committee for Forming a Plan of Defence for the Colony, in Gibbes, *Documentary History* 1: 203–206.

66. Drayton, *Memoirs* 2: 58–59.

67. Samuel Boykin to the Council of Safety, Granby, October 16, 1775, in Laurens, *Papers* 10: 471.

68. Henry Laurens to James Laurens, Charles Town, October 20, 1775, in Laurens, *Papers* 10: 477–478.

69. See Resolution of the Council of Safety, Charles Town, October 17, 1775, in Laurens, *Papers* 10: 472 n. 2. See also Proceedings of a Court Martial held October 13, 1775, William Gilmore Simms Collection, Kendall Whaling Museum.

70. Henry Laurens to James Laurens, Charles Town, October 20, 1775, in Laurens, *Papers* 10: 477–478.

71. William Moultrie to Henry Laurens, Charles Town, October 19, 1775, in Laurens, *Papers* 10: 476.

72. Council of Safety to William Moultrie, Charles Town, October 19, 1775, in Laurens, *Papers* 10: 473 n. 2.

73. Drayton, *Memoirs* 2: 70–71.

74. The *Defence*, the *Comet*, and the *Beaufort*, had been converted to armed ships in the beginning of September. On September 5, the Council of Safety wrote to William Henry Drayton and informed him that it "Resolved to equip three Schooners to be mounted with two Nine pounders each, for the defence of this Harbour." This operation was directed by Edward Blake, Clement Lempriere, and Benjamin Tucker. See Council of Safety to William Henry Drayton, Charles Town, September 5, 1775, in Laurens, *Papers* 10: 366; Drayton, *Memoirs* 2: 71.

75. Little River Committee to the Council of Safety, Little River, October 23, 1775, in Laurens, *Papers* 10: 499.

76. *SC AGG*, November 24–December 8, 1775, 3. John Allen (Alleyne) Walter(s) (1752–ca. 1787) is an interesting figure. A lawyer and later a lieutenant in Francis Marion's company of light infantry, Walter was employed as a messenger by the Council of Safety during the summer of 1775. On September 22 of that year, Walter attempted to resign his commission because of failing health (a reason that could, of course, reflect political anxiety and discomfort as well). See John Allen Walter to the Council of Safety, September 22, 1775, South Carolina Militia Papers, New York Public Library.

77. Council of Safety to Edward Thornbrough, Charles Town, October 28, 1775, in Laurens, *Papers* 10: 505.

78. Ibid., 504–506; Drayton, *Memoirs* 2: 62.

NOTES TO CHAPTER 5

1. This chapter has been much enhanced by the advice and input of Robert M. Calhoon. Sellers, *Charleston Business*, 25–36; Klein, *Unification*, 9–109.

2. Woodmason and Hooker, *Carolina Backcountry*, 67–84.

3. Fisher, *Albion's Seed*, 605–783; William Henry Drayton and William Tennent to Council of Safety, August, 7, 1775, in Laurens, *Papers* 10: 277–285.

4. See chapter 1 and below.

5. Weir, *Colonial South Carolina*, 322.

6. No one expressed the dynamic of the "powder" struggle better than Dr. George Milligen. In September 1775, he wrote:

The General Committee received sometime in the beginning of August orders from the Continental Congress to fit out such a number of armed vessels as they should find to be necessary for their schemes, and to send commissioners among the Indian tribes with presents to induce them to take their part in the dispute with the mother country. The plunder they got from the ships at Savannah and St Augustine will greatly assist them in their views with the Indians, who are all mercenary and will be of his side who gives them the last dram.

See Report by George Milligen, September 15, 1775, CO 5/396/208–216d, NAUK; Davies, *Documents* 10: 109–114.

7. Laurens to Fletchall, July 14, 1775, in Laurens, *Papers* 10: 214; Fletchall to Laurens, July 24, 1775, in Laurens, *Papers* 10: 244–246; quote from Morgan, *Slave Counterpoint*, 309.

8. Piecuch, *Three Peoples*, 53.

9. Drayton, *Memoirs* 2: 70.

10. Edward Thornbrough to Henry Laurens, Tamar, November 1, 1775, in Laurens, *Papers* 10: 507–508; Drayton, *Memoirs* 2: 94–95, 97.

11. Ibid., 507–508.

12. Hemphill and Wates, *Extracts*, 88–89.

13. Ibid., 89.

14. Ibid.

15. Ibid.

16. Hemphill and Wates, *Extracts*, 86–101.

17. Ibid., 92.

18. On April 27, 1769, Eden was found guilty of assaulting a white man. In the fall of 1772, the craftsman was involved in another altercation. On this occasion, he alleged that he had been attacked first by an individual named Thomas Robinson. It is difficult to ascertain whether such aggression was directed at his slaves; however, it may have played a role in his bondsman's departure. See Criminal Court Journal 1769–1776, microfilm, 4/27/1769, 10/23/1772, 10/24/1772, 2/17/1773, SCDAH.

19. On November 14, Eden placed an advertisement in the *South Carolina Gazette*: "JOSHUA EDEN, Chair-maker *in* King-Street, has for sale, Some extraordinary good SPINNING WHEELS, and will continue to make more if he is properly encouraged. He also has for sale some very good Straw-bottom Chairs." See *SCG*, November 14, 1775, 4. On November 28, Eden placed a notice in the same newspaper calling for the return of his runaway, Limus:

Absented himself from the Subscriber, the 4th of this Instant, A NEGRO Man, named LIMUS; he is of a yellow Complexion, and has the Ends of three of his Fingers cut off his left Hand; he is well known in Charles Town from his saucy and impudent Tongue, of which I have had many Complaints; therefore I hereby give free Liberty, and will be also much obliged to any Person to flog him (so as not to take his Life) in such Manner as they shall think proper, whenever he is found out of my Habitation without a Ticket, for though he is my Property, he has the audacity to tell me, he will be free, that he will serve no Man, and that he will be conquered or governed by no Man.—I forwarn Masters of Vessels from carrying him off the Province, and all Persons from harbouring him in their Houses or Plantations. JOSHUA EDEN

See *SCG*, November 28, 1775, 3.

20. Hemphill and Wates, *Extracts*, 95–99.

21. Andrew Williamson to Edward Wilkinson, Camp Near Long Cane, November 6, 1775, in Gibbes, *Documentary History* 1: 210.

22. Ibid.

23. Edward Wilkinson to Andrew Williamson, November 7, 1775, William Gilmore Simms Collection, Kendall Whaling Museum. See also Council of Safety to Andrew Williamson, Charles Town, December 2, 1775, in Laurens, *Papers* 10: 524 n. 5.

24. Hemphill and Wates, *Extracts*, 101, 102, 103, 107.

25. See Council of Safety to Richard Pearis, Charles Town, October 24, 1775, in Laurens, *Papers* 10: 502 n. 2.

26. The patriot Indian commissioners were appointed by the Provincial Congress on June 23, 1775. George Galphin, LeRoy Hammond, and David Zubly were the representatives for the Creeks, while Edward Wilkinson, Andrew Williamson, and John Bowie were the representatives for the Cherokee. See Henry Laurens to John Laurens, Charles Town, June 23, 1775, in Laurens, *Papers* 10: 190 n. 16; Council of Safety to Richard Pearis, Charles Town, October 24, 1775, in Laurens, *Papers* 10: 502 n. 2.

27. There was a certain irony in Pearis's accusation against Drayton. In 1769, Richard Pearis devised a land-swindling scheme of his own with fellow Virginian Jacob Hite. Pearis's son George was half Cherokee. As Woody Holton observed, "Métis, like George Pearis were viewed by Cherokee headmen as useful diplomatic bridges to British America whose interests should be promoted; so, when George asked headmen for a 150,000-acre tract just west of South Carolina, they gave it to him. George Pearis then sold the land to his father and Jacob Hite." Fearing that it might provoke the Cherokee to join an anti-British confederation that was then forming, a Crown official persuaded a South Carolina court to void the deal. Eventually, however, Richard Pearis managed to revive the claim. See Holton, *Forced Founders*, xiii–xiv; Hatley, *Dividing Paths*, 207–208; Richard Pearis's Affidavit, November 11, 1775, William Gilmore Simms Collection, Kendall Whaling Museum; Drayton, *Memoirs* 2: 116–117; Council of Safety to Richard Pearis, Charles Town, October 24, 1775, in Laurens, *Papers* 10: 502 n. 2.

28. Born in Virginia, Joseph Robinson (d. 1807) moved to South Carolina and eventually settled on the Broad River in the Camden District. In July 1775, Robinson penned the loyalist "Counter Association." The same year, he received an appointment as major of a militia. Andrew Wilkinson to William Henry Drayton, White Hall, November 25, 1775, in Laurens, *Papers* 10: 241 n. 5, 515 n. 4; *Collections of the South Carolina Historical Society* 3: 35 n. 1

29. Hemphill and Wates, *Extracts*, 111–113.

30. Henry Laurens to William Manning, Charles Town, November 14, 1775, in Laurens, *Papers* 10: 509–510.

31. On November 9, the Congress resolved that Colonel Moultrie would "detach and post a guard in the most proper place beyond Mr. Rugeley's store, to examine strictly all suspected wagons coming into or going out of Charles-Town, and also every person suspected of proceedings prejudicial to the welfare of the Colony, or the common cause." See Hemphill and Wates, *Extracts*, 109.

32. There is some confusion in the accounts of the Battle of Hog Island Creek. The extracts from the Journals of the Provincial Congress refer to Captain Blake as receiving the order rather than Tufts. However, from what would later transpire, this is likely a mistake. See Hemphill and Wates, *Extracts*, 117; Drayton, *Memoirs* 2: 72–73, 113.

33. Drayton, *Memoirs* 2: 70–77, 113–114; Hemphill and Wates, *Extracts*, 119–123.

34. Henry Laurens to William Manning, Charles Town, November 14, 1775, in Laurens, 10: 509.

35. Drayton, *Memoirs* 2: 78; Hemphill and Wates, *Extracts*, 126–131.

36. See Andrew Williamson to William Henry Drayton, White Hall, November 25, 1775, in Laurens, *Papers* 10: 515–516.

37. Henry Laurens estimated that there were "about five hundred" troops under Williamson's command and that they were attacked by a force of "one thousand five hundred." John Drayton believed that "the garrison including officers consisted of five hundred and sixty-two men: while the number of besiegers was about eighteen hundred and ninety." See Council of Safety to Richard Richardson, Charles Town, December 4, 1775, in Laurens, *Papers* 10: 534 n. 1; Drayton, *Memoirs* 2: 118–119, 150.

38. Andrew Williamson to William Henry Drayton, White Hall, November 25, 1775, in Laurens, *Papers* 10: 516.

39. Hemphill and Wates, *Extracts*, 137–138.

40. Ibid., 138.

41. Ibid., 138–139.

42. See Krawczynski, *William Henry Drayton*, 207.

43. Andrew Williamson to William Henry Drayton, White Hall, November 25, 1775, in Laurens, *Papers* 10: 516–517.

44. Drayton, *Memoirs* 2: 148–149.

45. The day after Moore's announcement to the Provincial Congress, Henry Laurens reported to his son John: "Accounts from our backcountry are very unfavorable." See Henry Laurens to John Laurens, Charles Town, November 26, 1775, in Laurens, *Papers* 10: 518–519.

46. Hemphill and Wates, *Extracts*, 151–152.

47. Henry Laurens to William Manning, Charles Town, November 26, 1775, in Laurens, *Papers* 10: 521.

48. Members of the Council of Safety included Colonel Charles Pinckney, Colonel Henry Laurens, Henry Middleton, Thomas Ferguson, Arthur Middleton, Thomas Heyward Jr., William Henry Drayton, Rawlins Lowndes, Thomas Bee, Benjamin Elliott, Colonel James Parsons, David Oliphant, and Thomas Savage. See Hemphill and Wates, *Extracts*, 132.

49. On Monday, November 20, Congress resolved that "the Colonels of the several regiments of militia throughout the colony, have leave to enrol such a number of able male slaves, to be employed as pioneers and laborers, as public exigencies may require. And that a daily pay of seven shillings and six-pence be allowed for the service of such slave, while actually employed." See Hemphill and Wates, *Extracts*, 141.

50. On Tuesday, November 28, George-Abbot Hall from the Commissioners of the Pilotage reported that he and his men had indeed cut down and destroyed the leading mark over the Charles Town Bar the previous day. See Hemphill and Wates, *Extracts*, 159.

51. On December 2, Henry Laurens wrote to Andrew Williamson:

The Scorpion Sloop of War together with a large Transport Ship are come to Anchor in Rebellion Road where our Enemies now make a formidable appearance the Transport has brought some heavy Cannon but no Troops yet we are threatened with an early attack on our part we have erected several new & strengthened our old Batteries, Fort Johnson is in very good condition & we are determined to the utmost of our Power to defend the Metropolis— the destruction of which is probably their Aim.

See Council of Safety to Andrew Williamson, Charles Town, December 2, 1775, in Laurens, *Papers* 10: 528, 528 n. 9.

52. Hemphill and Wates, *Extracts*, 160, 168.

53. *Collections of the South Carolina Historical Society* 3: 35.

54. According to Drayton's account, he first met Richard Pearis on Monday, August 21, 1775, while trying to counteract various "machinations by ministerial influence" among the Cherokee. Drayton claimed that he did not know Pearis previously but knew that he had "resided a considerable time among the Indians" and imagined that "he had some influence over them." Attempting to draw on the captain's expertise as a translator, Drayton asked Pearis if he would mind bringing over a group of headmen to hear one of his harangues against the British. Pearis reportedly responded that he could assist Drayton, but it would be "attended with some expence [sic], and some inconvenience to his private affairs." When asked what he meant by this, the translator explained that he needed to be home to receive a sheriff from Ninety-Six who was coming to collect a debt he owed to a Mr. Powell and a Mr. Hopton in Charles Town. The Indian agent then asked Drayton if he could be of any assistance in the matter. He reportedly told the Whig leader that "he had a large tract of land from the Indians," which he would gladly sell to Drayton if he would agree to pay off a portion of his debt. According to Drayton's account, the two men discussed the matter at great length (though not in the way Pearis alleged). The conversation purportedly concluded with Drayton telling Pearis that the price on the land "was too high" but that he would defray the expense the captain mentioned and "mediate with the Sheriff not to distress him while absent on public business." According to Drayton, Pearis seemed content with the agreement, and the two parted company. From there, things quickly fell apart. Drayton reportedly defrayed the

expense as promised but only spoke to the undersheriff and not his superior. As a result, Pearis's property was seized by creditors. An "indulgence was allowed about the middle of November," and, according to Drayton, none of Pearis's effects was removed from the estate. The captain reportedly returned home "long before the expiration of the indulgence." During the course of their interaction with the Cherokee, Pearis supposedly asked Drayton yet again if he would satisfy his debt to Powell and Hopton and agree to purchase part of his land. It was at this point that the captain allegedly asked Drayton if he would "procure him the superintendent's place." The Whig official admitted that he told Pearis that he would attempt to secure the position for him. But when Drayton returned from his mission in the backcountry, he discovered that Edward Wilkinson had already been nominated. Drayton conceded that he "neither mentioned Pearis for such a post, nor applied to Messrs. Powell & Hopton, relative to their demand on Pearis." For a full account of Drayton's address, see *Collections of the South Carolina Historical Society* 3: 53–56.

55. That day, George Gabriel Powell (possibly one of the men Pearis was indebted to) was assigned the task of commanding the schooner *Comet*, which had been armed and equipped for the protection of the harbor and the navigation of the seacoast. Perhaps out of response to this action, Captain Thornbrough seized the *Polly* and began to fit it out with a number of swivel guns. *Collections of the South Carolina Historical Society* 3: 39, 42–44, 46; Council of Safety to Andrew Williamson, Charles Town, December 2, 1775, in Laurens, *Papers* 10: 524–526.

56. Council of Safety to Richard Richardson, Charles Town, December 4, 1775, in Laurens, *Papers* 10: 533–535; *Collections of the South Carolina Historical Society* 3: 49.

57. Matthew Floyd was an Irish immigrant who had resided in Pennsylvania and North Carolina before settling in the Camden district of South Carolina. By 1775, Floyd had become a justice of the peace and owned an estate estimated to be worth 3,078 pounds sterling. His property included some 2,300 acres, nine slaves, numerous livestock, and other articles, which he later reported to the Loyalist Claims Commission. See Transcripts of the Manuscript Books 54: 469–478, New York Public Library; Council of Safety to Andrew Williamson, Charles Town, December 4, 1775, in Laurens, *Papers* 10: 536–537 n. 3.

58. Drayton, *Memoirs* 2: 123.

59. On December 2, Laurens wrote to Andrew Williamson that the fourth article of the Treaty of Ninety-Six:

> stipulates that dispatches from Contracting Parties shall be sent unsealed to "their Superiors" by which we understand that each Party is to be fully acquainted with the correspondence of the other, we therefore take it for granted that we have a right to know every verbal intercourse on the Enemy's part with Lord William Campbell, & for that purpose to accompany Major Robinson's Messenger whenever he appears by a Proper Agent, otherwise the plain sense of that article will be defeated & we shall be ensnared by the shew of a Letter to one purpose, perhaps altogether Innocent, while messages of a quite opposite & mischievous tendency may be secretly interchanged.

See Council of Safety to Andrew Williamson, Charles Town, December 2, 1775, in Laurens, *Papers* 10: 526.

60. *Collections of the South Carolina Historical Society* 3: 48, 57–58, 65, 66–68, 72.

61. McCrady, *History of South Carolina in the Revolution*, 94–97.

62. See "Extract of a Letter from Charlestown, South-Carolina, to a Gentleman in Philadelphia," February 7, 1776, in Force, *American Archives* 4: 949.

63. Ibid.

NOTES TO CHAPTER 6

1. John Murray, fourth Earl of Dunmore's proclamation declared "all indented [*sic*] Servants, Negroes, or others, (appertaining to Rebels,) free that are able and willing to bear Arms, they joining His MAJESTY'S Troops." See Holton, *Forced Founders*, 156.

2. On Sunday, November 26, Henry Laurens wrote to John Laurens and asked him to tell his uncle James that "his domestics are all well but... I know not what to do with them nor with my own." See Henry Laurens to James Laurens, Charles Town, November 26, 1775, in Laurens, *Papers* 10: 519.

3. In 1765, a visitor to the Sullivan's Island "Pest House" observed "2 or 300 Negroe's performing quarantine with the smallpox." Cited in Fraser, *Charleston!* 99.

4. See Isaac Motte to Henry Laurens, Fort Johnson, September 19, 1775, in Laurens, *Papers* 10: 409.

5. *Collections of the South Carolina Historical Society* 3: 63, 75.

6. On November 28, 1775, Captain John Allston's "Company of Foot Rangers" from Craven County was ordered by the Provincial Congress "to scour the Sea-Coast from the Sewee Bay to Haddrel's Point... to repel the Landing of Men from British armed Vessels, to prevent their Depredations." See William Henry Drayton to John Allston, Papers of Henry Laurens, SCHS.

7. See *SCGG*, Friday, November 24, to Friday, December 8, 1775; Clark, *Naval Documents* 3: 14; *Collections of the South Carolina Historical Society* 3: 51–52, 63.

8. On December 6, 1775, John Ashe informed the Council that "some boats from the British ships of War in Rebellion Road, had yesterday sounded and staked the Creek, leading to the place of his residence." See *Collections of the South Carolina Historical Society* 3: 52, 57.

9. Ibid., 62–65.

10. Moultrie, *Memoirs* 1: 114.

11. See *Collections of the South Carolina Historical Society* 3: 74–76, 80, 81.

12. Ibid., 74–76, 80–82.

13. According to Captain Edward Thornbrough's journal of the HMS *Tamar*, when the *George Town* packet was seized, it was carrying a cargo of beef, flour, wine, lumber, and other merchandise. See Clark, *Naval Documents* 2: 1015.

14. *Georgia Gazette*, October 25, 1775.

15. *Collections of the South Carolina Historical Society* 3: 84–85, 87–88.

16. Like Thomas Jeremiah, Scipio Handley was taken prisoner by Whig authorities and put into close confinement. He, too, received a sentence of death under the Negro Act of 1740. But unlike Jeremiah, Handley managed to escape after six weeks when he was smuggled a file "by the hand of a Friend." He somehow "acquitted himself of his Irons and broak out of Gaol." Unfortunately for the fisherman, he sustained a "Rupture" during a two-story fall to his escape. Despite his injury, Handley fled South Carolina and headed for Saint Augustine. After a brief stay, he made his way to Barbados and subsequently took up residence in Savannah when the British occupied the city in 1779. During the siege of Georgia, Handley was employed in an armory, "Running grape shot and Carrying them out to the Redoubts and Batteries." One Saturday in 1780, he was wounded by a musket ball in his right leg. At first, the surgeons thought they would have to amputate. Eventually, the wound healed, though not entirely. For his trouble, Handley received twenty pounds sterling the greatest amount that the Loyalist Claims Commission would award to a black applicant. Similar claims by poor white loyalists amounted to at least twenty-five pounds and usually more. See "Memorial of Scipio Handley," Transcripts 53: 166–167, New York Public Library; "Claims and Memorials Petition of Scipio Handley of South Carolina," AO,/13/119/43, NAUK; Norton, "Fate of Some Black Loyalists," 404.

17. *Collections of the South Carolina Historical Society* 3: 89.

18. Moultrie, *Memoirs* 1: 113.

19. See South Carolina Commons House Journal, January 14, 1766, SCDAH.

20. See Parish Transcripts, March 7, 1755, New York Historical Society. See also Willis, "Divide and Rule," 157–176.

21. *Collections of the South Carolina Historical Society* 3: 89–91.

22. The *Scorpion* and the *Palliser* arrived off the Charles Town Bar on November 27 and anchored in Rebellion Road on November 29. Clark, *Naval Documents* 2: 1226–1227, 1194–1195.

23. Davies, *Documents* 12: 28–30. See also Lipscomb, *South Carolina Revolutionary War Battles*, 19.

24. On January 2, 1776, Henry Laurens wrote as president of the Council of Safety to the North Carolina Provincial Council: "The Scorpion man-of-war has been here, and sailed again about a fortnight ago, with two Bermuda sloops and a coasting scooner [sic], together with, as we are informed, thirty or forty negroes which Capt. Tollemache was pleased to seize while he was in Rebellion Road." See Council of Safety to North Carolina Provincial Council, Charles Town, January 2, 1776, in Laurens, *Papers* 10: 608–610. For information on Martin's flotilla, see Clark, *Naval Documents* 2: 1227.

25. *Collections of the South Carolina Historical Society* 3: 94–95.

26. According to Terry Lipscomb:

Allston's company—an elite volunteer unit of the Craven County militia— was sometimes referred to as the "Raccoon Company," perhaps in allusion to the Raccoon Keys, which marked the coastal boundary between Berkeley and Craven counties; it was also known as the "Indian Company." Although the company's rank and file certainly were not all Indians, contemporary records say the soldiers scouted "in the Indian manner" and sometimes disguised themselves as Indians. It has also been suggested that Allston may have recruited a few genuine Indian scouts from Catawba-affiliated tribes such as the Pedees, Waccamaws, and Cheraws.

See Lipscomb, *South Carolina Revolutionary War Battles*, 19; Brown, *Catawba Indians*, 262.

27. This is my estimate based on the 500 "negroes" who were on the island at the time minus the forty who had been carried off by Governor Martin.

28. See Council of Safety to Richard Richardson, Charles Town, December 19, 1775, in Laurens, *Papers* 10: 576; Josiah Smith Jr. to James Poyas, Charles Town, January 10, 1776, Josiah Smith Letterbook, UNCSHC; *SCGG*, December 15–22, 1775, 1; *Collections of the South Carolina Historical Society* 3: 40, 47, 62–63, 66, 84, 89, 90, 94–95, 103, 105, 106, 128; Drayton, *Memoirs* 2: 163–164.

29. For an account of the skirmish, see Hume, *1775*, 402–411.

30. Laurens wrote this portion of the letter on December 20. See Council of Safety to Richard Richardson, Charles Town, December 19, 1775, in Laurens, *Papers* 10: 576.

31. *Collections of the South Carolina Historical Society* 3: 103–106.

32. See *SCGG*, December 15–22, 1775, 1.

33. *Collections of the South Carolina Historical Society* 3: 116, 124, 126, 128, 130. William Tweed is an interesting yet mysterious figure. He may have actually been involved in the Jeremiah affair as he was the owner of the runaway slave Dewar. Dewar was accused by the witness Jemmy of being an accomplice to Jerry the pilot earlier that spring. Four years after the Jeremiah episode unfolded, Tweed himself was hanged by Whig authorities on suspicion of plotting to set Charles Town on fire. See Report of John Coram, CO 5/396/237 RH, NAUK; Piecuch, *Three Peoples*, 142.

34. In late December 1775, it appeared that the Georgians would refuse to comply with the terms of the Continental Association. In a letter to Colonel Stephen Bull, Laurens wrote:

> The seeming apostacy of Georgia, and the ingenuity of some of our associates, in finding out a law for a cloak to their transgressions, are subjects of real grief to us. 'Tis true, there is a resolution of the general committee, that an intercourse with Georgia should be opened, but that resolution was founded upon an assurance that Georgia had united with her sister colonies. Whenever, therefore, she had departed from that union, first by chicane and finesse, and at length openly and flagrantly acting in direct opposition to the resolves of the representative body of those colonies, by an exportation, flattering and beneficial to our enemies, disgraceful to us, and offensive in the highest degree to our friends, every true lover of liberty and his country should have determined to forgo his own interest, to take no advantage of a resolution, which, however glaring the causes may appear to individuals,

cannot be repealed, before the formality of proof has been complied with; in the mean time much evil may be done, and, according to your accounts, much has been done by men whose avarice has triumphed over patriotism... we hope we will check the evil complained of, and we are now coming to an ecclaircissement with our suspected sister. We shall in a few days, if she persists in attempts to ruin us, be obliged to speak in plain terms of resentment. There is no middle way, if she will not be a friend, an honest, faithful friend, she must be held to be an enemy.

See *Collections of the South Carolina Historical Society* 3: 127–128.

35. In a letter to Georgia patriot leader Archibald Bullock, Laurens speculated that Campbell and James Wright had "a concerted plan between the two Great Men for covering the Loading of all the Ships which now are & which may come into your River, for overawing the friends of Liberty, & for giving energy to the projects for our Enemies, in a word every mischievous & no good purpose towards the former." Henry Laurens to Archibald Bulloch, Charles Town, January 2, 1776, in Laurens, *Papers* 10: 606–607.

36. *Collections of the South Carolina Historical Society* 3: 141, 145–146.

37. Ibid., 148, 151–153; Henry Laurens to Stephen Bull, Charles Town, January 6, 1776, Laurens, *Papers* 11: 1–2.

38. Mercier secretly sailed the *William* from South Carolina to Georgia, thinking that enforcement of the Association in Savannah would be more lax. His vessel was seized on January 4 while sailing near Cockspur Island. See *SCGG*, January 26, 1776.

39. Also on that day, Laurens wrote to the Committee for St. Peters:

As the Continental Congress at Philadelphia have resolved, that vessels ought not to load with the produce of colonies to trade even from one colony to another, but under the inspection of committees; and as we are now very well assured that too much illicit trade has been carried on from this colony to Georgia, and that attempts are daily in hand to spread the evil still wider: we find it necessary to take every step in our power to put an end to its progress. For this end, we desire you will be very watchful in every part of your district, and suffer no vessel to take on board any of the produce of this colony under any pretence whatsoever, without your permission first obtained, and, that you are well satisfied such produce is intended to be transported only from one part of the colony to another, and that no vessel attempt to load or take produce on board for any other colony without a special licence.

See *Collections of the South Carolina Historical Society* 3: 163.

40. On Monday, January 12, 1776, the Council of Safety resolved that:

Mr. Daniel Cannon [leader of the Sons of Liberty] do forthwith provide all materials, workmen and labourers, that shall be necessary for erecting and completing the intended works upon Sullivan's Island, under the direction of Col. Roberts, with the utmost expedition: That, if the said works should be unavoidably discontinued, the public will indemnify Mr. Cannon, for all the materials that shall have been purchased at the time of such discontinuance; and that the public will make good any loss that may be sustained in boats, or by negroes killed, maimed, or lost in this service, by means of the enemy.

Whig leaders voted to provide Cannon with 4,000 pounds out of the colony treasury "for the more expeditious carrying on the works intended upon Sullivan's Island." See *Collections of the South Carolina Historical Society* 3: 167–168.

41. Drayton, *Memoirs* 2: 164–166; *Collections of the South Carolina Historical Society* 3: 170.

42. Henry Laurens to John Laurens, Charles Town, January 16, 1776, in Laurens, *Papers* 11: 32–36; *Collections of the South Carolina Historical Society* 3: 170. See Clark, *Naval Documents*, 3: 778, 1399.

43. Drayton, *Memoirs* 2: 165.

44. Henry Laurens to Richard Richardson, Charles Town, January 13, 1776, in Laurens, *Papers* 11: 26; *Collections of the South Carolina Historical Society* 3: 173–179.

45. Henry Laurens to Charles Cotesworth Pinckney, Charles Town, January 14, 1776, in Laurens, *Papers* 11: 29–31; *Collections of the South Carolina Historical Society* 3: 176.

46. Henry Laurens to John Laurens, Charles Town, January 16, 1776, in Laurens, *Papers* 11: 35.

47. Josiah Smith Jr. to Alexander Taylor, Charles Town, January 10, 1776, Josiah Smith Letterbook, UNCSHC.

48. In *SCGCJ*, September 13, 1774, Morelli tried to raise money for his own debts by giving notice "to all persons indebted to him; and whose Accounts have been a long time standing, unless they discharge the same within Fifteen day from this Date, they will positively be put in the hands of an Attorney at Law to be sued for."

49. *Collections of the South Carolina Historical Society* 3: 187, 190, 194, 196; Smith and Salley, *Register of St. Philip's Parish*, 203; Judgment Rolls, SCDAH; *SCG*, October 11, 1773.

50. *Collections of the South Carolina Historical Society* 3: 187, 190, 194, 196.

51. Henry Laurens to Stephen Bull, Charles Town, January 19, 1776, in Laurens, *Papers* 11: 41–44; *Collections of the South Carolina Historical Society* 3: 196–197; Memorial of Lord William Campbell to Lord North, Read July 2, 1778, Treasury 1/541, NAUK.

52. South Carolina Council of Safety to Georgia Council of Safety, Charles Town, January 19, 1776, in Laurens, *Papers* 11: 44–45; *Collections of the South Carolina Historical Society* 3: 198–199.

53. Tom may have tried to run away in the fall of 1774. An ad placed by a white slaveowner named Joseph Wigfall called for the return of a "stout Negro fellow" with the same name who had escaped from his Christ Church parish plantation. Tom was described as being "about 5 feet 9 inches high, Jamaica born, had on when he went

away, white Negro cloth trowsers, and robin trimmed with blue, a gold laced hat, branded on each temple with a small R; he is very artful, and will endeavor to pass for a free man, and get off the province. All masters of vessels are hereby cautioned not to carry him off. A reward of Ten Pounds will be given to any person who will deliver him to the warden of the workhouse, or to Joseph Wigfall." *SCGCJ*, November 22, 1774.

NOTES TO CHAPTER 7

   1. *Georgia Gazette*, December 7, 1774; Grand Jury Presentments, December 7, 1774, SCDAH; Wood, *Slavery*, 191–192.
   2. Candler, *Revolutionary Records* 1: 39, 41–42.
   3. Wood, *Slavery*, 201–202; Jackson, "'American Slavery.'"
   4. Lipscomb, *South Carolina Revolutionary War Battles*, 20.
   5. Clark, *Naval Documents* 4: 493–495.
   6. Drayton, *Memoirs* 2: 206; Clark, *Naval Documents* 3: 1239.
   7. Quoted in Killion and Walker, *Georgia*, 162–163.
   8. Clark, *Naval Documents* 4: 246–249, 460.
   9. For information about the vital North Carolina encounter known as the Battle of Moore's Creek Bridge and the related events described in the following paragraphs, see Rankin, "Moore's Creek Bridge"; Frech, "Wilmington Committee"; Ready, *Tar Heel State*, 111–115; Drayton, *Memoirs* 2: 215–218. For information pertaining to North Carolina Royal Governor Josiah Martin, see Strumpf, *Josiah Martin*; Sheridan, "West Indian Antecedents."
   10. Drayton, *Memoirs* 2: 215–218; Ready, *Tar Heel State*, 111–114.
   11. On February 22, Laurens wrote to his son and told him that Gadsden had introduced Thomas Paine's *Common Sense* to Charles Town.

> I know not how the Doctrines contained in it are relished in the Northern Colonies, nothing less than repeated & continued persecution by Great Britain can make the People in this Country subscribe to them, I have already borne my testimony against them in open Congress & more against those indecent expressions with which the Pages abound. However the Author's reasoning, tho not all original; is strong and captivating & will make many converts to Republican principles, if, as I have said above, the present scene of Kingly persecution is much longer continued. Mr Gadsden introduced the Book into this Colony, he is wrapped up in the thought of separation and independence, & will hear nothing in opposition.

See Henry Laurens to John Laurens, Charles Town, February 22, 1776, in Laurens, *Papers* 11: 115. According to John Drayton, Gadsden returned to Charles Town also carrying the famous yellow American naval flag with a rattlesnake in the center: "DON'T TREAD ON ME." The standard was ordered to be carefully preserved and displayed in the central meeting room of the State House where Congress met.

From the time it was presented by Gadsden, the flag was placed in the southwest corner of the room at the left hand of the president's chair. See Drayton, *Memoirs* 2: 172–174.

12. Krawczynski, *William Henry Drayton*, 215.

13. Fraser, *Charleston!* 149; Starr, "Conservative Revolution," 36–37.

14. Drayton, *Memoirs* 2: 175–177.

15. On March 20, a report from Georgia stated that "a Number of Negroes have been taken off a Gentleman's Plantation, lying on the Savannah River, and carried on board the Men of War." *SCGG*, March 8–20, 1776. See Henry Laurens to Martha Laurens, Charles Town, March 14, 1776, in Laurens, *Papers* 11: 160; Schama, *Rough Crossings*, 88.

16. Clark, *Naval Documents* 4: 246–249, 372.

17. Stephen Bull to Henry Laurens, Savannah, March 14, 1776, in Laurens, *Papers* 11: 163–164.

18. Ibid.

19. Henry Laurens to John Laurens, Charles Town, March 16, 1776, in Laurens, *Papers* 11: 174.

20. Henry Laurens to Stephen Bull, Charles Town, March 16, 1776, in Laurens, *Papers* 11: 172–173.

21. Clark, *Naval Documents* 4: 636.

22. See entry of September 24, 1775, in Adams, *Diary* 2: 182–183.

23. Clark, *Naval Documents* 4: 515–516, 636, 1437.

24. Recently, Cassandra Pybus asserted:

There appears to be no evidence of so large a runaway encampment on Tybee Island. British officials including Governor Wright, and refugee loyalists with some of their slaves were using the houses on the island as an alternative to the cramped conditions on the fleet. The Committee of Safety ordered local militia, aided by Creek Indians to attack these houses on March 25. In the process of *attacking the island* [emphasis mine], they arrested the loyalists and burned their houses but found no runaway encampment, only a party of marines landed to cut firewood.

But as Simon Schama remarked:

Whether the slaughter was then carried out is not known; but given the state of hysteria prevailing throughout the South in the spring and summer of 1776, there is no reason to rule it out. (Since Tybee Island now enjoys a happy reputation as a prime spring and summer resort, complete with Beach Bum Festival and birding amidst the woodstorks and herons, it seems safe to say that no one is going to go poking round the dunes looking for the remains of African Americans.)

See Pybus, "Jefferson's Faulty Math"; Schama, *Rough Crossings*, 89.

25. Clark, *Naval Documents* 4: 515–516, 636, 1437; Schama, *Rough Crossings*, 89.

26. Maier, *American Scripture*.

27. Copies of the constitution are published in Drayton, *Memoirs* 2: 186–197; and Hemphill and Wates, *Extracts*, 256–263.

28. Edgar, *South Carolina*, 12–121.

29. By referring to the "twinkling of an eye," Laurens was making a Biblical allusion to 1Cr 15:52 foretelling the transformation of the saints to occur upon Christ's return; John Adams to Mrs. Adams, May 17, 1776, in Force, *American Archives* 6: 488–489; Drayton, *Memoirs* 2: 243; SCGG, April 3, 1776; Hemphill and Wates, *Extracts*, 267; quoted in Krawczynski, *William Henry Drayton*, 220.

30. Cooper, *Statutes at Large* 4: 343–346.

31. Drayton, *Memoirs* 2: 251–252.

32. Ibid.

33. Ibid.

34. Lipscomb, *South Carolina Revolutionary War Battles*, 20–21.

35. Fraser, *Patriots*, 80–84.

36. Drayton, *Memoirs* 2: 279–280.

37. Krawczynski, *William Henry Drayton*, 227.

38. McCrady, *History of South Carolina in the Revolution*, 138–139.

39. Fraser, *Patriots*, 84; Krawczynski, *William Henry Drayton*, 229.

40. Lipscomb, *South Carolina Revolutionary War Battles*, 26–27.

41. Force, *American Archives* 6: 1206; Drayton, *Memoirs* 2: 328.

42. Lipscomb, *South Carolina Revolutionary War Battles*, 26–27.

43. Drayton, *Memoirs* 2: 328.

44. According to Terry Lipscomb:

Sir Henry Clinton's soundings off Sullivan's Island in 1780 confirmed the general consensus that the ships could have anchored within 150 yards of the shore, and perhaps even as close as seventy. British sources variously imputed the behavior of the pilots to ignorance, fright, or deception, and even the *Annual Register* commented on their "strange unskillfulness." The pilots may have been more familiar with the harbor than their performance during the battle suggests. According to a claim against the state arising from the British seizure of one Harry, "most valuable Negroe man pilot," Harry had been trained by his master William Stone, who was one of the most able pilots on the Carolina coast.

See Lipscomb, *South Carolina Revolutionary War Battles*, 50 n. 51. See also Audited Account of William Stone, SCDAH. The South Carolina treasury also reimbursed Jacob Waldron 800 pounds S.C. currency for a black pilot who had been seized by a British man-of-war. The amount Waldron received illustrates just how invaluable slave pilots were thought to be. Moreover, the sum shows that the slave was highly skilled and possessed an expert knowledge of Charles Town Harbor. See Cash Book, SCDAH.

45. Drayton, *Memoirs* 2: 303. In the aftermath of the rousing American victory, a number of newspapers poked fun at British misfortunes. One of them, in a question and answer format jested:

Q. By whom should a Commodore be directed?
A. By a pilot, so skillful as to discern a sand-bank, and so industrious as to run the fleet athwart it.

See *Providence Gazette and Country Journal*, Novemeber 30, 1776; Quoted in Lipscomb, *South Carolina Revolutionary War Battles*, 44.

46. See Claim of Jeremiah Harrold, NAUS.

47. Unfortunately for the commodore, when British deserters spread the news of this strange occurrence, Parker became the brunt of numerous "breeches" jokes for some time to come. See Lipscomb, *South Carolina Revolutionary War Battles*, 33–34, 51–52 n. 62.

48. Drayton, *Memoirs* 2: 328.

49. Lord William Campbell, South Carolina's last royal governor, died at Southampton, England, on Friday, September 4, 1778, The cause could have also been tuberculosis. See *General Evening Post*, September 8, 1778; Lipscomb, *South Carolina Revolutionary War Battles*, 34.

50. Henry Laurens to John Laurens, Charles Town, August 14, 1776, in Laurens, *Papers* 11: 232; Fraser, *Patriots*, 96.

51. Henry Laurens to John Laurens, Charles Town, August 14, 1776, in Laurens, *Papers* 11: 242–227.

NOTES TO CONCLUSION

1. Patriots successfully fended off the combined loyalist-Cherokee attack and pursued their assailants deep into the backcountry. Thirteen white men, "some of whom were painted and dressed in the Indian manner," were captured and promptly consigned to the Ninety-Six jail. Included in their ranks were ringleader Hugh Brown and a number of Tories who had been paroled earlier in the year by Whig authorities. Reportedly, the public wished to see them hanged immediately for "having associated with Savages." John Drayton observed, "it was thought by the best informed statesmen at that time, that the public would have received an essential piece of service, had they been all instantly hanged, by the right of martial law, and the law of nations. And that the same would have been consistent with justice, and policy." Drayton, *Memoirs* 2: 338–339, 342 n.; Laurens, *Papers* 11: 231 n. 16.

2. Raphael, *People's History*, 224.

3. William Henry Drayton to Francis Salvador, July 24, 1776, in Gibbes, *Documentary History* 2: 29.

4. Andrew Williamson to William Henry Drayton, August 22, 1776, in Gibbes, *Documentary History*, 2: 32; Raphael, *People's History*, 224.

5. Ibid., 224; Hatley, *Dividing Paths*, 219.

6. Fraser, *Patriots*, 95; Drayton, *Memoirs* 2: 314–315, 396.

7. Henry Laurens to John Laurens, Charles Town, August 14, 1776, in Laurens, *Papers* 11: 223–225, 228–232. The following paragraphs draw on this famous letter.

NOTES TO EPILOGUE

1. See the December 16, 1775, edition of the *Public Advertiser* (London). See Laurens, *Papers* 10: 450 n. 2. It is impossible to know what black opinion was regarding the matter, but news traveled quickly through the black community. In September 1775, for example, two Low Country whites remarked that the "Negroes have a wonderful art of communicating Intelligence among themselves." Apparently, African-American communication networks could "run [news] several hundreds of miles in a week or a fortnight." The case of Thomas Jeremiah may have been an important topic of discussion for African-Americans up and down the coast. See Adams, *Diary* 2: 182–183.

2. John Laurens to Henry Laurens, London, October 4, 1775, in Laurens, *Papers* 10: 450.

3. Hutchinson, *Diary* 1: 543.

4. See Simmons and Thomas, *Proceedings* 4: 365, 369.

5. Henry Laurens to John Laurens, Charles Town, August 20, 1775, in Laurens, *Papers* 10: 321–322. Needless to say, such attitudes were later replicated in the Jim Crow South, where supposedly "uppity blacks" such as Thomas Jeremiah became prime targets for lynch-mob violence. See Litwack, *Trouble in Mind*.

6. Henry Laurens to John Laurens, Charles Town, August 20, 1775, in Laurens, *Papers* 10: 321, 322, 334.

7. Peter Timothy to William Henry Drayton, Charles Town, August 22, 1775, in Middleton, "Correspondence," 132.

8. According to John Laurens, Englishmen had the wrong opinion about the Jeremiah trial: "The affair of the negro man Jerry has been quite differently represented here. I shall set it in a proper light whenever it occurs here in conversation, for according to the prevailing story the character of our countrymen for justice and humanity would suffer very much." See John Laurens to Henry Laurens, London, October 4, 1775, in Laurens, *Papers* 10: 450.

9. Campbell to Dartmouth, August 31, 1775, CO 5/396 folios 225RH start to 230LH end, NAUK; Davies, *Documents* 10: 93–98. Returning to England on the *Eagle*, Milligen also may have spread word of the story in the fall of 1775.

10. Ibid.

11. Report by George Milligen, September 15, 1775, CO 5/396/208–216d, NAUK; Davies, *Documents* 10: 109–114; Campbell to Dartmouth, August 31, 1775, CO 5/396 folios 225RH start to 230LH end, NAUK; Davies, *Documents* 10: 93–98. Whether Campbell was simply trying to shift responsibility away from himself or actually believed that blacks were incapable of raising an insurrection of their own is unclear. However, the notion of a "spillover," which he ostensibly espoused, and the idea that

blacks only learned revolutionary ideologies by white example is a concept that continues to color much of the recent historiography. This tendency is especially evident in the writings of "consensus" historians. Popularized in Bailyn, *Ideological Origins*, chapter 6, the trickle-down theory has been taken up in Wood, *Radicalism*, 4; rearticulated in Bailyn, *Voyagers*, 17–19; modified in Nash, *Forging Freedom*, 39; and critiqued in Wood, "'Liberty Is Sweet,'" 150–152.

12. Ultimately, the British proved to be unreliable as slave liberators. Although some Afro-Carolinians were well treated, as Berlin notes, many blacks who sought British protection were eventually used, abused, or sold back into bondage. Berlin does concede that "despite contradictory policies and inconsistent practices, slaves clung to the belief, however uncertain or misguided, that the enemy of their enemy was their friend.... If the British were unreliable friends, slaves knew what to expect from patriots." See Berlin, *Many Thousands Gone*, 296–298. Black runaways were treated extremely cruelly by the British in 1779. When thousands of slaves fled to the Low Country in hopes of obtaining their freedom, the maroons were either enslaved or abandoned. Hundreds perished, and it was reported that Otter Island was scattered with their remains as late as 1785. See McCrady, *South Carolina in the Revolution, 1775–1780*, 392–394. I am grateful to an anonymous OUP reviewer for this latter reference.

Bibliography

PRIMARY SOURCES: ARCHIVAL

Kendall Whaling Museum, Sharon, Mass. William Gilmore Simms Collection of Laurens Papers, formerly in the Long Island Historical Society.

NAUK: National Archives, United Kingdom. Records of the Auditor 1783–86.

———. Records of the Colonial Office 1774–1801.

———. Records of the Treasury 1776–87.

NAUS: National Archives, United States. Claim of Jeremiah Harrold (S17467), Roll 1209, Revolutionary War Pensions.

New York Public Library. South Carolina Militia Papers, 1775–1779.

———. Transcripts of the Manuscript Books and Papers of the Commission of Enquiry into Losses and Services of the American Loyalists held under Acts of Parliament of 23, 25, 26, 28, and 29 of George III preserved amongst the Audit Office Records in the Public Record Office of England, 1783–1790, made for the New York Public Library.

New York Historical Society. Daniel Parish Jr. Transcripts relating to South Carolina.

SCDAH: South Carolina Department of Archives and History. Judgment Rolls, 1774, Nos. 64A, 69A, 70A, 100A; 1775, No. 126A.

———. Audited Account of William Stone (AA-7432).

———. Cash Book, 1775–1777, Commissioners of the Treasury, Records of the State Treasurer (SC Archives Microcopy No. 4).

———. Grand Jury Presentments, Court of General Sessions, 1769–1776.

———. South Carolina Commons House Journal, January 14, 1766.

———. Miscellaneous Records, Books OO and RR.

SCHS: South Carolina Historical Society. Ball Family Papers, 1631–1858.

UNCSCH: University of North Carolina, Southern Historical Collection. Josiah Smith Letterbook.

————. Preston Davie Collection.

USCSCL: University of South Carolina, South Caroliniana Library. Manigault Family Papers.

Westminster College, Cambridge, England. Countess of Huntingdon's American Papers.

PRIMARY SOURCES: PUBLISHED

Adams, John. *Diary and Autobiography of John Adams.* 4 vols. Ed. by L. H. Butterfield. Cambridge, Mass.: Harvard University Press, 1961.

Bargar, B. D., ed. "Charles Town Loyalism in 1775: The Secret Reports of Alexander Innes." *South Carolina Historical Magazine* 63 (1962): 125–136.

Barry, J. Neilson, ed. "An Almanac of 1776." *Oregon Historical Quarterly* 15 (1914): 147–152.

Barnwell, Joseph W, ed. "Correspondence of Hon. Arthur Middleton." *South Carolina Historical and Genealogical Magazine* 26 (October 1925): 183–213.

Barnwell, Joseph W, ed. "Correspondence of Hon. Arthur Middleton." *South Carolina Historical and Genealogical Magazine* 27 (July 1926): 107–137.

Bartram, William. *Travels through North & South Carolina, Georgia, East & West Florida, the Cherokee Country, the Extensive Territories of the Muscogulges, or Creek Confederacy, and the Country of the Chactaws; Containing an Account of the Soil and Natural Productions of Those Regions, Together with Observations on the Manners of the Indians. Embellished with Copper-Plates.* Philadelphia: James and Johnson, 1791. Documenting the American South, University of North Carolina—Chapel Hill Library http://docsouth.unc.edu/nc/bartram/menu.html.

Burke, Edmund. *The Speeches of the Right Honourable Edmund Burke, in the House of Commons, and in Westminster-Hall.* 4 vols. London: Longman, Hurst, Rees, Orme, and Brown, 1816.

Candler, Allen D, ed. *The Revolutionary Records of the State of Georgia.* 3 vols. Atlanta: Franklin Turner, 1908.

Clark, William Bell, ed. *Naval Documents of the American Revolution.* 10 vols. Washington, D.C.: U.S. Government Printing Office, 1964–1996.

Collections of the South Carolina Historical Society, 5 vols. Charleston: South Carolina Historical Society, 1857–1897.

Cooper, Thomas, ed. *The Statutes at Large of South Carolina.* 22 vols. Columbia, S.C.: A. S. Johnson, 1836–1898.

Davies, K. G., ed. *Documents of the American Revolution 1770–1783.* 21 vols. Shannon, Ireland: Irish Academic Press, 1972–1981.

De Vorsey, Louis B. Jr., ed. *De Brahm's Report of the General Survey in the Southern District of North America.* Columbia: University of South Carolina Press, 1971.

Dickens, Charles. *All the Year Round.* London: Charles Dickens, 1861.

Donnan, Elizabeth, ed. *Documents Illustrative of the History of the Slave Trade to America.* 4 vols. Washington, D.C.: Carnegie Institution, 1930–1935.

Douglass, Sir Robert. *The Peerage of Scotland.* 2 vols. Edinburgh: G. Ramsay, 1813.

Drayton, John. *Memoirs of the American Revolution Relating to South Carolina, from its Commencement to the Year 1776, Inclusive; as Relating to the State of South-Carolina: And Occasionally Referring to the States of North-Carolina and Georgia.* 2 vols. Charleston, S.C.: A. E. Miller, 1821.

Edgar, Walter B. *South Carolina: A History.* Columbia, S.C.: University of South Carolina Press, 1988.

"Entries in the Bible of Robert Pringle." *South Carolina Historical and Genealogical Magazine* 21, no. 1 (1920): 26–27.

Force, Peter, comp. *American Archives: A Collection of Authentick Records, State Papers, Debates, and Letters and Other Notices of Publick Affairs,* 4th Series. 6 vols. Washington, D.C.: U.S. Congress, 1837–1846.

Gadsden, Christopher. *The Writings of Christopher Gadsden, 1746–1805.* Ed. by Richard Walsh. Columbia: University of South Carolina Press, 1966.

Gibbes, R. W., ed. *Documentary History of the American Revolution: Consisting of Letters and Papers Relating to the Contest for Liberty, Chiefly in South Carolina, from Originals in the Possession of the Editor, and Other Sources, 1764–1776.* 3 vols. New York: D. Appleton, 1853–1857.

Glen, James, and George Milligen-Johnston. *Colonial South Carolina: Two Contemporary Descriptions.* Columbia: University of South Carolina Press, 1951.

Hemphill, William Edwin, and Wylma Anne Wates, eds. *Extracts from the Journals of the Provincial Congresses of South Carolina, 1775–1776.* Columbia: South Carolina Archives Department, 1960.

Howe, Mark A. DeWolfe, ed. "Journal of Josiah Quincy, Junior, 1773." *Proceedings of the Massachusetts Historical Society* 49 (1916): 424–481.

Hutchinson, Thomas. *Diary and Letters of His Excellency Thomas Hutchinson, Esq.* 2 vols. Ed. by Peter Orlando Hutchinson. Boston, 1884–1886; New York: Houghton Mifflin, 1973.

Izard, Ralph. *Correspondence of Mr. Ralph Izard, of South Carolina, from the Year 1774 to 1804; with a Short Memoir.* Anne Izard Deas, ed. New York: Charles S. Francis, 1844.

Johnson, Samuel. *Taxation No Tyranny.* London, 1775.

Laurens, Henry. *The Papers of Henry Laurens,* ed. by Philip Hamer. 16 vols. Columbia: University of South Carolina Press, 1968–2003.

Madison, James. *The Papers of James Madison,* ed. by William T. Hutchinson and William M. E. Rachal. 17 vols. Charlottesville: University Press of Virginia, 1962–1991.

Manigault, Gabriel. "The Papers of Gabriel Manigault." *South Carolina Historical Magazine* 64 (January 1963): 1–12.

Moultrie, William. *Memoirs of the American Revolution, So Far as It Related to the States of North and South Carolina, and Georgia.* 2 vols. New York: David Longworth, 1802.

Ramsay, David. *The History of South Carolina, from Its First Settlement in 1670, to the Year 1808.* 2 vols. Charleston, S.C.: David Longworth, 1809.

Simmons, R. C., and P. D. G. Thomas, eds. *Proceedings and Debates of the British Parliaments Respecting North America, 1754–1783.* Vols. 5 and 6. White Plains, N.Y.: Kraus International, 1986.

Smith, D. E. Huger, and A. S. Salley Jr., eds. *Register of St. Philip's Parish, Charles Town, or Charleston, S.C., 1754–1810.* Charleston: South Carolina Society, Colonial Dames of America, 1927.

Smith, James Edward. *A Selection of the Correspondence of Linnaeus, and Other Naturalists, from Original Manuscripts.* 2 vols. London: Longman, Hurst, Rees, Orme and Brown, 1821.

"Viator" [Sir William Draper]. *The Thoughts of a Traveller upon our American Disputes.* London, 1774.

Washington, George. *The Papers of George Washington: Revolutionary War Series,* ed. by W. W. Abbot and Dorothy Twohig. 7 vols. Charlottesville: University of Virginia Press, 1985.

Wells's Register Together with an Almanack for the Year of Our Lord 1775 by George Andrews, Esq., 12th ed. Charleston, S.C., 1775.

Woodmason, Charles. *The Carolina Backcountry on the Eve of the Revolution: The Journal and Other Writings of Charles Woodmason, Anglican Itinerant.* Ed. by Richard J. Hooker. Chapel Hill: University of North Carolina Press, 1969.

PRIMARY SOURCES: NEWSPAPERS

General Evening Post
Georgia Gazette
Massachusetts Gazette and News Letter
Morning Chronicle and London Advertiser
Pennsylvania Evening Post
Providence Gazette and Country Journal
Public Advertiser (London)
South Carolina American and General Gazette (SCAGG)
South Carolina Gazette (SCG)
South Carolina Gazette and Country Journal (SCGCJ)
South Carolina General Gazette (SCGG)

SECONDARY SOURCES

Alden, John R. "John Stuart Accuses William Bull." *William and Mary Quarterly* 2 (July 1945): 315–321.

———. *John Stuart and the Southern Colonial Frontier: A Study of Indian Relations, War, Trade, and Land Problems in the Southern Wilderness, 1754–1775.* New York: Gordian Press, 1966.

Ammerman, David. *In the Common Cause: American Response to the Coercive Acts of 1774.* Charlottesville: University Press of Virginia, 1974.

Ashe, Samuel A' Court. *History of North Carolina.* 2 vols. Greensboro, N.C.: Charles L. Van Noppen, 1908.

Bailyn, Bernard. *The Ideological Origins of the American Revolution.* Cambridge, Mass.: Harvard University Press, Belknap, 1967.

———. *Voyagers to the West: A Passage in the Peopling of America on the Eve of the Revolution*. New York: Knopf, 1986.

Ball, Edward. *Slaves in the Family*. New York: Ballantine, 1998.

Baranowski, Maciej. *Phonological Variation and Change in the Dialect of Charleston, South Carolina*. Durham, N.C.: Duke University Press, 2007.

Berlin, Ira. *Many Thousands Gone: The First Two Centuries of Slavery in North America*. Cambridge, Mass.: Harvard University Press, Belknap, 1998.

Blumrosen, Alfred W., and Ruth G. Blumrosen. *Slave Nation: How Slavery United the Colonies and Sparked the American Revolution*. Naperville, Ill.: Sourcebooks, 2005.

Bolster, W. Jeffrey. *Black Jacks: African American Seamen in the Age of Sail*. Cambridge, Mass.: Harvard University Press, 1998.

Bonds, John B. "Opening the Bar: First Dredging at Charleston, 1853–1859." *South Carolina Historical Magazine* 98, no. 3 (July 1997): 230–250.

Borick, Carl P. *A Gallant Defense: The Siege of Charleston, 1780*. Columbia: University of South Carolina Press, 2003.

Bridenbaugh, Carl. *Cities in Revolt: Urban Life in America, 1743–1776*. New York: Knopf, 1955.

Brown, Douglas Summers. *The Catawba Indians: The People of the River*. Columbia: University of South Carolina Press, 1966.

Bullard, Mary R. *Cumberland Island: A History*. Athens: University of Georgia Press, 2005.

Carp, Benjamin L. "Fire of Liberty: Firefighters, Urban Voluntary Culture, and the Revolutionary Movement," *William and Mary Quarterly* 58, no. 4 (October 2001): 781–818.

———. *Rebels Rising: Cities and the American Revolution*. New York: Oxford University Press, 2007.

Cashin, Edward. *William Bartram and the American Revolution on the Southern Frontier*. Columbia: University of South Carolina Press, 2007.

Cheves, Langdon. "Izard of South Carolina." *South Carolina Historical Magazine* 2 (July 1901): 205–240.

Coclanis, Peter A. *The Shadow of a Dream: Economic Life and Death in the South Carolina Low Country, 1670–1920*. New York: Oxford University Press, 1989.

Coker, P. C. III. *Charleston's Maritime Heritage 1670–1865*. Charleston: Coker Craft Press, 1987.

Cole, Arthur Harrison. *Wholesale Commodity Prices in the United States, 1700–1861, Statistical Supplement: Actual Wholesale Prices of the Various Commodities*. Cambridge, Mass.: Harvard University Press, 1938.

Côté, Richard N. *Mary's World: Love, War, and Family Ties in Nineteenth-Century Charleston*. Mount Pleasant, S.C.: Corinthian, 2000.

Crary, Catherine S. *The Price of Loyalty: Tory Writings from the Revolutionary Era*. New York: McGraw-Hill, 1973.

Crow, Jeffrey J. "Slave Rebelliousness and Social Conflict in North Carolina, 1775 to 1802." *William and Mary Quarterly* 37, no. 1 (January 1980): 79–102.

Estes, Rosemary Niner. "Charles Town's Sons of Liberty: A Closer Look," Unpublished Ph.D. dissertation, University of North Carolina at Chapel Hill, 2005.

Fischer, David Hackett. *Albion's Seed: Four British Folkways in America.* New York: Oxford University Press, 1989.

Fraser, Walter J. Jr. *Charleston! Charleston! The History of a Southern City.* Columbia: University of South Carolina Press, 1989.

————. *Patriots, Pistols, and Petticoats: 'Poor Sinful Charles Town' during the American Revolution,* 2nd ed. Columbia: University of South Carolina Press, 1993.

Frech, Laura Page. "Wilmington Committee of Public Safety and the Loyalist Rising of February, 1776." *North Carolina Historical Review* 41 (January 1964): 21–33.

Frey, Sylvia. *Water from the Rock: Black Resistance in a Revolutionary Age.* Princeton, N.J.: Princeton University Press, 1991.

Gayle, Charles J. "The Nature and Volume of Exports from Charleston, 1724–1774," *Proceedings of the South Carolina Historical Association* (1937): 25–33.

Gipson, Lawrence Henry. *The British Empire before the American Revolution.* 13 vols. New York: Knopf, 1958.

Greene, Jack P. *Pursuits of Happiness: The Social Development of Early Modern British Colonies and the Formation of American Culture.* Chapel Hill: University of North Carolina Press, 1988.

Hatley, M. Thomas. *The Dividing Paths: Cherokees and South Carolinians through the Era of Revolution.* New York: Oxford University Press, 1993.

Haw, James. *John & Edward Rutledge of South Carolina.* Athens: University of Georgia Press, 1997.

Heitzler, Michael J., and Nancy Paul Kirchner. *Goose Creek: A Definitive History.* Charleston, S.C.: History Press, 2005.

Hendrix, M. Patrick, and Christopher Nichols. *Down and Dirty: Archaeology of the South Carolina Lowcountry.* Charleston, S.C.: History Press, 2007.

Higginbotham, Don. "Some Reflections on the South in the American Revolution," *Journal of Southern History* 3 (August 2007): 659–670.

————. *The War of American Independence: Military Attitudes, Policies, and Practice, 1763–1789.* London: Macmillan, 1971.

Hoffman, Ronald. "The 'Disaffected' in the Revolutionary South." In *The American Revolution: Explorations in the History of American Radicalism,* ed. by Alfred F. Young, 275–316. De Kalb: Northern Illinois University Press, 1976.

Holton, Woody. *Forced Founders: Indians, Debtors, Slaves, and the Making of the American Revolution in Virginia.* Chapel Hill: University of North Carolina Press, 1999.

Hood, Graham. *The Governor's Palace in Williamsburg: A Cultural Study.* Williamsburg, Va.: Colonial Williamsburg Foundation, 1991.

Hume, Ivor Noël. *1775: Another Part of the Field.* New York: Knopf, 1966.

Jackson, Harvey H. "'American Slavery, American Freedom' and the Revolution in the Lower South: The Case of Lachlan McIntosh." *Southern Studies* 19 (Spring 1980): 81–93.

Jenrette, Richard H. *Adventures with Old Houses.* Layton, Utah: Gibbs Smith, 2005.

John, Richard R. *Spreading the News: The American Postal System from Franklin to Morse.* Cambridge, Mass.: Harvard University Press, 1995.

Jones, Alice Hanson. *Wealth of a Nation to Be: The American Colonies on the Eve of the American Revolution.* New York: Columbia University Press, 1980.

Klein, Rachel N. *Unification of a Slave State: The Rise of the Planter Class in the South Carolina Backcountry, 1760–1808.* Chapel Hill: University of North Carolina Press, 1992.

Knepper, David Morgan. "The Political Structure of Colonial South Carolina, 1743–1776." Unpublished Ph.D. dissertation, University of Virginia, 1971.

Kossman, Ernst. *The Low Countries, 1780–1940.* New York: Oxford University Press, 1978.

Krawczynski, Keith. *William Henry Drayton: South Carolina Revolutionary Patriot.* Baton Rouge: Louisiana State University Press, 2001.

Laurie, Peter B., and David Chamberlain. *The South Carolina Aquarium Guide to Aquatic Habitats of South Carolina.* Columbia: University of South Carolina Press, 2002.

Linebaugh, Peter, and Marcus Rediker. *The Many-Headed Hydra: Sailors, Slaves, Commoners, and the Hidden History of the Revolutionary Atlantic.* Boston: Beacon Press, 2000.

Lipscomb, Terry W. *South Carolina Revolutionary War Battles 1: The Carolina Lowcountry April 1775–June 1776 and the Battle of Fort Moultrie*, 2nd ed. Columbia: South Carolina Department of Archives and History, 1994.

Litwack, Leon. *Trouble in Mind: Black Southerners in the Age of Jim Crow.* New York: Knopf, 1998.

Maier, Pauline. *American Scripture: Making the Declaration of Independence.* New York: Knopf, 1997.

———. "The Charleston Mob and the Evolution of Popular Politics in Revolutionary South Carolina, 1765–1784." *Perspectives in American History* 4 (1970): 173–196.

———. *From Resistance to Revolution: Colonial Radicals and the Development of American Opposition to Britain, 1765–1776.* New York: W. W. Norton, 1972.

Matthews, Marty D. *Forgotten Founder: The Life and Times of Charles Pinckney.* Columbia: University of South Carolina Press, 2004.

May, W. E. "His Majesty's Ships on the Carolina Station." *South Carolina Historical Magazine* 71 (July 1970): 162–169.

McCrady, Edward. *The History of South Carolina in the Revolution 1775–1780.* New York: Russell and Russell, 1901.

———. *The History of South Carolina under the Royal Government 1719–1776.* New York: Russell and Russell, 1899.

McCusker, John J., and Russell R. Menard. *The Economy of British America, 1607–1789.* Chapel Hill: University of North Carolina Press, 1985.

McDonnell, Michael A. *The Politics of War: Race, Class, and Conflict in Revolutionary Virginia.* Chapel Hill: University of North Carolina, 2007.

McDonough, Daniel J. *Christopher Gadsden and Henry Laurens: The Parallel Lives of Two American Patriots.* Selinsgrove, Pa.: Susquehanna University Press, 2000.

Morgan, Philip D. "Black Life in Eighteenth-Century Charleston." *Perspectives in American History* 1 (1984): 187–232.

————. *Slave Counterpoint: Black Culture in the Eighteenth Century Chesapeake and Low Country.* Chapel Hill: University of North Carolina Press, 1998.

Mullin, Gerald W. *Flight and Rebellion: Slave Resistance in Eighteenth-Century Virginia.* New York: Oxford University Press, 1972.

Nash, Gary B. *Forging Freedom: The Formation of Philadelphia's Black Community, 1720–1840.* Cambridge, Mass.: Harvard University Press, 1988.

————. *Red, White, and Black: The Peoples of Early North America.* Upper Saddle River, N.J.: Prentice-Hall, 1974.

————. "Social Change and the Growth of Prerevolutionary Urban Radicalism." In *The American Revolution: Explorations in the History of American Radicalism,* ed. by Alfred F. Young, 3–36. De Kalb: Northern Illinois University Press, 1976.

————. *The Unknown American Revolution: The Unruly Birth of Democracy and the Struggle to Create America.* New York: Viking, 2005.

————. *The Urban Crucible: Social Change, Political Consciousness, and the Origins of the American Revolution.* Cambridge, Mass.: Harvard University Press, 1979.

Nash, R. C. "Urbanization in the Colonial South: Charleston, South Carolina, as a Case Study." *Journal of Urban History* (November 1992): 3–29.

Norton, Mary Beth. "The Fate of Some Black Loyalists of the American Revolution." *Journal of Negro History* 68 (October 1973): 402–426.

Olwell, Robert. "'Domestick Enemies': Slavery and Political Independence in South Carolina, May 1775–March 1776." *Journal of Southern History* 55 (February 1989): 21–48.

————. *Masters, Slaves and Subjects: The Culture of Power in the South Carolina Low Country, 1740–1790.* Ithaca, N.Y.: Cornell University Press, 1998.

Palmer, Gregory, ed. *Biographical Sketches of Loyalists of the American Revolution.* Westport, Conn.: Meckler, 1984.

Pearson, Edward. "'Planters Full of Money': The Self-Fashioning of the Eighteenth-Century Planter Elite." In *Money, Trade, and Power: The Evolution of Colonial South Carolina's Plantation Society,* ed. by Jack P. Greene, Rosemary Brana-Shute, and Randy J. Sparks, 299–321. Columbia: University of South Carolina Press, 2001.

Piecuch, Jim. *Three Peoples, One King: Loyalists, Indians, and Slaves in the Revolutionary South, 1775–1782.* Columbia: University of South Carolina Press, 2008.

Poston, Jonathan H. *The Buildings of Charleston: A Guide to the City's Architecture.* Columbia, S.C.: University of South Carolina Press, 1997.

Pybus, Cassandra. *Epic Journeys of Freedom: Runaway Slaves of the American Revolution and Their Global Quest for Liberty.* Boston: Beacon Press, 2006.

————. "Jefferson's Faulty Math: The Question of Slave Defections in the American Revolution." *William and Mary Quarterly* 62, no. 2 (2005): 243–264.

Rankin, Hugh F. "Moore's Creek Bridge Campaign, 1776." *North Carolina Historical Review* 39 (January 1953): 23–60.

Raphael, Ray. *A People's History of the American Revolution: How Common People Shaped the Fight for Independence.* New York: New Press, 2001.

Ready, Milton. *The Tar Heel State: A History of North Carolina.* Columbia: University of South Carolina Press, 2005.

Rediker, Marcus. *Between the Devil and the Deep Blue Sea: Merchant Seamen, Pirates and the Anglo-American Maritime World, 1700–1750*. New York: Cambridge University Press, 1989.

Rogers, George C. *Charleston in the Age of the Pinckneys*. Columbia: University of South Carolina Press, 1980.

Ryan, William R. "'Under the Color of Law': The Ordeal of Thomas Jeremiah, a Free Black Man, and the Struggle for Power in Revolutionary South Carolina." In *George Washington's South*, ed. by Tamara Harvey and Greg O'Brien, 223–258. Gainesville: University Press of Florida, 2003.

Schama, Simon. *Rough Crossings: Britain, Slaves and the American Revolution*. London: BBC Books, 2005.

Sellers, Leila, *Charleston Business on the Eve of the American Revolution*. Chapel Hill: University of North Carolina Press, 1934.

Sheridan, Richard B. "West Indian Antecedents of Josiah Martin, Last Royal Governor of North Carolina." *North Carolina Historical Review* 52 (January 1975): 20–36.

"Sir John Pringle (1707–1782): Military Physician and Hygenist." *Journal of the American Medical Association* 890 (1964): 849–850.

Starr, Raymond G. "The Conservative Revolution: South Carolina Public Affairs, 1775–1790." Unpublished Ph.D. dissertation, University of Texas, 1964.

Strumpf, Vernon O. *Josiah Martin: The Last Royal Governor of North Carolina*. Durham, N.C.: Carolina Academic Press, 1986.

Taylor, George R. "Wholesale Commodity Prices at Charleston, S.C., 1732–1791," *Journal of Economic History* 4 (1932): 356–377.

Van Ruymbeyke, Bertrand. "The Huguenots of Proprietary South Carolina: Patterns of Migration and Immigration." In *Money, Trade, and Power: the Evolution of Colonial South Carolina's Plantation Society*, ed. by Jack P. Greene, Rosemary Brana-Shute, and Randy J. Sparks, 26–48. Columbia: University of South Carolina Press, 2001.

Wallace, David Duncan. *The Life of Henry Laurens, with a Sketch of the Life of Lieutenant-Colonel John Laurens*. New York: G. P. Putnam's Sons, 1915.

Walsh, Richard. *Charleston's Sons of Liberty: A Study of the Artisans, 1763–1789*. Columbia: University of South Carolina Press, 1959.

Weir, Robert. *Colonial South Carolina: A History*. Columbia: University of South Carolina Press, 1983.

Williams, George W. *Early Ministers at St. Michael's, Charleston*. Charleston, S.C.: Dalcho Historical Society, 1961.

Willis, William S. "Divide and Rule: Red, White and Black in the Southeast." *Journal of Negro History* 48 (July 1963): 157–176.

Wood, Betty. *Slavery in Colonial Georgia, 1730–1775*. Athens: University of Georgia Press, 1984.

Wood, Gordon S. *Radicalism of the American Revolution*. New York: Knopf, 1992.

Wood, Peter H. *Black Majority: Negroes in Colonial South Carolina from 1670 through the Stono Rebellion*. New York: Knopf, 1974.

———. "The Changing Population of the Colonial South: An Overview by Race and Region, 1685–1790." In *Powhatan's Mantle: Indians in the Colonial Southeast*, ed.

by M. Thomas Hatley, Gregory A. Waselkov, and Peter H. Wood, 35–103. Lincoln: University of Nebraska Press, 1989.

————. "'The Dream Deferred': Black Freedom Struggles on the Eve of White Independence." In *Resistance: Studies in African, Caribbean, and Afro-American History*, ed. by Gary Y. Okihiro, 166–187. Amherst: University of Massachusetts Press, 1986.

————. "'It Was a Negro Taught Them': A New Look at African Labor in Early South Carolina." *Journal of Asian and African Studies* 9 (July/October 1974): 160–179.

————. "'Liberty Is Sweet': African-American Freedom Struggles in the Years before White Independence." In *Beyond the American Revolution: Explorations in the History of American Radicalism*, ed. by Alfred F. Young, 149–172. DeKalb: Northern Illinois University Press, 1993.

————. "'Taking Care of Business' in Revolutionary South Carolina: Republicanism and Slave Society." In *The Southern Experience in the American Revolution*, ed. by Jeffrey J. Crow and Larry E. Tise, 268–293. Chapel Hill: University of North Carolina Press, 1978.

Zele, Adam. "Becoming Sensible: David Margate and Colonial Calvinist Methodist Attitudes toward Slavery." Unpublished graduate seminar paper, Duke University, April 2001.

Zornow, David. "A Troublesome Community: Blacks in Revolutionary Charles Town, 1765–1775." Harvard College honors thesis, March 1976.

Index